BLACK MARKET

BLACK MARKET

AN INSIDER'S JOURNEY INTO THE HIGH-STAKES
WORLD OF COLLEGE BASKETBALL

MERL CODE

HANOVER
SQUARE
PRESS

HANOVER SQUARE PRESS™

Recycling programs
for this product may
not exist in your area.

ISBN-13: 978-1-335-42577-5

Black Market

Hanover Square Press
22 Adelaide St. West, 41st Floor
Toronto, Ontario M5H 4E3, Canada
HanoverSqPress.com
BookClubbish.com

Printed in U.S.A.

I'd like to dedicate this book to all those who refuse to stay silent so that others can remain comfortable. The truth makes people uneasy because it complicates the lie they live.

BLACK
MARKET

AUTHOR NOTE

This memoir is grounded, first and foremost, in my own experiences and memories. My stories were cross-referenced against interviews and correspondence with former teammates, families, coaches, colleagues and friends, and, where relevant, court documents. This specific narrative may be mine alone, but it illuminates the struggles of countless young athletes across multiple generations. I hope it inspires change.

PROLOGUE

Zion shifts his weight from side to side, looking around the room with a hint of shyness, almost embarrassment, as a man sings his praises to the cameras and a small crowd assembled to watch. It's part interview, part hype session. But when the man nudges him to introduce himself, he hesitates.

"I'm Zion," the boy says, taking in a deep breath. "And I like to ball."

"You're the number one player in your class," the man proclaims, clearly feeling like Zion is being a bit too understated. And the man is probably right. Zion is, after all, starting to build quite a buzz for himself in the basketball world.

"Ain't nobody can hold you in your class," the man continues. "Nationally, you're on the map!"

"I definitely ain't backing down," Zion finally says, showing a hint of the self-confidence he exudes on the court.

At this point you are probably thinking to yourself, *I know who Zion is. The number one pick in the 2019 NBA draft. As a rookie with the New Orleans Pelicans he was already an NBA megastar and one-man ratings bonanza who'd secured a $75 million sponsorship deal with Nike's Jordan Brand. His highlight videos got hundreds of millions of views online before he even set foot on Duke's campus or was named college basketball's player of the year. In only his second year as a pro, he became an NBA All-Star and one of the league's most marketable faces.*

All of that is true. But actually, you probably don't know Zion. Not *this* Zion, anyway. Because this isn't Zion Williamson we're talking about. It's Zion Lawson. *This* Zion is the number one player in the class of 2029. If you're doing the math in your head, you're right. He's eleven years old. He's on a Nike-sponsored travel team. They've already got highlights of their players splashed across various social media accounts. It's on.

And if you want to know how this game really works, you've gotta understand what the next eight years of this kid's life—scratch that, all of these kids' lives—are going to be like.

Now that they've been identified as top-tier players in their class, they're going to be shuttled through a system of branded basketball camps and clinics every spring and summer that are run by Nike, adidas and Under Armour.

And Puma, who is trying to reestablish itself in the basketball market on the back of sponsorship deals with young up-and-comers like Deandre Ayton, Michael Porter Jr., Marcus Smart and the 2021 NBA Rookie of the Year LaMelo Ball, will have something to say as well, along with New Balance, which recently inked a footwear-and-apparel deal with Boston College to outfit all of its athletic teams, and has Kawhi Leonard and young, emerging NBA talent like Darius Bazley in the fold.

Staffers from the brand their team is associated with, who are geographically positioned around the country, will interact with these kids or their people constantly. And depending on how highly ranked they are, that same staffer is shipping them product—shoes, shirts, shorts, sweat suits, socks, backpacks, whatever—on a weekly, monthly or quarterly basis. The FedEx deliveryman knows what's up, even though the names on the packages often change. That sneaker rep is like a year-round Santa Claus whose elves do nothing but make the hottest basketball gear, sometimes including stuff that hasn't, and may never, hit retail stores open to the general public.

That's their job. That was *my* job.

By the time they were in their midteens and college coaches came knocking, I knew damn near everything there was to know about a kid's family. I knew if Dad drank and flew off the handle. I knew if he was cheating. I knew if Mom needed a job because her company hit a rough patch and had to lay folks off. I knew who else was in their life—uncles, cousins, random hangers-on hoping the talented kid might be their meal ticket.

Mom wanted some new shoes? Done. The young man needed some winter clothes? I had you. By the time these kids were sixteen and starting to consider where they wanted to go to college, nobody had a better relationship with them than I did.

So now you can begin to understand why college coaches call sneaker reps when they're trying to start a relationship with a kid and his family. They've already been in there for years by then. And they know who's influential in the kid's life, who's got the juice.

What? You thought these kids just magically show up at

these camps, the coaches see them, they start being recruited and next thing everybody knows they're on campus?

Think about it.

If you're that kid and his family, which school are you more likely to choose? One that's sponsored by the brand that's been outfitting you for years and helping your family, right? Not always, but definitely more often than not.

When I was at Nike, we wanted them at Kentucky, Duke, North Carolina or Oregon. At adidas? We wanted them at the University of Kansas, Indiana, Louisville, North Carolina State or Miami. Over at Under Armour? South Carolina, Auburn or Wisconsin. The list could go on for each of those brands, but you get the idea. We're pumping hundreds of millions of dollars into sponsoring these programs, so we need them suiting up the best players, right?

And then, when they turn pro a year or two later, it's time to make it official. Welcome to the family. Of course, you've been part of the family for a long time. And hopefully you were taken care of along the way, because you deserved it, no matter what the money-hoarding NCAA said.

And there you have it. A decade-long process in which people drop in and out of a kid's life, but the sneaker rep is there for the entire journey. That's why the shoe companies have leverage at every pivotal moment. Sure, it's the money. But like everything in life, it's all about relationships. And that, more than anything else, was what my job was about. Relationships.

Which is why I found myself being introduced to the step-dad of another Zion, Zion Williamson, at a Clemson University football game in 2015, even though they are a Nike school and I was working for adidas at the time. But more on that story in a minute.

★ ★ ★

When the FBI shocked the college basketball world with its 2017 announcement of charges in a corruption scandal, I was caught in the cross fire.

That morning, I was in bed. It was a Tuesday. September 26. Early, around 6:15 a.m. My wife, Candance, who has a PhD in occupational therapy and was pregnant with my son August at the time, and I had just returned from a surprise trip to Canada for her birthday. She was in the bathroom, getting ready to go to work. I heard somebody knocking at the door. It was still dark outside. Nobody in their right mind would be knocking that early in the morning. I jumped up out of the bed, still half asleep, and rushed downstairs to see what all the commotion was about.

Aggravated, clad only in a T-shirt and underwear, I opened the door and was greeted by the shocking sight of close to twenty FBI officers on my porch, lawn, driveway and the adjacent street. About twelve of them were outfitted in tactical gear, assault rifles raised and at the ready, the rest in plainclothes with handguns drawn. You would have thought that I was an international drug lord and murderous fugitive from justice. It was a bizarre scenario that seemed more like a horrific dream.

The lead agent barked, "Are you Merl Code? You're under arrest!"

"For what?"

"I'll tell you when you get in a car."

"Nope. Tell me why I'm under arrest now."

"No, I'll tell you when you get in the car."

"Listen, man, I know enough about the law to know that you have to tell me why I'm under arrest."

"Money laundering."

"From whom? What are you talking about?"

The next thing I knew, one of the officers was playing a recording of me talking to Christian Dawkins, a young up-and-coming sports agent that I'd mentored in the past. "That's not a decision that I can make—that's an adidas decision and I will certainly ask Gatto and see what they want to do."

That was the first and last time I ever heard evidence of that call.

"You were involved in money laundering," said the officer.

Then he started talking about wire fraud, and whatever else. Shit, okay, whatever.

An ensuing *Yahoo! Sports* column said the federal charges had me facing a maximum of eighty years in prison.

Adidas executives Merl Code and Jim Gatto were widely known in the basketball industry as benevolent deal-makers, behind-the-scenes shakers and confidants of the sport's boldfaced names… That changed when Code and Gatto became two of the 10 basketball industry figures arrested in a federal probe that's shaken the sport to its core.

Wait, what? Shaken the sport to its core?

That's when it began, the nightmare. The bullshit.

My name, my picture and video footage of me were splashed across every major newspaper, online outlet and television news program throughout the country. I was mentioned alongside some of the biggest college coaches in the game. Louisville's Rick Pitino, Auburn's Bruce Pearl, Arizona's Sean Miller, LSU's Will Wade. But none of them ultimately faced any charges and only Pitino lost his job as the head coach at the University of Louisville at the time. Sean Miller survived the initial storm, but was ultimately fired by the University of Arizona following the 2021 NCAA Tournament for not winning enough games.

Pitino has since returned to stalking the college basketball sidelines at Iona, despite two separate sex scandals prior to the FBI investigation that have littered his legacy as one of the greatest coaches of all time.

So why would a small, private, Catholic college in New Rochelle, New York, with approximately three thousand undergraduates hire a coach who was seemingly so toxic a few short years ago? Because what happened at Louisville is par for the course in major college basketball, and it's been going on for over a century and not too long after Dr. James Naismith invented the game in 1891.

And toxic or not, Rick Pitino wins games and gets his teams to the NCAA Tournament, which he accomplished in just his first year on the job in 2020–21. That translates into big money flowing in from television and proud alumni donors, not to mention lucrative sponsorship deals from sneaker and apparel companies, other revenue streams and a chance to put Iona on the national basketball map. In essence, it's all about the money. Big money. And the machine doesn't stop; it just keeps on churning as the financial stakes continue to get bigger and bigger.

So what was Pitino's final straw at Louisville, where he lorded over the most profitable college basketball program in the country for a university that monetized hoops better than any institution in America?

The NCAA ruled that Louisville basketball recruit Brian Bowen, a certified future star who could single-handedly elevate the fortunes of the program, was ineligible because of payments that I helped facilitate at the request of his father and the Cardinals basketball program with the approval of both the Louisville and adidas hierarchies.

The NCAA has sold the myth of "amateurism" for decades. If you go to the NCAA website, they lay out the myth for everyone to see:

> *Below are some situations that may impact a prospective student-athlete's amateur status...*
> - *Receiving payment from a sports team to participate.*
> - *Receiving funds or money to offset training expenses.*
> - *Accepting prize money based on performance/finish at a competition.*
> - *Being represented or marketed by a professional sports agent.*
> - *Promoting or endorsing a commercial product or service.*

A moneymaking scheme to rake in billions of dollars, while the workers producing the product aren't allowed to profit themselves? Students of American history, or world history for that matter, will be tempted to say they've heard of this type of arrangement before. *Indentured servitude* is a nice way of calling it what it actually is: a form of slavery.

So was I involved in breaking the rules of the NCAA's absurd system? Man, all of us were tiptoeing around, and at some points stomping on those rules—the players, the families, the coaches, the agents, the sneaker reps. It's all in the game—a dirty game, some would say.

But answer me this: Who's really dirty?

Is it the guy who goes out and helps a kid's family cover their rent by getting them paid under the table for their work and their talents? Or is it the coaches, universities and supposed nonprofits that collectively bring in billions of dollars on the backs of flat broke kids, then tell them to shut up and dribble because they're getting an "education"?

I know which side of that argument I take, but I'll also

concede that it's not black-and-white. I lived my entire professional life in the gray.

But a felon? A criminal who required an entire tactical team of federal agents to arrest me at the crack of dawn? Come on!

And that's a window into why that judge could call me a "very decent human being" before sentencing me to prison time for doing things that he conceded are "prevalent in college basketball and other college sports."

I do not think it was an accident that the famous, mostly white, head coaches and university administrators were shielded from the legal implications, and even the public scrutiny, that came from the FBI investigation.

But should paying talented athletes something approaching a fair living wage be a crime? Is it really so wrong for the NCAA student athletes to get a small piece of the wealth they generate for their schools and apparel outfitters? Judge Edgardo Ramos, who sentenced me, didn't seem to think so.

It appears that all this type of conduct is prevalent in college basketball and other college sports. The money is there. There's a lot of it and it's so easy to take it. It doesn't make it right, but it explains how an individual like Mr. Code ends up in this courtroom today.

That's why I only got a three-month sentence for charges that in other circumstances merit much longer sentences under federal guidelines.

Even the NCAA itself doesn't seem to think so anymore, as the organization that controls amateur college athletics is now letting athletes explore endorsement deals for their name, image and likeness. We'll see how that goes, but even healthy endorsement deals are just a fraction of the money athletes earn for the athletic departments they play for.

The overwhelming majority of major Division I basketball and football players are African Americans from underprivileged backgrounds. I've sat in their living rooms and heard their stories. I've consoled single mothers crying as they struggled to provide for their children. I've seen the look in a sixteen-year-old's eyes when he gets the first truly new, not-passed-down set of clothes he's ever worn. And I've seen the amount of money that everyone else is making as those families struggle to get by. I do not regret a single thing I did to help those kids and families.

My story is the definitive insider's guide to the high-stakes world of competitive basketball. As a former director of grass-roots basketball at Nike and as a consultant with adidas, it's a world that I can talk about like very few can. And like no one else has ever dared.

No one has ever fully revealed what goes on behind the scenes in the high-stakes, big-money world of amateur basketball. Some people have tried, but for someone who has actually lived it, most of their efforts have been laughable. This is mainly because the people who have the access to actually see it all are incentivized to keep quiet and maintain the status quo.

Hell, if I hadn't found myself getting caught up in a bizarre set of circumstances, I probably would not be ready to peel back the curtain either. But I believe there's a plan for everyone's life, that every twist and turn, no matter how unexpected, has a purpose. So now that I've survived the fire, I believe I've been brought here to tell this story.

I hope my experiences and recollections force people to really see up close, in real terms, the kids and families who are being taken advantage of by the companies and schools that profit off their talent. It's those kids and families who are often overlooked in all of this. It is a profound injustice that billions of dollars are made from the talents of young men, usually underprivileged young Black men, who are prohibited from participating in the revenue they generate.

And if they do, they, or the people helping them, are vilified for being rule breakers, or even lawbreakers. I believe the stories I have, the human, often heartbreaking ones, will help build on the growing public demand for change.

When the most recent abuses in collegiate athletics first came to light in 2017, people were outraged. And yet nothing really changed. No major schools suffered serious sanctions. No major corporations suffered. Business as usual just continued. We didn't learn a damn thing. Even at the height of the COVID-19 outbreak, the efforts to put basketball players back on our TV screens to entertain the masses took on far more urgency than concerns about the health risks to the players and their families.

My story will shed more light on one of the most compelling social justice issues in modern American life: the systematic manipulation of young Black men and their loved ones for the love of money.

I should know. I've been part of this pattern of abuse for most of my career.

For most of my adult life I lived in a world most people know exists, but can't really see. My job was part politics, part big business, part hustle, part social work. The multibillion-dollar machine I helped run can be seen all over the world. It plays out on TV screens and on social media, in arenas and stadiums, and in the dreams of kids of every race, color and creed.

But most of the work I did took place far from any bright lights, in dimly lit hotel rooms and nightclubs, in inner-city neighborhoods, on private jets and in penthouse suites. And as it turns out, on wiretapped phone calls.

So what did I do? What cog was I, in what giant wheel?

"Amateur athletics," they call it, although it's hard for anyone involved to say that phrase with a straight face these days. And that's how I first came to know an adolescent Zion Williamson and his family. Again, more on that later.

I've lived every angle of this story. I was recruited as a high school basketball player. I played in the ACC and as a pro. I've worked at the highest levels of the two most powerful shoe brands on Earth. I've worked with the most famous NBA players and the most ruthless agents. I've been a resource for the biggest college programs and an adviser to the most highly recruited kids and their families. I've lived my entire adult life at the intersection of amateur athletics, major college programs and the pros, through which a swollen river, overflowing with billions of dollars, flows on by.

I want to tell the truth. And I want to do it without an agenda. I am not coming from a place of anger or frustration. Sure, there have been times over the last couple of years when I've been furious. Even now, there are days when I cannot believe my life was upended and my livelihood was taken away from me. I believe the justice system failed me.

If everyone who ever committed an NCAA violation that left a kid ineligible is guilty of a crime, they'd have to build a whole lot of new jails. And why didn't they lock up the dozens of other people who fit that description, including the famous coaches?

But putting the thought and effort into chronicling my journey has been a cathartic experience. And more importantly, it has given me a sense of purpose. Change is coming. I want to be a part of that. I've got a story to tell. The world will hear it.

So, I ask again, what did I do to wind up here?

I did my job, plain and simple.

1

Littlejohn Coliseum, the Clemson University basketball arena, sits right across the street from Memorial Stadium, more popularly known as Death Valley and home to one of the nation's most dominant and profitable college football programs. In October of 2019, Clemson's board of trustees approved a $70-million renovation project for Death Valley, including the addition of premium seating and club spaces, modifications to the locker rooms, a new LED lighting system and the installation of a massive new video board.

The basketball coaching staff often entertains recruits, their families and a carefully curated assortment of other individuals there during home football games, basking in a swollen sea of orange pomp and pageantry, where the energy and electricity generated by close to eighty-six thousand rabid fans is off the charts. It's a pretty convincing setting for a seventeen-year-old aspiring college athlete to dream about their future and envision themselves becoming part of the university's athletic family.

On one particular beautiful autumn day in 2015, a handful of basketball recruits were in town with their families. They played some pickup ball with guys on the team at Littlejohn while parents and coaches watched and got to know each other. After the pickup run, the coaches showed the recruits around the offices and the weight room, then we went outside to enjoy the weather and some catered food before the big football game. It was a nice little setup.

"You're the guy I've been wanting to meet," a voice from behind me said.

When I turned around, a bald-headed Black man, probably in his fifties and wearing wire-rimmed glasses, was walking up to me with his hand out. He was well-built, probably about six-two, and was smiling.

"Really?" I said, shaking his hand.

"Yessir, I'm Lee Anderson," he replied. "One of the assistant coaches told me that I need to get to know you."

He went on to explain that he had played at Clemson in the 1970s, but was now focused on guiding his stepson, an up-and-coming high school sophomore named Zion Williamson.

Zion. Great name.

This was before Zion became a social media sensation and the most dynamic, celebrated, marketable and explosive prep hoops phenom since LeBron James was wrecking rims at St. Vincent–St. Mary High School in Akron, Ohio, nearly twenty years ago. This was before he became the most telegenic, seemingly impregnable and balletic above-the-rim force of nature in the college game since Shaq's individual dominance at LSU back in the late '80s and early '90s.

The Williamsons had recently moved twice after living in Marion, South Carolina, a tiny town of about seven thousand people that had nonetheless produced at least two NBA players from the area, the late Boston Celtic Levern Tart and recent fifteen-year vet Raymond Felton. From Marion, they had moved to nearby Florence in search of a better situation for Zion.

"We're in Spartanburg now, though," Lee said, explaining that they had made the three-hour move west so that Zion could attend Spartanburg Day School. There would be better competition there, and more opportunities to develop and get attention. "But I'm still his trainer," Lee insisted.

Then he cut straight to the chase.

"Zion's a superstar in the making." He said it like it was an indisputable matter of fact. "But I need some guidance on how to maneuver this system."

"Listen," he continued, leaning in a little closer. "I've been around this game a long time. I kinda know how it works. I had my own AAU program. We had a relationship with adidas too. But this is my stepson. So, you know, we're going to be having some real conversations with schools and I need someone to lean on through that process."

The Clemson coaches had told him I could help him navigate the uncharted waters ahead. And I was happy to help.

"That's not a problem at all," I told him.

We exchanged cell phone numbers, shook hands again, and Lee said he'd call me soon. About three days later my phone rang and Lee's number popped up on the screen. I answered right away, and there was a sense of urgency in his voice.

He wanted me to make the half-hour drive from Greenville to Spartanburg to meet with him right away. I could tell it was important to him, so I agreed, and it wasn't long before we were sitting across from each other in a booth at McDonald's. Lee had come with his infant son, Noah, in tow.

After some pleasantries, Lee got to the point of the impromptu meeting. "The Clemson staff likes you a lot and I feel comfortable with you," he began. "But I need some help."

I told him I was glad to help any way I could, and asked if there was anything specific he needed. Of course, I assumed there must be, since he'd asked me to come on such short notice.

"I'm trying to be the man of my house," he said, glancing away. "But I don't have any money."

Those are difficult words for any man to say. And he carried it with dignity. But as he sat there with his baby boy in his arms, I could feel a sense of desperation rising in him. And I wanted to help.

The vulnerability of his plight spoke to me. But let's be clear, as an adidas consultant, my job was to build and nurture relationships with kids like Zion and their families, i.e., players that had the potential to be something special at the next levels. There was no universal benevolence there. Had Zion been a nice kid who played chess, I would not have been sitting across from his father and baby brother that afternoon at McDonald's.

I asked if he had discussed his financial issues with any of the schools that were starting to recruit his stepson. He said there had been some conversations about helping him find a job, but he was needing something to help him get by until it came together.

"I just need $100 so I can put some groceries on my family's table," he said. "Can you help me?"

"That's not a problem," I said without hesitation. At this point it wasn't really about basketball. It was about humanity. About doing the right thing, the decent thing. I figured it took a lot for him to make that ask, and it was only a hundred bucks anyway. But I'd be lying if I said that it wasn't about basketball and my job as well.

There was a BP Fast Fuel right next door to the McDonald's. In bright green lights I could see ATM through the front window of the gas station, so I told Lee to hang tight while Noah crawled around on the McDonald's playground and I walked over to get some cash. A few minutes later, the money was in Lee's pocket, and we went our separate ways.

That night I told my wife what happened. I figured she needed to know the deal if I was going to be taking cash out of random out-of-town ATMs. "That's really nice," she said. "Tell me about his stepson."

"He's a little overweight, but he's an incredible athlete," I told her. "And he seems like a really smart, good kid too."

The next day, I called the Clemson coaching staff and told them what was going on. They're a Nike school and I was an adidas guy, but it's a relatively small world we're all operating in. Yeah, I'm trying to send my kids to adidas schools. But these relationships will last forever. I was at Nike, now I'm at adidas, and who knows where I'll be next? Wherever it is, I'll know everybody. And ultimately, this was about helping a kid. That's not always the case in a lot of these situations. And if we're being truthful, it was also a low-cost opportunity to get welcomed into his orbit and for adidas to be in the mix.

Don't get it twisted. This ain't an altruistic industry. It's big business. The money generated from mostly lower-income, big-time college football and basketball athletes keeps the revenue faucets flowing, allowing schools like Clemson to celebrate a $70-million expansion to its football stadium, the construction of new dorms, academic buildings, luxury suites and the sparkling, ostentatious locker rooms and practice facilities that put NBA and NFL teams to shame. As far as I'm concerned, these kids and families deserve everything that comes to them in the process, and usually a helluva lot more.

I think that came through in my interactions with families like Zion's. Sincerity goes a long way in any relationship. They knew I had a job to do. But they also knew I was going to take care of them if I could, even though in all likelihood we'd go our separate ways at some point. So we started interacting on a constant basis from that point forward.

Not long after our meeting at McDonald's, Lee and I were together and we stopped by their place in Spartanburg. The family of four—Lee, his wife and Zion's mother, Sharonda Sampson, Zion and baby Noah—lived in a nine-hundred-square-foot apartment on the ground floor of the Willows at North End apartments. The complex is populated mainly by blue-collar folks, with some Section 8 tenants sprinkled in as well. It wasn't the projects, but they hadn't quite moved on up like George and Weezie just yet.

The entire family was unfailingly polite, especially Zion. The open door to his bedroom revealed a scene familiar to any parent, shoes and clothes strewed haphazardly across the floor. Their tiny dining room table had room for three, with the fourth side pressed against the wall. A TV sat on a small stand in the living room.

But there weren't any family photos on the wall or many decorations. It had the feel of a place that someone didn't anticipate living in for very long.

Sharonda was reserved, even a bit guarded, but clearly very smart. She explained that she was studying to get her master's degree, and from that point forward I rarely saw her without her books.

The better I got to know Zion, the more I liked him. He had an easy way about him and an infectious smile. At that point it was too early in the process to know if the blue blood programs like Duke, North Carolina, Kentucky or Kansas would be clamoring for him.

He was attracting a lot of interest, no doubt. Barring something unforeseen, he would definitely be playing big-time college basketball; otherwise schools like Clemson wouldn't be sending him my way to get help. But he was still young.

Not long after that, Lee invited me over to Northwood Middle School, where Sharonda was teaching, to watch Zion work out. When they were done, I invited the entire family to dinner at the nearby Green Tomato Buffet. And this time it was clear that Lee had been spending a lot of time thinking about what was next for Zion. And himself.

"Let's talk about the summer circuit," Lee said, referencing the summer basketball tournaments that showcase the top players in each class. I was happy to talk about it.

"You're going to have a lot of options because of Zion's abilities," I said. "But he's still relatively unknown outside the state. Let me call around and see who's got room on their team."

"Yeah, that's good," Lee said. "But listen, I want to coach." *Coach? Aw hell.*

For anybody in the business, this is a giant red flag. The last thing the guys running top AAU programs want is a parent who thinks they're a coach. It's a recipe for disaster. Next thing you know you've got issues with parents complaining and other kids getting frustrated. It rarely works out well for anybody involved.

Lee was adamant. But I had another idea.

"What do you think about getting him down to Atlanta and letting him play in a bigger market?" I asked. "That could be really good for him. Everyone's seen what he can do here locally, but if he goes down there and puts in work, he's going to get a lot of people's attention."

Lee was intrigued, and I told him about coach Ryan Faulkner and trainer Desmond "Dez" Eastman, who run a top AAU program in Georgia called Game Elite. These are high-level guys. They're running a factory that produces nothing but real hoopers. I'm talking about big-time D-I players, even NBA guys like Jaylen Brown from the Boston Celtics. He came up under Ryan and Dez. They know what they're doing. And more importantly, they're genuine. They'll always tell you the truth, whether it's what you want to hear or not. And for that reason, parents, players and college coaches all respect them.

As I was telling Lee this, I remembered the good-natured competition I had with Dez when I was at Nike. They were an adidas program back then too.

I was running a Nike camp and I wanted Jaylen Brown to come play in it. So I called Dez up and made my pitch.

"You gonna let him come?" I asked.

"Nope," he said. "You ain't stealing my kid!"

We both burst out laughing. He knew what was up. That's how the business works. Nike's trying to take adidas's kids and they're trying to take Under Armour's kids. It never stops.

And these camps are where that work gets done. If I could bring you into my world, put you in the atmosphere I could create? Forget about it. You want access to LeBron and Kevin Durant at these camps? Come on over to Nike.

Ultimately Dez relented and allowed Jaylen to come to my

camp, but not without an escort. "If he's coming, I'm coming!" he said. And so they did. And I was glad to have them. Because for me it really wasn't about stealing him away, and Dez knew that.

"That's not what I'm here for," I told them both.

"But when he turns pro," I said, turning my attention to Jaylen, "he'll have options."

That's the kind of rapport I wanted with my competition. It was respectful. It's not always like that. But now that I was at adidas, Dez and I were on the same side of the fence, and I thought bringing Zion into his orbit would be a win for everybody involved.

Before long we had Zion in the gym with the Game Elite crew and the feedback was instant. "He's got to get in better shape," Dez said. "But man, talent-wise he's off the charts!"

That summer, Zion torched opponents, proving he could swim with the bigger fish in a much bigger pond. But Lee wasn't satisfied.

"They don't know how to coach him like I do," he'd say. "He needs to be the playmaker. Everything needs to run through him. They don't get it."

When a parent has a kid as talented as Zion, it's hard not to get tunnel vision. "Okay, okay," I told Lee. "But have you thought about the possibility that you may not know how to coach the other kids as well as they do?"

There were some other high-profile kids in the Game Elite program. So in Lee's defense, Zion wasn't out there getting twenty shots a game. But truthfully it didn't matter. His raw athleticism and talent were shining through anyway. He was a burgeoning social media phenomenon, and the attendance at his games was growing along with his buzz in college basketball circles. He had played himself into becoming a consensus five-star recruit.

Ryan and Dez had done right by Zion, but at the end of the summer, I knew he would never suit up again for Game Elite.

"They're good guys, but I want my own thing," Lee said.

I had some friends who were running an AAU program back home in South Carolina, Karolina Khaos, on the adidas circuit. What about having a conversation with them?

"I'm not talking to anyone unless I'm coaching," Lee snapped. I gave it a shot, but my guys weren't having any part of that, no matter how talented Zion was.

So I knew it was finally time to have a conversation with my boss, Chris Rivers, who was the adidas executive in charge of all youth basketball. Rivs had been in the game a long time. He came up under the legendary Sonny Vaccaro, who signed Michael Jordan to his groundbreaking signature sneaker deal with Nike. He'd done stints at both adidas and Reebok in the late '90s and early 2000s, and had been running youth basketball and the adidas NBA players portfolio for much of the last decade.

I told him all about the situation with Lee, and as much as it pained me, I recommended we give him what he was asking for, his own program. "Rivs, this kid is too good to lose," I said. "If we don't find him a home, he's going to end up playing for Nike or Under Armour. I don't care how it looks, but we need to get them taken care of."

Rivs agreed, and before you knew it Lee and Sharonda were both pacing the sideline as coaches of South Carolina Supreme, passing baby Noah back and forth during games. We set them up with a $60,000 "travel team budget," but in reality we kept paying for the travel directly, so that money basically went into their pockets.

And by this time I had been told a Clemson alum had set Lee up with a job as a maintenance supervisor, and Sharonda was working as a physical education teacher at Northwood Middle School, while still working on her master's. Oh, and by the way, adidas had also started sponsoring Zion's official high school team over at Spartanburg Day School. So as his social media views skyrocketed into the millions, he performed most of his gravity-defying dunks with the three-stripes logo on his chest.

I was doing my job. But it wasn't easy. College coaches started telling me that Nike was in hot pursuit. Of course they were. I would have been too. But I also knew that Nike wouldn't outspend adidas, not on this one, anyway.

They had a much bigger budget, sure. But they were also messing with a lot more kids than we were. For every one Zion they didn't yet have under their umbrella, they had five or six others already lined up. We needed Zion in our system more than they did. But they were smart, and they did what I would have done. Throw a dart out there, see if it hits the target. If it doesn't, move on. There will be another chance to make a run at him after college anyway.

And to Lee's credit, Zion's stock was soaring. With no other notable players on his AAU team, he was the undeniable center of attention and focus of the entire operation, both on and off the court. If he was my son, I can't say I'd do it any other way. And his family's situation was steadily improving too.

On the day of the Clemson vs South Carolina football game in the fall of 2016, I got a call from one of the Clemson assistant coaches, who immediately said, "You're not going to believe this one."

Lee, he explained, had called them up and asked for six

tickets—six!—to the biggest annual rivalry game in the state, just hours before kickoff.

Now, by this point, Clemson was all-in on Zion, so in the grand scheme of things, this was a cheap, albeit annoying, request. So after a conversation with the school's compliance department, a mad scramble ensued to round up six tickets. There's no telling how many arms they had to twist and whose dream of seeing the rivalry up close was dashed. But somehow they found six tickets and called Lee back to inform him that Zion and the family could all come to the special entrance for recruits to get their tickets.

At that point Lee shocked him by explaining that no one in the family was planning to come.

The coach was taken aback. *What? Why not?*

As it turned out, Lee just wanted to give some of his friends and coworkers tickets to the big game and figured he'd call in a quick favor. He and his family would be watching the game on TV, if at all.

The work had already been done, so the coach begrudgingly agreed to let them all come, took down their names and had the tickets waiting for them at the recruiting entrance.

A couple of hours later, every single one of them showed up dressed head to toe in South Carolina gear. In a sea of orange, surrounded on every side by Clemson recruits and their family members, Lee had sent a half-dozen SC fanatics. It wasn't a half hour in before they had caused such a ruckus, arguing with kids and parents alike, that security had to remove them and seat them in a different area for fear of an actual fight breaking out.

The coach relayed the entire story to me, alternating between laughter and outrage.

Plus Lee was pushing for them to help the family get into a

larger apartment, or perhaps even a house. I heard that someone close to the program was checking with alumni to find a spot that might work at a nominal price.

This didn't surprise me at all, of course. How do you think these underprivileged families move with their kids when they go to school? Coaches get boosters to give parents jobs, or give them discounted rent, or whatever else makes sense for the situation. There's really no difference between that and just giving them cash, but it's easier to get it done. The way I saw it, these kids and parents should make the most of it. Otherwise everybody involved is cashing in except for them. And what if they never make it to the NBA? Believe me, most of them don't. So if this was their chance to improve their lives, I hoped they'd take full advantage of the opportunity.

In this particular situation, all I know is that it wasn't long before Zion's family was living in a four-bedroom house. And they had some other plans in mind as well.

Clemson's coaching staff called me again to let me know that Zion's mother, Sharonda, was asking for her older son, Tyriek, to be taken care of as well. At the time, Tyriek was running track at the University of South Carolina Upstate, a lower-tier Division I school in Spartanburg. But Sharonda apparently wanted him to become a package deal with Zion. Whatever school signed him to play basketball would also have to sign his brother to run track.

Fortunately, one of my wife's best friends happened to be tight with one of the Clemson track coaches. She agreed to help set up a dinner with the coach. We started building a relationship, and she was willing to explore the possibility of bringing Zion's brother into the program. At least at first. Then she actually saw him in action.

"He can't run worth a shit," the coach said with a mixture

of amusement and exasperation. "Even my girls are out here kicking his ass!"

We had a good laugh, but that wouldn't be the end of it. Before long, word came down from on high inside the Clemson athletic department that they would indeed make some room on the team for Tyriek, whether his ass could run worth a shit or not.

In the middle of all of this, the rumor that I kept hearing was that Lee had also approached the South Carolina coaches about helping them pay their rent.

Just pause for a moment to think about that request.

He wants SC to pay the rent on the house that Clemson supposedly helped them move into!

Apparently everyone involved knew that SC had very little shot of actually landing Zion, so to my knowledge they smartly stayed on the sidelines.

But that didn't change the fact that my guys at Clemson were trying to figure out what to do since allegedly Lee hadn't paid his massively discounted rent in months.

"Look, man," I began, "a few more months and this is all over with. Whatcha gonna do, put them out on the street?"

Of course they weren't. Especially not after all the work they'd put in to get to this point. Around that same time, Zion was in the middle of entertaining the most famous college basketball coaches in America in their family's house, the one Clemson had allegedly helped put them in. Think about that one for a minute as well.

I was with Zion the night North Carolina coach Roy Williams was scheduled to come to the house. He'd won three NCAA championships and was inducted into the Naismith Memorial Basketball Hall of Fame in 2007.

"Do I really have to go?" Zion asked, sincerely. Really he

just didn't want to waste everyone's time, including coach Williams's. "I really don't want to do this and I know I'm not going to North Carolina."

Do you understand the level of high school stardom you have to achieve to be completely disinterested in Roy Williams coming to your house?

And it wasn't arrogance. He was that good, that famous, that clear-eyed about his future. There were really only two schools that had a chance. Clemson had put in the work. They'd built the relationship. But I also remembered what he told me at the adidas Nations event in Houston earlier that summer. "Duke's my favorite school," he said. "Always has been, like, since I was little."

Zion was never an overly talkative kid, so the fact that he volunteered that little piece of information always stuck with me. And here's where you've got to understand that it's not my job to convince a kid where to go to school. I'm here to maintain the relationship, no matter where he ends up going. Other than nudging him toward one of the best AAU teams in the country the year before, I never tried to get in the way of what Lee was doing with Zion. And by that point, Lee was doing, well, a lot.

Capitalizing on Zion's now unprecedented online following, Lee was fielding offers from the organizers of various dunk contests. Want Zion to come? Lee could make that happen for a few thousand bucks. With that, you're guaranteed to pack the gym, get some viral highlights and raise the profile of your event. It was probably a good investment for the event organizers, and as I've already made clear, I never begrudge any of these families for getting paid what they're worth.

But it was all becoming a bit more than I felt like handling. Zion was now a nationwide phenomenon, a generational talent with a stepdad who was, to put it politely, high maintenance.

So I decided it was time to transition the day-to-day handling of the Williamsons to Chris Rivers. For the rest of the year, I got ongoing updates, but was much more hands-off. I later learned that there were records showing that Rivs and adidas had made thousands of dollars of payments to Zion's family.

There was discussion of moving Zion out to Prolific Prep, an adidas-sponsored hoops juggernaut in Napa, California. Sharonda wasn't interested. Rivs told her he was just trying to help any way he could, and wanted to make sure the relationship was still solid from a company standpoint. She said it was, but made it clear that she was disinterested in the business side of things. For that, adidas should continue to deal with Lee.

Unbeknownst to us at the time, and what would later come out in court documents, Sharonda had worked out a deal for Nike to pay her as a consultant. It turns out that Lee was doing the most, but Sharonda had the real juice. And Zion had his own mind. Props to him for that.

The morning of April 20, 2018, over two years since I first met Lee at that Clemson football game, Clemson got word that Zion would announce that afternoon that he would be officially signing to play for them. A brief moment of euphoria broke out of the hoops offices on campus, where football success had far exceeded basketball in recent years. Maybe Zion was going to change that.

A few hours later at a press conference at Spartanburg Day, flanked by his mother, stepfather, track-running older brother and baby Noah, Zion reached under the table, pulled out a blue hat and announced to the world, "I will be joining the brotherhood of Duke University."

When I saw it, I leaned back in my chair and smiled. *Well played*.

During an interview with reporters eager to get the inside scoop on how it all went down, Lee told them, "At first, I thought Clemson was the ideal place for Zion… I still believe that, I really believe that. But it wasn't me making that decision." As for what he told Clemson, Lee remarked, "You all had a mile-and-a-half lead on the situation. I don't know what happened along the way."

So what really happened in the end? I don't know for sure. But here's what we do know: Sharonda Sampson had a job at Duke University during her son's tenure there, and it was rumored that the family moved into a $950,000 mansion in a gated community in Durham.

And everything worked out lovely for Zion. With Duke. With the NBA. And in the end, with Nike and Jordan Brand. Get yourself paid, young man. You deserved it all along.

The most powerful names in my world aren't coaches like Krzyzewski, Calipari or Self; or institutions like Duke, Kentucky or Kansas; or even "non-profits" like the ACC, SEC or Big 12; or even the NCAA itself.

If you want to know who has the power, ignore the millionaire coaches. Don't bother following the ten-figure TV rights deals.

You'll find some of it in the venerable hoops palaces with names like Rupp Arena, the Dean Dome or Allen Fieldhouse, but that's not where it starts.

No, if you're trying to find out who really has the juice, the *real* power, you'd do better to show up at venues like the LakePoint sporting complex in Atlanta, the Riverview Park Activities Center in North Augusta, the Hoover Metropolitan Complex in Birmingham or the Boo Williams Sportsplex in Hampton.

Follow the signs that say EYBL, adidas Gauntlet or The Under Armour Association.

If this is starting to sound like an underground fight club, don't worry. It's all out there for the public to see. But much like the fictional Fight Club, the first rule is that nobody talks about what's really going on.

So when you show up at one of these venues on a weekend in April, May or July, find a seat or stand along the wall, close your eyes and listen. You hear that? Those quick, high-pitched squeaks are something like the unofficial soundtrack of basketball. The friction of rubber soles against a hardwood floor. It's a beautiful thing. There's a purity to it. That sound happens everywhere the game is played. It's ubiquitous. You don't need a scoreboard, or referees, or announcers, or TV crews. All you need is a ball, a basket and the shoes.

Those shoes, man. Everyone needs them. *Everyone.*

Now open your eyes and look at every player's feet, and you'll see who's got the juice. It's symbolized by a check mark, or three stripes, or sometimes by an interlocked *U* and *A*. Nike. adidas. Under Armour. A combined market capitalization upward of $160 billion. Yeah, check that number again real quick.

Now look around you. You'll see the familiar logos of your favorite college athletics programs, probably even your own alma mater, on the polos and jackets of almost everyone there. And among them you'll see someone who doesn't appear to be aligned with any particular team, probably dressed head to toe in one particular shoe brand or another.

That's me. This is my world. The rest of these guys are just passing through.

At one point for me it was Nike. At another point it was adidas.

In both instances I was a get-it-done guy. Get what done, you may ask?

It.

Whatever it was.

As long as it meant that the best teenage basketball players suited up for the youth basketball teams we sponsored, signed to play for the universities we had deals with, and ultimately turned pro, preferably as first-round draft picks going to major-market NBA teams, and did it all while wearing our logo on their shoes, and socks, and shorts, and jerseys, and headbands, and…well, you get the idea.

But long before a Zion Williamson becomes a household name, he's just a kid, usually a Black kid, and more often than not he's flat broke. So before he can ever worry about putting a ball in a hoop, he's gotta survive. Shit, his whole family's gotta survive.

So it was almost with a sense of poetic irony that during Zion's tremendous one-and-done season at Duke—in which he was named the ACC Player of the Year, a consensus All-American, won both the Naismith and Wooden Awards among a much longer list of remarkable accolades for a mere freshman—the lasting memory of him on the court wasn't the twenty-eight points he scored in his ballyhooed debut against Kentucky in only twenty-three minutes of action. Nor was it the thirty-five he banged on the collective heads of the Syracuse Orangemen. It wasn't leading the Blue Devils to within two points of the Final Four after a crushing one-point loss to Michigan State in the Elite Eight, or his otherworldly, Bill Russell–esque shot-blocking prowess or the thunderous compilation of dunks that made folks believe that their eyes had the capacity to lie.

No, the moment most remembered came in February 2019. It was the blowout heard around the sports world, when his foot ripped through the Nike, Duke-specific PG 2.5, NBA star Paul George's signature shoe model as he planted his left foot on the shiny hardwood of Cameron Indoor Stadium against the rival North Carolina Tar Heels in one of the most viewed college basketball games ever aired on ESPN.

I say poetic irony because it was a season following what was supposed to be one of the most "explosive" scandals in the history of college hoops. The one I got snagged up in by the FBI. The FBI!!!

But in the same way that Zion returned shortly with no ill effects, continuing his reign atop the game while serving as an unofficial billboard for Nike every time he appeared on television, the college game moved forward with no ill effects, save for the few individuals, myself included, the majority being Black men, middlemen and assistant coaches being cast as some type of rogue organized crime figures who were threatening the so-called sanctity of the game. Which is all utter bullshit.

Michael Sokolove, in the epilogue of his recent book, *The Last Temptation of Rick Pitino*, when reflecting on Zion's lone season at Duke, wrote,

To watch Zion play at the end of such a dreary year of college basketball, after all the layers of sleaze that were exposed—after the coaches who talked like gangsters and the self-interested NCAA suits who stayed in duck-and-cover mode—was to be reminded that there is actually some good left in the center of it. It was proof that if you could clear away the corruption, even for a moment, something like pure, joyous competition comes into view.

The statement was absurdly hilarious to me, given that he speaks as if he's in a pulpit, not knowing what the hell he's talking about, without the slightest clue as to what went into Zion's recruitment and the dollars swirling around the young man, a mere pittance of which flowed into his family's coffers before he cashed in big in the NBA.

Does that make him or his family sleazy gangsters? Of course not. Neither he nor his family created the environment that was designed to exploit them. They were simply playing the game according to the real rules, the Fight Club rules, grabbing what they could off the margins.

And, happily, the best-case scenario happened for him. But that is a rarity, and far-fetched from the reality of most poor Black kids that play college basketball.

That phrase Sokolove used, if I'm being honest, still irks me. "After all the layers of sleaze were exposed…"

I was obviously lumped into those "layers of sleaze." At various junctures I was called not only sleaze, but an undesirable and corrupt. These were, among others, the terms used to describe me since the entire ordeal came to light in various media outlets.

It's typical of those who are so comfortable in their spaces of privilege as it relates to the space of elite college athletics. It's typical of the uninformed, uneducated and inexperienced, specifically those writers and journalists and other media members pecking away at their computers who are oblivious to how the whole machine operates, casting aspersions about an environment, one in which they cling to the absurd concept of "amateurism" and the facade that allows young Black athletes to be exploited and taken advantage of by the NCAA and universities that falsely claim to have their best interests at heart.

My credibility and reputation were attacked, which was to be expected. My life was upended; my ability to provide for my family was severely compromised. All of this despite the fact I committed no crimes and simply played loosely, as everyone does in this space, from the Rick Pitinos to the Will Wades to the Bill Selfs and countless others, with the Byzantine and exploitative NCAA rules.

Yes, I was in the business of giving the companies that employed me a competitive advantage in the marketplace. But I was also in the business of helping kids and their families.

These young men were athletes first and students a very far second. Many were directed toward recreation management majors or other easy, less rigorous courses of study meant to keep them eligible, not educate them. I was dealing with them as people, not property, as well as their families' real-world issues.

We put groceries in the kitchens of families that didn't know where their next meal was coming from. We supplied winter coats against bitter winters. We covered doctor and dentist bills out of our own pockets when the situation was dire. Sometimes we personally paid families' heat, gas or electric bills, so they wouldn't go without. We ensured mortgage or rent payments got covered, giving athletes and their families a respite from the haunting specter of foreclosure or eviction. So yes, let's have an honest conversation. Not one based on some fictional fantasy that has Luther Vandross singing "One Shining Moment" in the background right after Baylor has kicked Gonzaga's ass in the national championship game as the nets are being cut down.

I'm ready to tell my story. And it is my sincere hope that you are ready to listen.

2

During the whole FBI ordeal and ensuing media coverage I was, at various points, portrayed as a shady criminal preying on vulnerable kids and their families. I was part of those "layers of sleaze." I was erroneously referred to as some rogue grassroots coach. When people read my name in articles, there was an overall assumption of guilt in terms of the way the coverage was slanted. Whenever I was seen on television, it was a brief glimpse of me walking into a courtroom to face up to the "crimes" I'd supposedly committed.

Unless you actually knew me, I was some shadowy figure, some outsider, some gangster outfitted from head to toe in slick adidas gear making backroom deals with a shady assortment of Black assistant coaches for the sole purpose of lining our own pockets.

Let me tell you the truth.

My family has a long, entrenched history as it relates to higher education and its intersection with elite athletics.

My dad, Merl Code Sr., is from Seneca, South Carolina, a small city with a population of roughly eight thousand in Oconee County, about eight miles from the Clemson campus. He was a phenomenal high school football player in the early '60s. Back in those days, the best Black prep talent in the south wasn't welcome at most of the big white SEC, ACC and old Southwest Conference schools. So the rosters of the historically Black colleges and universities were supremely stocked and overflowing with an embarrassment of riches.

Big Merl, as he's referred to, had an exceptional college career, both in the classroom and on the gridiron. He's in the Hall of Fame as a defensive back at North Carolina A&T, where he met my mom and graduated cum laude with a bachelor of science in mathematics.

Many years later, when I was working for Nike, I was attending some opening-round NCAA Tournament games in Greenville and bumped into my former high school teammate and friend since the earliest days of elementary school, Shammond Williams, who was a phenomenal player that had starred at the University of North Carolina. He introduced me to Hall of Famer Bob McAdoo, a UNC alum. In basketball circles, McAdoo is an all-time great, revered for being one of those dudes with superfluous skills that helped usher in the modern game. At six-foot-nine and skinny, he was a forerunner in terms of scoring the rock and the overall magnificence of what we're seeing today from the majestic Kevin Durant.

As we were walking out of the arena, Mac, who was born and raised in Greensboro, where his father was a custodian at North Carolina A&T, stopped in his tracks, lowered his chin and looked down at me with eyes that had suddenly come alive. "Merl Code? Is your daddy Merl Code that played football at A&T?" When I confirmed that I was indeed his son, he let out a wide smile and said, "Boy, your daddy was a bad, baaaaad man!"

My grandfather, Allen L. Code, played pro baseball in the Negro Leagues. I'd long heard the stories about the vicious beatings he'd receive because he wanted to play baseball and would often choose to practice over working in the fields.

He went on to become one of the first Black educated men from the area who'd attained advanced degrees, receiving his master's from the University of Michigan. He was the long-time principal at the segregated, all-Black Blue Ridge High School and there was an elementary school later named after him. His wife, my grandmother Sedalia, played basketball at South Carolina State.

My mother, Denise, who hails from Roanoke, Virginia, played tennis in high school and played competitively long into her adult years. Her mom played basketball. Till this very day, you can walk into her house and hear my grandmother yelling at the TV while watching NBA and college hoops.

So we were all about education and sports. I came from a family of achievement, where a commitment to educational success was paramount.

My dad played pro ball in the Canadian Football League in the early '70s and won two Grey Cup championships, the CFL's equivalent of the Super Bowl. He also won a championship in the defunct World Football League for the Memphis Southmen, where his teammates included the likes of NFL

Hall of Famers Paul Warfield and Larry Csonka, along with former Dallas Cowboys quarterback Danny White.

When reflecting on his experiences in Canada, he often cites those years as being among his most enjoyable, not because he was playing pro ball, but because it was his first time outside of the explosive powder keg of the South. For the first time in his life, he felt celebrated for his talents and thoughts in a place where race was not an issue.

But football, as much as I'm sure he loved it, was a means to an end for him. While playing pro ball, he also owned the Ghana, a nightclub in Greenville that could seat close to six hundred people.

He was also a promoter and an investor in the music business, partnering to finance national tours for groups like the Jackson Five, Gladys Knight, the O'Jay's, Santana, the Average White Band, Teddy Pendergrass, Marvin Gaye and others. He used his earnings from all these endeavors to pay his way through law school as soon as he retired from professional athletics.

When he graduated from the University of South Carolina's law school, my dad and one of his classmates immediately set up their own practice, specializing in criminal defense, which they built from scratch.

My mother was holding things down as well, working as an office manager for General Electric.

My parents were very loving and supportive of my academic and athletic endeavors. Books came first. Bringing anything other than As and Bs into my house was not tolerated. Dad would take me to the park at an early age, teaching me how to throw and catch a football and baseball, how to dribble and shoot. Mom would teach me how to play tennis.

My father is a very cerebral, intelligent dude. A masterful

storyteller with the oratorical skills of a mesmerizing preacher, he's accomplished great things as an attorney and judge in the state of South Carolina. His reputation is impeccable. He strongly believed in being a community servant, helping folks that look like us to elevate into better circumstances. He's adamant about creating opportunities, pursuing education and helping folks down the path of economic empowerment and ownership.

One of the first things he did when he passed the bar exam and opened his practice, in addition to his concentration in criminal law, was to establish himself as an NFL agent.

He often said that any decent lawyer could negotiate a contract. But he was interested in clients that wanted to use football as a stepping-stone, the personal aspect where he could help others set themselves up for later success away from the gridiron. He'd stress that the average career for a pro football player was merely three years, so he wanted to set those guys up for life after football in the same way that he set himself up through law school.

He was ahead of his time because if you look at the rookie orientation programs that are now instituted by the NFL and the NBA, they mirror what he did for his clients. His thing was, *Let's prepare for when the air goes out of the ball, let's understand how to take care of your money and make it grow, let's get that degree so when you're ready, you're a viable candidate for some really good jobs when this sports thing is over.*

He had a few clients that bought into that philosophy and he enjoyed the work, bringing a unique perspective as an agent with a law degree who a few years prior was playing pro ball himself. But the enterprise wasn't worth the amount of money that he was investing and after a few years, as his criminal law practice had really taken off, he decided to exit the sports agent business.

I absorbed what he was trying to accomplish and later incorporated those leanings into my dealings with the families and elite athletes that I'd work with down the line. One of the most exhilarating aspects of my job, in addition to doing it well and achieving my own personal successes, was being a conduit, a sounding board, an adviser to kids and their families in terms of using their blessings to achieve something higher, and that had nothing to do with making it to the NBA.

My mom comes from a long line of some of the most beautiful women you've ever seen. She's a dancer, a singer, the life of the party, a superb cook, very compassionate, concerned, a worrier and a nurturer who's always there to take care of others. And she has a very playful sense of humor. She also handled her business as a professional woman before recently retiring, so my parents do a great job of balancing each other out. I could not have asked for better role models in terms of parents and seeing what a loving partnership looks like.

Saturday was cleanup day in my house. Mom would be blasting Luther Vandross or the Whispers, so that was the soundtrack that propelled me through my household chores of mopping, sweeping, vacuuming and cleaning the bathrooms. Before you went to play or do anything, you got your work done. It was about discipline, and that always stayed with me.

I watched as my father built up his practice over the years and would sit in on some of the meetings he had with colleagues at our house, which had a huge impact on me. I wasn't interested in law per se as much as I was in the business aspect, how people made money and the different avenues they pursued to make that happen.

I grew up in a small, two-bedroom, one-bath, single-level

house on the Black side of town, 30 Old Augusta Road in Greenville, South Carolina, which is the approximate midway point between Atlanta and Charlotte. Greenville was once a Cherokee hunting ground in the 1700s, later known as a booming summer resort town by the mid-1800s after the Native Americans had been expelled and exterminated.

While my father was building his practice, he wasn't making a whole lot of money. Don't get me wrong—we were doing okay; we weren't worrying about where our next meal was coming from. Our light bill was gonna get paid. We had cars. But we weren't killing it.

I did have plenty of friends, though, who were worried about that next meal. Spending time with them in their home, I learned to appreciate what I did have and what my parents were able to provide.

So growing up in the less affluent area, I was considered the rich kid, even though we weren't rich. Which meant I learned that some people don't like the fact that you have and they don't. We had a saying in our house, "Everybody that's with you ain't always for you." I learned early on that just because people are around you and act like your friend, they don't always want the best for you.

As I started getting into the athletic space in youth sports, playing on my first football, basketball and baseball teams, I'd hear people, older folks along with those who were my own age who'd mimic them, saying stuff like, "Aw, he's only on the team because his daddy paid for the uniforms."

As a youngster, you don't know how to deal with or handle that. But my father had already been through that with his own experiences of my grandfather having advanced degrees and being a high school principal. So he'd just tell me, "Listen, you can't be just as good—you gotta be better. And

sometimes, better ain't good enough. You gotta be exceptional. You gotta dominate. Whatever they're saying about
you, go prove them wrong. And you don't even have to open
your mouth to prove them wrong. But you gotta prove 'em
wrong."

By the time I got to middle school, I became passionate
about hoops. I knew that's what I wanted to do. My father's
response was, "If you wanna get better at it, I'll take you as far
as I can. I'll show you what I know and if you wanna work at
it, I'll get up with you." So I started getting up before school
every morning at five thirty to put in some extra work.

His one stipulation was, "You get out of the bed and come
get me because I'm not getting up to come and get you. This
is for you, not me." So every morning, Monday through Fri-
day, we'd be in the backyard at the crack of dawn getting up
two hundred shots.

He then sent me to train with my godfather, Johnny Jones.
Johnny, whose son is the actor Orlando Jones, had been one
of the best high school coaches in the state of Alabama and an
assistant at a number of colleges such as Florida State, Florida
A&M and Furman. He'd also been the head coach at South
Carolina State. After his coaching career, he settled in nearby
Mauldin, which is Kevin Garnett's hometown.

When people think about basketball hotbeds, the state of
South Carolina may not immediately come to mind if you're
not from this area. The aforementioned KG may have been
named the National Player of the Year by *USA TODAY* and
the MVP of the McDonald's All-American game while attending Farragut Academy on the west side of Chicago for his
senior year, but he was born in Greenville, went to Hillcrest
Middle School and balled out for three years at Mauldin High.

Kevin wound up in Chicago due to a racially charged incident in which he was arrested after a brawl between a group of white and Black students. The charges were expunged through a pretrial intervention, but the foul stain of that episode, with him seen as a target because of his athletic prowess and the color of his skin, still lingers back at home.

The Milwaukee Bucks' Khris Middleton along with Ja Morant and Zion Williamson are repping the state to the fullest at the highest levels of the game right now. The Nets' Nick Claxton, whose parents are neighbors with my parents in Greenville, is beginning to emerge as an exceptional NBA role player as well, along with the Denver Nuggets' P. J. Dozier.

And if we want to take a walk down recent memory lane, the state also produced the likes of Hall of Famer Alex English, Shammond Williams—my homeboy since we were seven or eight years old who forged a legendary college career as a North Carolina Tar Heel—Larry Nance, Jermaine O'Neal, Xavier McDaniel, Tyrone Corbin, Raymond Felton, Willie Anderson, Stanley Roberts and a slew of others.

Johnny Jones was an incredible teacher who helped me develop my skills. It was the first time I'd ever done two-ball drills: simultaneously dribbling with my left hand and shooting with my right, him timing me, increasing my pace and speed as we went along. I didn't understand the purpose in all of that, thinking to myself, *I'll never have to do this in a game.* But I later came to recognize that he was on that Mr. Miyagi shit from *The Karate Kid*—"Wax on! Wax off!" Pretty soon, the ball became an extension of me and I could get to any spot on the floor that I wanted to as a point guard, while developing skills as an accurate shooting guard as well.

As I mentioned earlier, my mom's family is from Roanoke, Virginia, so I'd go there during the summer months to spend time with her side of the family. There were so many good players in that area. Where my grandmother lives, if you walk down the alley and pass two houses, that's where Curtis Staples lived. He was a high school All-American and was named Virginia's Mr. Basketball during his senior year at Patrick Henry High School. He had a great career at the University of Virginia, where his number is now retired.

George Lynch lived in the area as well. Both of his parents had gone to high school with my mother. George, who was a few years older, had also been named the state's Mr. Basketball, won a national championship at North Carolina and wound up being a first-round draft pick that played twelve seasons in the NBA.

There was also Curtis Blair, who was a helluva player at Richmond and is now an NBA referee, the twins Ramon and Damon Williams, who tore it up at VMI, and my guy Troy Manns, who played at George Mason and Virginia Tech.

The CORD summer basketball camps in Roanoke, that was my incubator, where I started to learn the fundamentals and acquired the ability to think the game at a young age, how to utilize jab steps, pump fakes, head fakes, ball fakes, how to simply be crafty with the rock. That was my real hoops foundation, where the hunger really started.

Eureka Park may have had some beautiful rolling hills and stunningly large trees, but it was also where the dope boys conducted their business, so some of my games of one-on-one against Troy Manns out there would be interrupted when the bullets started flying. We'd scamper, wait for the coast to clear and then hop right back on the court. Those summers in Roanoke, playing with and against some really good players in the park and at camp, made me realize that I could really play.

My favorite players back then, the guys whose games spoke

to my soul, were Isiah Thomas, Joe Dumars and Kenny Anderson. It wasn't simply about scoring the ball with them; it was about facilitating, sharing, elevating the collective to much more than the individual parts of a team. Little did I know that I'd later get to spend time with Joe when I was working at Nike and he was the general manager of the Pistons. Same with Isiah when he was working with the New York Knicks.

These were some fun days for me, matching up against some of the best dudes in the area—the local legends who were now working nine-to-fives, the college guys, the top high schoolers—at a spot called the Armory. In the same way that the Fonde Recreation Center in Houston was the incubator where iron sharpened iron, that's what the Armory was for us in Greenville.

It was where the older guys lumped you up, where you dared not set foot on that court unless you had some serious game, where you fought for every inch and every basket, where you had to knuckle up sometimes and shoot some hands to prove that you weren't no punk. And as a young teenager in the formative stages of your hoops journey, nothing made you feel better than one of the local legends nodding at you, patting you on the back and saying, "Good game, young fella."

On the outside, it was just a brick-and-cinder-block eyesore. Inside, it was a sweatbox with low rafters and no air-conditioning, the industrial-sized fans doing nothing but circulating blistering, scorching air. But for us, it was an oasis, the place where you established and maintained your rep, where you earned your stripes as a real baller. In the summer of '96, after Stephon Marbury was drafted and before playing his first season with the Minnesota Timberwolves,

Kevin Garnett brought the kid from Coney Island to the Armory to hoop.

I wasn't overly athletic but I was really good with the ball, could get to where I wanted to and either hit the open man or make my own shot. I was a good little point guard as a sophomore, but I was only five-foot-six. The summer before my junior year at Southside High School, I had a six-inch growth spurt. By the end of that season, the head coach at South Carolina, George Felton, told me, "Hey, we really like you and we want you to come." I was ecstatic. I'd been getting calls and letters from some midmajor programs, but this was my first offer from a major D-I school. In my mind, I screamed, *I'm coming!*

But my parents were basically like, "Look, South Carolina is great. Is that what you wanna do?"

"I guess."

"Don't guess. If you're not sure, just tell the coach you wanna play out your senior year and see what happens. Don't jump at the first thing that comes along, especially if you only think it MIGHT be what you wanna do."

Coach Felton was like, "Cool. We want you. We're not going anywhere. We think you'll fit in great with our program."

So I had a scholarship from an SEC school heading into my senior year. But I was soon to get my first taste of how big-time college athletics works on the business side.

Turns out that coach Felton got fired prior to the start of my senior season and Steve Newton was brought in from Murray State to take over the program. Before suiting up for my final year, my high school coach, Mark Huff, pulled me out of class and we walked to his office. Coach Newton was there. "Hey, just wanted to make the trip up and do this face-to-face," he said. "We've seen you and we just don't think you're good enough to play for us."

My disappointment did not last long, however, because Virginia Tech soon started recruiting me. But that excitement was soon tempered when I learned that they'd already signed five guards who'd be sophomores when I got there. *Ain't no way I'm going there if they just recruited five guys that can play one of the two positions that I can play*, I said to myself. So that wasn't a good look.

Clemson would come to see me at least once a week, but they never offered a scholarship. Tons of schools would come to watch us practice because my teammate, Mike Minniefield, a six-foot-eight-inch, 230-pound forward was being heavily recruited and we also had my guy Shammond Williams. Mike, after a stint at JUCO, would go on to play for St. John's in the Big East. We were a very nice inside-outside combo that would go on to win a state championship, with me being named the state player of the year in my division. And yet, my college basketball future still looked murky.

What was a good look was one school that was showing a ton of interest, Northwestern. I liked the coaching staff and took a visit, where my host was the team's point guard, Pat Baldwin. Pat is currently the head coach at the University of Wisconsin–Milwaukee. His son, Patrick Baldwin Jr., is a ridiculously talented six-foot-nine prospect projected to be a top-five pick in the 2022 NBA draft. He recently chose to play for his dad at Milwaukee over offers from the likes of Duke, Kansas, Kentucky, Michigan and a slew of others.

So I loved my visit to Northwestern and was on the verge of committing. My parents were like, "Are you sure that's what you want to do? They haven't won a conference game in like four years."

I loved the campus, it was one of the top academic institutions in the country, but I was stuck on what I should do. Another option was going to Anderson Junior College, one of the top JUCOs in the country, which was only twenty minutes from my house. The coach there promised that after one year, I'd have my pick among offers from the top programs that I wanted to attend. The only drawback was I'd only have three years of eligibility to play D-I if I went the JUCO route.

After one of my high school games, I came home and there was a short, slim white man with some receding white-blondish hair who looked to be in his forties sitting in my living room. His name was Dan Peterson and he was the scout for one of the top prep basketball programs in the country, Fork Union Military Academy. It is also considered one of America's top military boarding schools.

He was very convincing in telling me and my parents what a postgraduate year there could do for me in terms of visibility, maturation, building up my body and improving my understanding of the game. He said I'd be a perfect fit and urged me to go check the campus out to see if it was something that I might consider. He was an honest man, very charismatic, but he wasn't there for a song and dance or a sales pitch.

Three weeks later, I was in a car with him, riding seven hours toward Fork Union, a town of about a thousand people that had one post office, one grocery store, one supermarket, one bank, one restaurant and one pizza shop.

During the ride, I was thinking, *What am I getting myself into?*

I'd just played in an all-star game that McDonald's sponsored—not the prestigious McDonald's All-American game but a regional affair—in Atlanta, where my teammates included Kevin Garnett, Jerry Stackhouse and Jeff McInnis, among some of the other best players from the North Carolina–South Carolina–Georgia region. And yet, the colleges that were calling me wouldn't pull the trigger and offer me a situation that felt right.

So I watched the Fork Union squad practice, and they were really good. I saw how strong those dudes were, how they played together as a team, how crisply they moved the ball, how precise they ran their offense, how hungrily they played D. It was an entirely different level than the South Carolina high school basketball that I was accustomed to playing. From a strictly hoops perspective, it felt like the best route for me to take.

You can't drive and accidentally stumble across Fork Union. You can only get there if you're intentionally trying to. During that long ride, I was feeling uncertain. I knew that I loved basketball, that I wanted to play on TV in the ACC. I also knew that this wasn't a recruiting visit. I was going up there to try out.

I didn't have a muscle on my body and the Fork Union guys were rocked up. They played some grown-man, physical ball. That first back screen when we scrimmaged, I got hit so hard I thought I broke my back. I was like, *Damn! This is what big-time basketball looks like.*

On the ride back to South Carolina I asked Coach Pete, "How'd I do?" He just looked at me and said, "You'll be alright." I didn't know what that meant but about three weeks later, I got a call from the head coach, Fletcher Arritt, telling me how he ran his program and asking me if I wanted to come and be a part of it.

Coach Arritt, who recently passed away, was a legendary figure on the prep basketball scene, the best type of man you'll ever come across. He coached every kid the same way, whether they were heading to North Carolina or a Division III school. It was never about your feelings, but always about the game. He was tough, but it wasn't personal with him; it was about what your responsibilities were and being there for your teammates. He instilled a pride about wearing that uniform, about being part of something unique and special.

Coach Arritt, despite being on the opposite end of the cultural and age spectrum, had something in common with his players in that he too came to Fork Union as a postgraduate cadet. He went on to play basketball at the University of Virginia, where he also lettered in track and cross-country. Close to two hundred of his former players went on to play major D-I college ball, with seven of those making it to the NBA.

The guys I played with at Fork Union could really get down, and they were a really good group of dudes. Harold Deane would go on to become a three-time All-ACC player at Virginia. Sydney Johnson had an exceptional college career at Princeton and would later become the head coach at his alma mater and Fairfield. We played against junior colleges, other high-profile prep schools and some Division I schools' JV programs. Being there provided a quick lesson in terms of how many talented dudes were out there, how deep the pool was of guys who could really play the game, who were desperately scraping and fighting for scholarships.

At my high school in South Carolina, I was a big fish in a very small pond. At Fork Union, I got to see and play against some of those dudes from Detroit, from Cali, from New York, from DC, from Chicago.

And even though I came from a disciplined household, I was totally unprepared for the school's military aspect. Having the time to do what you want, whether it be listening to music or watching TV, is not prevalent in a military school setting. That damn trumpet starts blaring at the crack of dawn and you better jump out of that bed and get to moving, wash up, brush your teeth, shine your shoes and you better be outside and in formation by 7:00 a.m.

The food was horrible, awful, but you ate it because you were hungry. Class started at eight, lunch was at noon and you had formation before every meal. We'd practice from three until five, then run down to the cafeteria to eat dinner. Then you had study hall, taps at 10:00 p.m. and then lights out.

I hated it, so basketball became even more meaningful; it was my refuge.

I'd try to get out of some of the more mundane commitments, whether it was marching or cleaning, by getting some extra shots up in the gym or using the phones in the coaches' office to call my parents and friends back in Greenville. I'd pretend like my life depended on calling back some assistant coach at some college that was recruiting me.

But Coach Arritt saw through all of that. He'd see me in the gym trying to be slick and a playful twinkle would permeate his face as his gravelly voice would shout out, "Code! You're hiding from your responsibilities!!!" or "Code! You're ducking out on your duty!!!"

Playing against Harold Deane in practice was an eye-opener. He was a strong, physical specimen and I quickly learned what I'd be dealing with on the college level. My body started to fill out; I was in the weight room getting stronger, learned the importance of the dietary and strength and conditioning pieces. That day-to-day combat in practice was no joke, and whenever I stepped on the court I had to be ready to bring it.

Coach Arritt would always say, "You're playing for your money every day!"

Initially, I didn't know what he was talking about, but I came to understand. He wasn't talking about cold hard cash to put in our pockets, but rather getting someone else to pay for us to attend their school on scholarship. If you were playing horrible, he'd say, "You're losing money today!" That was when I first started to equate college basketball as more than just a simple game.

And our gym was filled with high-profile coaches sitting in on our practices. As a kid who grew up dreaming about playing in the ACC, do you know what it's like to have Dean Smith in the bleachers smiling at you?

In high school, I went to practice to laugh and have fun, to joke around and giggle with my guys, playing practical jokes like putting crushed-up cookies in people's shoes, throwing hot water into the bathroom stall while a teammate was on the toilet.

But at Fork Union, there wasn't any of that. You stepped on that court to compete. I realized that it wasn't a joke, that we can have some fun but that excelling and reaching your potential in between those lines was work, and that we had a job to do. In my high school league, I did well because I was simply better than mostly everybody else. But if I wanted to play in the ACC, and not just be there but be a factor, I was going to have to deposit some sweat equity into the bank of hard work and commitment.

And no disrespect to my high school coach, but the learning curve was steep. I began to learn the nuances of what being a point guard at the higher levels meant. And when you're cramped in vans for twelve-hour drives and the highlight of your culinary experience is a stop at McDonald's on the way home, knowing no matter how late you get back you have to be in formation in the morning and be prepared for class, you quickly learn to prioritize and allocate the necessary time to getting all of your work done, to taking care of your responsibilities.

As difficult as it was, it paid off. I remember my dad being in the stands for the only game he saw me play at Fork Union. It was a triple-overtime thriller against a monster squad from Maine Central Institute, which was led by Cuttino Mobley, a future ten-year NBA pro. And I played my ass off. I'll never forget the look on my dad's face after that game. It was mischievous, an excited sparkle in his eye telling me, *I see you, son.* He saw my growth, my development, my maturation. He saw it and I felt it. It was exhilarating. And it was intoxicating and addictive, because I kept wanting to have that feeling.

It was early in the season but I was ready to make my college decision and get that out of the way. I was tiring of the recruiting process, tired of hearing the same worn pitches from the coaches. Among the schools most heavily involved were West Virginia, Southern Cal and Cincinnati.

My academics were never an issue and one day Coach Arritt, with his distinctive gravelly voice and unhurried, mountainous country twang he'd acquired growing up near the scenic cliffs of New River Gorge in Fayette, West Virginia, said, "Code, are you interested in the University of Pennsylvania? Because they're interested in you."

I said, "Nah, not really," and he quickly slapped back with, "Yes, you are!"

"Damn," I giggled, "I guess I am then!" I didn't know anything about Ivy League basketball at the time, but he was letting me know about the weight those prestigious institutions carried later on in life.

But I have to admit, I wanted to be in the ACC and it felt good to have a list of programs clamoring for me, and me, unlike the previous year, not having to beg them and tell them that I was good enough. Shoot, North Carolina told me I was good enough, but they'd just signed Jerry Stackhouse and Jeff McInnis out of Oak Hill Academy. The Tar Heels said they'd welcome me as a walk-on. Growing up where I did, UNC was the pinnacle that every kid who played basketball aspired to. But I wasn't going to settle for being a walk-on. I knew my worth and believed in myself, especially after how much my game had blossomed at Fork Union.

The best-case scenario for me was being close to home because I wanted my family to be able to see me play. And Clemson had gotten back in the mix after being noncommittal toward me for close to a year. One of the assistants at Clemson was a brother named Eugene Harris. Gene had played for my godfather, the man who trained me when I began to take hoops seriously, Johnny Jones, when he was playing high school ball in Alabama.

Gene and I had a history together. When I was in the seventh and eighth grade, I'd ride with him to go to the legendary B/C camp in Carnesville, Georgia. We had that family connection. But college scholarships don't come a dime a dozen. He couldn't offer me simply off the relationship we had.

But after my season at Fork Union, he said, "Hey, man, we'd love to have you, we love the improvements you've made, you're so much better now and ready to step in and play for us right away."

I was hyped-up, and Gene basically sold me on the bullshit. It never occurred to me that I hadn't had a single conversation with the head coach, Cliff Ellis. Chris Whitney had just gone to the NBA, so I signed early with Clemson. They told me they had a senior point guard that I'd apprentice under, that I'd get some consistent minutes off the bench my first year and would be prepared to run the show over the ensuing three years. I was like, *I'm gonna get on the floor as a freshman and then they're gonna hand me the keys! Let's do it!!!*

Gene said, "If you sign early, we won't bring in another guard in this class. You're our guy."

When I told Coach Arritt that I was gonna sign with Clemson, he glanced at me with a look of genuine concern. He took his time before responding, seeming to choose his words carefully. He pursed his lips into a half smile, half frown and said, "Code, you sure you wanna do that?"

Took me a couple of years to decode the tone of his voice and his body language. He was basically trying to tell me that they weren't some trustworthy dudes. But I guess, for whatever reasons, he didn't want to say it to me straight.

So I signed my letter of intent, the pressure was off my shoulders, and I'd reached my goal of becoming an ACC basketball player. A few weeks later I walked into practice and Coach Arritt, his words seeming to roll off an assembly line of sandpaper with a hint of disappointment, said, "Code! You see the newspaper today?"

Clemson had signed another guard as well, a JUCO player out of Mississippi. I felt like they lied to me.

Now I was pissed and wanted to get out of my letter of intent. I didn't know Cliff Ellis, the head coach. My relationship was with Eugene and I trusted everything he was selling me. I kept calling Cliff and Gene, but there was radio silence. They didn't return my phone calls; after all the letters and calls during the courting stage, now that they had me, they moved on.

They already had me in pocket, wouldn't release me, and I was stuck. That really put a damper on how excited I was, the way they handled that. My days of basketball innocence were now over.

And instead of showing up on the Clemson campus for my freshman year with the excitement that I'd dreamed of, I started my college basketball career with a taste in my mouth that would continue to grow more sour.

I later came to learn that the institution that would be known as Clemson University was built on the former antebellum slave plantation of John C. Calhoun. It was known as Fort Hill and was home to approximately two hundred slaves in its heyday. Calhoun's daughter inherited the 1,341-acre property when he and his wife passed away. When she died, the estate was willed to her husband, Thomas Greene Clemson, who later bequeathed three-fourths of the Fort Hill plantation and $80,000 to the state of South Carolina for the establishment of a public scientific and agricultural college.

Enslaved African Americans built and were responsible for Fort Hill's and the Calhoun and Clemson families' attendant economic engine. All of that physical and financial growth was a direct result and byproduct of the forced physical labor of those folks who cultivated the land's cotton. John C. Calhoun was often cited for his political defense of America's peculiar institution of slavery, saying that owning slaves in the antebellum South was "a positive good."

Later on, when I realized the amount of cash pouring into the university's coffers off the backs of their Black football and basketball players and their respective unpaid labor, I was struck by some glaring and sobering similarities.

3

It's crazy how fast one's world can get turned upside down.
The morning of my arrest, right before the handcuffs bit into
my wrists like shark teeth, everything just felt surreal.

While standing outside my town house, before being placed
in a standard dark blue unmarked car, the lead agent, a short
white guy, started barking at me.

"Do you know Jim Gatto? Do you know Christian
Dawkins? Do you know Jill such and such?"

I told him point-blank, "Yeah, I know Jim and Christian,
but I don't know no Jill."

Listen, my father's a damn judge and I know better than to
lie to the FBI, especially since I had nothing to hide.

Turns out that Jill was the fictitious name of one of the

FBI agents that had set us up. Now, I hadn't met this lady but once, and the agent plays me a recording of my voice saying, "That's not a decision that I can make, that's an adidas decision and I will certainly ask Gatto and see what they want to do."

As he's placing me in the car, he starts woofing again, "You knew them and you knew that you were money laundering!"

I'm thinking to myself, *What the hell?*

Sitting next to me in the back seat as the car begins to pull out of my driveway, he asks, "Are you going to cooperate?"

"I am cooperating," I said incredulously. His eyes glinted with joy, like he'd just captured Bonnie and Clyde.

At this point, I realized that it was best for me to keep quiet. So for the rest of the short ride, as he blabbered on about what I'd done and what I was facing, I slouched down in the leather seat, resting my head against the window, trying to figure out what the hell was going on.

As I looked out of the window on the way to the federal courthouse, a bizarre juxtaposition hit me. We passed the Bon Secours Wellness Arena, formerly known as the BI-LO Center. It's where Clemson played their home basketball games the season prior when the campus arena, Littlejohn Coliseum, was undergoing renovations. It's also where I played my last professional basketball games while winning the inaugural championship of the NBA's D League with the Greenville Groove.

Basketball had taken me all around the world on a fantastic journey. The symbolism of passing the arena on the way to be arraigned was not lost on me. I kept thinking to myself, *These guys can't be serious. They're taking me to jail? Talking about fraud? Conspiracy? Money laundering? For some basketball shit, some run-of-the-mill stuff that happens every day in my business, and has been happening since college sports became big business damn near a hundred years ago?*

When we got to the courthouse, they placed me in a holding cell. A bunch of guys in there started looking at me. One of them said, "You look familiar." A few others chimed in with the same sentiment.

"Are you from around here?" another asked.

"Yeah," was the only response I could muster.

My father arrived not long after I did and I felt a wash of relief. He'd help us get this mistake sorted out. I'd be fine.

"CODE!" shouted the guard, who came to escort me to the meeting room where I'd be able to sit down with my dad prior to the arraignment.

"Yeah, that's me."

"C'mon."

They proceeded to shackle my feet and wrists, and as they escorted me out the chains ominously echoed, announcing my every shuffle. One guy yelled out, "Gaaaaaaahdayumn, motherfucker! WHAT THE FUCK DID YOU DO!!!???"

I looked at the shackles, the jail bars, the guards and then down at the adidas shower shoes I was wearing and asked myself the same damn thing.

The first ten games or so of my freshman year at Clemson had somewhat lessened the lingering bitterness of how my recruiting process wrapped up. I was getting some decent playing time off the bench, had actually started a few games and was contributing.

After an up-and-down start to the 1993–1994 season where we'd gotten blown out by a good Minnesota squad led by Voshon Lenard and then won a close one against a very good Oklahoma State squad headlined by Big Country Reeves at the Rainbow Classic in Honolulu, we were hosting number three Duke at our place.

It was Grant Hill's senior year. Cherokee Parks was a junior. The team was really good. They'd later go on to lose a nail-biter to Arkansas in the national championship game. So this was a good test of where we stood. I was excited to test myself against their backcourt of Jeff Capel and Chris Collins. But ultimately, though I played some decent minutes, we wound up losing by six.

Despite the loss, we proved that we could play with anybody. We had two exceptional big men in Devin Gray and Sharone Wright and thought we had a chance to make some noise. But it never really came together. We finished the year at 18–16 and didn't make the tournament. My personal highlight was against West Virginia in the NIT, where I came close to getting the first triple-double in Clemson history.

That season was also disappointing in another way.

At Fork Union, I learned so much about the game from Coach Arritt. Things were different at Clemson under Cliff Ellis. At practices we essentially played one-on-one and then scrimmaged. The offense was primarily, "Get the ball to Sharone."

But something about my relationship with Coach Ellis was messing with my head. If he saw you on campus, outside of basketball-related activities, he would not speak to you. He'd just look at you and keep it moving.

There were very few guys, if any, who had a real relationship with the dude. I don't know if he was socially awkward or shy, but as a young Black man, I felt hurt, like I wasn't worthy of a simple greeting, like I was simply one of his faceless slaves putting money in his pocket, like the only purpose I served in his life was to help win games and get him to his next contract. It was as if my humanity didn't exist.

This might not have been how he felt, but all I can tell you is how I felt about it.

But as my minutes dropped and my disappointment gave way to anger, it was my father who snapped me out of it. "Make the practices your games. You can't control how much playing time you get, but what you can control is how you practice every day."

So that's what I did, concentrated on being the best player on the scout team. If we were playing against Georgia Tech, I was Travis Best. If it was Wake Forest, I was Randolph Childress. That shift in thinking actually allowed me the freedom and flexibility to start exploring and expanding my own game and built up my confidence. And by my sophomore year, I'd wind up starting every game I played for the next three years.

I also learned something else my freshman year. And that was that some of my teammates were getting paid.

My roommate would often say, "Hey, man, they're taking care of me." I never pressed and he never went into specifics, but I later learned that he was getting between three and five grand a month. He didn't come from much, but he always had a handful of cash and a nice car that always had a full tank of gas.

He wasn't buying Rolex watches or anything, but for a poor college kid who came from some challenging circumstances, he was in decent shape. Sometimes we'd take some road trips to visit girls at other schools and he made sure we ate well at some nice restaurants. And it wasn't some top secret stuff either, more like an unspoken truth. Some guys were getting cash under the table, plain and simple.

I don't know if it was from Clemson boosters, the actual coaching staff or agents that were hoping to rep them once they made it to the league, but the fact of the matter was that dudes were getting money.

David Falk, Michael Jordan's agent and widely considered the most successful NBA agent ever, was in my dorm room, as was Fred Whitfield, who worked as an attorney for Falk at the time and who would later go on to hold executive positions with the Jordan Brand, the Washington Wizards and is now a minority owner and the NBA's only Black chief operating officer, a post he currently holds with the Charlotte Hornets. And really, it wasn't a big deal. It was an accepted part of big-time college athletics.

I also learned during my freshman year that some of my teammates were literally stealing food on the weekends because they didn't have anything to eat.

Prior to the 2014 NCAA Championship game, UConn's Shabazz Napier shocked some people when he was asked about being a scholarship athlete during Final Four weekend. He said,

> We're definitely blessed to get a scholarship to our universities but at the end of the day that doesn't cover everything. We do have hungry nights where we don't have enough money to get food… Sometimes there are hungry nights where I'm not able to eat and I still gotta play up to my capabilities… When you see your jersey getting sold and things like that, you feel like you want something in return. There are hungry nights where I go to bed starving. Something could change, something should change.

And I knew exactly what he was talking about. Shabazz was about to play on college basketball's biggest stage, where he'd eventually go on to win his second national championship.

A writer for *SB Nation* mentioned how 79,000 people paid an average of $500 to watch the Final Four, how the event would be broadcast by CBS, which paid approximately $800 million a year for the rights to show the tournament. He summed it up best when he wrote:

In full, the tournament is among the most profitable things in sports. And here's one of the star players on one of the teams in its most important game saying he can't eat sometimes.

The writer also touched on another problematic issue, UCONN's abysmal graduation rate for its male basketball players, pointing out that, according to the most recent NCAA statistics at the time, that the program only graduated 8 percent of its so-called student-athletes.

I suppose in a hypothetical world where every college athlete got a meaningful education, I would understand a system where athletes didn't receive any monetary compensation. Instead, we have hungry players at schools that sometimes fail to even put in enough effort to cook up diplomas, and NCAA leadership that accuses players of greed while raking in billions.

And I felt every bit of what Shabazz and that writer were saying. Their words shone a light on the fact that college athletes are nothing but indentured servants who get little more than scraps while other people are making millions of dollars off of our work.

Some of my teammates had children. Back then, before Shabazz's words eventually led to an overhaul where players now have twenty-four-hour access to meals at the training table or increased food stipends, we got three meals a day during the week in the cafeteria, and we got one meal a day on Saturday and Sunday, which was breakfast only.

And guys would be stealing food on the weekends because they didn't have money to eat lunch or dinner. One of the cafeteria ladies would look out for our team during the week, sliding bags of food to take home at night or letting us come back through the line again to get another plate, but she didn't work on the weekends. So on some weekends, I'd bring teammates to my house to eat and my mom would cook a big meal. But otherwise, guys would have to fend for themselves.

That's why I laughed when Jameis Winston, the Heisman Trophy winner who delivered a football national championship to Florida State, was accused of stealing $32 worth of crab legs from a Tallahassee grocery store during that same year in 2014. When I saw it on the news, I simply shrugged and chuckled, saying to myself, "The dude was hungry."

But the SB Nation writer touched on an element worse than hungry weekend nights, and that was the inherent graduation rates at some of the big-time athletic programs, specifically around football and basketball.

Schools bend the rules every day to get top recruits to come and play for them, often arranging for them to get the qualifying scores on their SATs by having a proxy sit in to pass the exam for them, then they stick them in bullshit majors to keep them eligible. At Clemson, it was Parks, Recreation and Tourism Management. Players were kept eligible so they could win games and generate revenue. And when guys exhausted their eligibility and hadn't fulfilled their requirements to graduate, the school didn't give a shit. They were done with you.

After my freshman year, I was ready to be a starter. And with Cliff Ellis being fired, I was excited about our new head coach, Rick Barnes, who went on later to coach Kevin Durant at Texas and is now the head coach at the University of Tennessee. From a teaching perspective, the difference was night and day. Rick was a helluva teacher and my understanding of the game blossomed under his tutelage.

When a new coach takes over at a major college basketball or football program, he immediately wants to put his own stamp on it. Out with the old philosophies and in with the new. They don't want even the slightest bit of residue from the prior regime. That often pertains to the players who are already in the program too.

Rick exposed me to another facet of the business side of the game when he tried to run everybody off the team—literally. The minute he took over that spring, he instituted a series of gruesome workouts. The strength-and-conditioning coach's job during summer school was literally to run us into the ground and to make guys quit. It would be over one hundred degrees and we'd be running those steps in Death Valley until guys vomited or passed out.

On the one hand, yes, he was trying to get us into great condition. But he was also trying to run guys off to free up their scholarships and bring in more of his own recruits. Ultimately he was successful in doing so. A number of players bounced up out of there. Rick brought in some new guys to fill those gaps, and then ran some of them off the next year, including a six-foot-nine forward named Mike Tabb, who transferred to Temple and would eventually marry Kobe Bryant's sister.

Rick drove us so hard that by the time fall practices got underway we had to have registered nurses at every session. They administered intravenous fluids because guys were passing out regularly, or catching full-body cramps. I'd never seen anything like it.

Early that fall the media started calling us the Slab Five. Some preseason prognosticators said we'd possibly be the worst team in ACC history. No one expected anything from us. On paper, we didn't have an intimidating, let alone a serviceable roster that could compete in the conference.

But what we did have was a bunch of guys who were smart and could shoot the ball. We spread the floor, incorporated some of the Princeton offense, milked every bit of the shot clock and hoisted threes. And we were superdisciplined and feisty. We might have been undermanned, but with Rick's coaching and the competitive fire we had, we surprised a lot of people.

Despite everything, Rick really was a helluva coach and teacher. The practices, preparation and his approach to teaching the game were great. Unlike under Cliff Ellis, Rick's practices were clinics in the art of motion, rotations, floor spacing, down screens, curl screens, fade screens and team dynamics. I honed my on-court knowledge, my feel for the game, and I was the one with the ball in my hands. I was the one running the show. I needed that, fed off that, and as my game grew, so did my confidence.

Yet some aspects of Rick's coaching style didn't sit well with me. College hoops has long been littered with coaches who denigrate their players and engage in abusive behaviors that would not be tolerated in any other workplace. And when I played for him at Clemson, Rick was often one of those coaches. The old-school mentality, exemplified by Bob Knight's bullying antics at Indiana, was that it built character. But I can tell you from firsthand experience that it doesn't. It only causes harm and resentment. In practice, we were regularly referred to as "stupid motherfuckers," "pieces of shit" and "pussies." I don't care who you are; when another person has the green light to treat you like shit and you can't respond in kind, some very real animosity festers.

In practices, there were no out-of-bounds, so running teammates into the bleachers or into a wall was encouraged, as well as fighting with one another if it came to it. As a result we became a very tough team physically, but there was a nastiness to it. We anticipated practices with dread. Christmas break was the worst because if we didn't have games, we practiced three times a day. And those practices were brutal.

We had a teammate who, during one game, should have taken a charge and didn't. That next practice, Rick lined him up under the basket with the rest of the team in a single file at half court. There was no ball involved. Instead we were instructed to run him over. Teammates who were six-foot-eight and over, close to 250 pounds, running at full speed, a forty-seven-foot sprint, lowering their shoulder while he took it square in the chest. He was only six foot, maybe 190 pounds, and he had to take that beating fifteen times.

"If any of you motherfuckers slow down," Rick said, "you're gonna take his place."

The NCAA had a rule that you were only allowed to do anything basketball related—whether it was practice, film sessions, games, lifting weights, individual workouts, etc.—for twenty hours per week. We were forced to sign paperwork every week that confirmed that we were in compliance, knowing that we were falsifying information because twenty hours wasn't even half the real amount of time spent on basketball. In essence, we weren't simply encouraged to lie; we were instructed to.

But we had a great staff with Larry Shyatt, who was considered one of the best assistant coaches in the country, along with Dennis Felton, who'd later become the head coach at

Western Kentucky, Georgia and Cleveland State. And by the time the season started, I was ready to become a player to be reckoned with on a national level.

No one expected anything from us, and the ACC was loaded. Jerry Stackhouse and Rasheed Wallace were putting in work at North Carolina, Tim Duncan was a man among boys at Wake Forest, Joe Smith was a monster at Maryland, and Virginia had some outstanding depth with my boys Harold Deane, Curtis Staples and guys like Junior Burrough and Cory Alexander.

We weren't expected to win a single game in the ACC, but we exceeded all expectations. We beat Duke twice that year and qualified for the NIT. I went from playing sparingly as a freshman to starting every game as a sophomore, played thirty-three minutes per game and averaged twelve points, four rebounds, four assists and two steals. It was a huge step up from my freshman year.

So heading into my junior season, my confidence was sky-high, not only because of the individual success of my sophomore season, but also because of what happened the summer prior.

The Clemson coaching staff had picked me, coming off being voted the team MVP that year, to play on an ACC All-Star squad that would be traveling to Brazil. We played against the teams that Dream Team II would be going up against in the opening pool of the Olympics that next year—Angola, Paraguay, Uruguay and Brazil.

Dave Odom from Wake Forest was the head coach. Todd Fuller, a very good big man from North Carolina State who would later play a few years in the NBA, was on the squad, as was Georgia Tech's Drew Barry, Hall of Famer Rick Barry's kid, a skilled six-foot-six guard who is still the Yellow Jackets' all-time assists leader.

But the headliner was Wake's Tim Duncan, the coolest of dudes who was already being touted as the future number one pick in the NBA draft whenever he decided to leave college. And as most people know, Timmy would later go down as the greatest power forward to ever play the game.

We practiced for a few days in Winston-Salem, then got on a plane and flew to Orlando, had dinner, then hopped on a plane back to Rio. Tim and I roomed together for two legs of the trip. We traveled throughout the country, playing games in Belo Horizonte, Curitiba and Brasília, spending three or four days in each city. Being able to stand at the base of the incredible Cristo Redentor statue, at the peak of the Corcovado mountain in the Tijuca National Park overlooking Rio, was a feeling of awe that I'll never forget.

That was my first international experience in dealing with language barriers. It was also the first time I saw Black folks that looked like me that didn't speak English. Growing up in South Carolina, I thought I'd seen people living in poverty. But those poverty-stricken areas in Brazil were on an entirely different level.

I realized that the world was much bigger than the US and Canada, and that I was ignorant of many things that I'd never been exposed to. We were riding on the bus, and I saw four people living in a cardboard box eating rotten fruit for dinner. In that area there was no running water, no electricity.

Everywhere we stayed, we were told, "Don't leave this hotel at night, you WILL get robbed." I remember running out onto the floor that very first time for warm-ups and seeing uniformed soldiers around the perimeter of the court holding AK-47s. I was like, *WTF!!!???*

The exposure to international basketball was phenomenal. It was an entirely different game than the one we were playing in college. Those guys were huge; they were some grown-ass men who could shoot the shit out of the ball. It was an adjustment, to put it mildly. They were strong and physical, and it was the first time I saw the game played European style, where everyone on the court was highly skilled, where the game wasn't predicated on athleticism. It was about ball movement and skills. I had never seen seven-footers shooting threes, putting it on the floor, running the break and handing out assists all in one package like that.

The experience was eye-opening, and I came back a different player. And getting to know Tim Duncan off the court was great. He was an extremely humble, really hardworking, genuinely caring person. But on the court, playing with him and really watching him go? My goodness!

We were playing these grown-ass men out there, and I remember one game when they were really pushing him around. Dave Odom called a time-out and told him something. I don't know what it was, but he just took over and started busting everybody's ass. I was like, *Oh damn! Okay, Timmy.*

Tim was quiet, not introverted. He was smart, would talk and giggle, but he was about his business. While some of the guys were trying to find a club to go to or a spot where they could meet some women, Tim just wanted to get some ice cream after a game and head back to the room. He wanted to get his rest so he'd be ready to play.

A year and a half later during our senior season, we were playing Wake and Tim was wearing our ass out. We couldn't do a damn thing with him. I started yelling, "Push him off the box! Push him off the box!" Sure enough, he got the ball on the box, went into his Kevin McHale bag of tricks, our guy fouled the shit out of him and he still got the and-one. Tim just looked at me and calmly said, "That shit ain't gonna work, Merl."

In late July, early August, after the Brazil trip, Lynn Merritt, an executive at Nike, invited me to work as a counselor at Jason Kidd's and Tim Hardaway's summer basketball camps out in California. They were star players under the Swoosh umbrella at the time. And there was a connection there, as Lynn had been college football teammates and roommates with an older cousin of mine, Ron Blasingame, while they were students at both the College of Marin, where they played with future Hall of Fame coach Pete Carroll, and later at San Francisco State. Ron and my dad were closer to one another than they were to their own actual brothers.

The best parts of those camps were the pickup games with the pros and other college players during the evenings. I was playing with and going up against guys like Jason Kidd, Brian Shaw, Mike Bibby, J. R. Rider, Richard Jefferson, Shareef Abdur-Rahim, Hardaway and others. My game had evolved, my body was strong, my jumper was wet, I could get to my spots, was scoring and facilitating and even surprising myself with what I was doing, raising more than a few eyebrows in the process. I was feeling like a pro.

That feeling carried over into my junior year. We got out of the gate strong and as an individual, I was killing it. My ball handling, vision, pull-up game and deep ball were all clicking. NBA scouts started calling the coaching staff at Clemson, asking, "Is he gonna stay in school?"

I'd reached another level and it showed. And we raced out to an 11–0 start. In that eleventh game, we were hosting Virginia at our place. It was a night game and the atmosphere in

Littlejohn Coliseum was electric. The house was packed and my juices were flowing.

The year prior, they'd beaten us both times we played them. And there had been a healthy amount of trash talking leading up to the game with the guys over there that I was close to: Harold Deane, who was my prep school classmate; Curtis Staples, who I'd grown up playing with during my childhood summers in Roanoke; and Jamal Robinson, who I played with on that ACC All-Star squad that had toured Brazil the previous summer.

And right from the tip-off, I had it cooking. I was getting to my spots with ease, coming off curl screens and knocking down my jumpers, swinging the ball to the open man and running the show with the ball in my hands. I felt unstoppable. I felt like a pro.

But early in the second half, I was driving baseline with a defender on my hip. I made a quick jump stop and was about to raise up when I heard it. Pop!

My adrenaline was still flowing and I was able to walk to the bench. After a few minutes, I told the coaches I was ready to go back in. As soon as I got back into the game, I tried to turn and run after a free throw and that's when the pain hit me. I crumpled to the ground and felt like I'd been shot in my leg.

Here I was, playing the best ball of my life and in an instant, everything changed.

My ACL was torn and I wound up missing the rest of the year. Here I was, establishing myself as a legitimate NBA prospect and now, for the first time in my career, I had a serious injury that required surgery and a lengthy, painful rehabilitation process.

And while I was going through those arduous physical

therapy sessions, with my knee in excruciating pain and swollen to the size of a grapefruit, Rick came to check on me. He told me, "I don't know what you're working so hard for. You're not gonna play when you come back if we get Oded Kattash. You might as well transfer."

Kattash was an excellent guard from Israel that Rick was in hot pursuit of. Was Rick trying to motivate me? Perhaps. But it didn't work. I knew he was telling me the truth too because if we did manage to land Kattash, who eventually wound up staying in Israel and had an excellent pro career in the Euroleague, somebody was going to have to transfer.

After ACL surgery your body naturally develops scar tissue to protect the injured area. You have to break up the scar tissue in order to regain full range of motion. It's an extremely painful process. At least once a week, when I'd be rehabbing with our trainer, Reno Wilson, Rick would come in and tell him, "Hey, Reno, I'm pushing on his knee today." He may have thought he was encouraging me in my rehab, but to me it almost looked like he took joy in seeing me in pain.

To this day, I'm still conflicted about my time with Rick because the actual basketball and being able to study the game under him was great, but not the other stuff we had to deal with from him. Maybe he's mellowed over time and that's no longer a part of his coaching or motivational philosophies today. But back then, he'd say some things to you that, had you been in any other setting, say just two guys on the street, there would have been some physical consequences and repercussions.

And it wasn't just limited to the players. We were playing at Duke once and Coach Felton was in charge of the scout for that game. Meaning he was responsible for breaking down every aspect of Duke's offense, defense, inbounds plays, personnel and all of the details we needed to know.

Felton had papers everywhere and when we were done, it was taking him a long time to get all of his materials gathered and organized. The whole team was on the bus waiting for him, and as he emerged out of the building, Rick told the driver, "Close the doors and leave his ass."

The bus started pulling away, and Coach Felton was running behind it. Rick laughed and said, "Stop the bus. Open the doors." And as soon as Coach Felton got within ten yards, Rick said, "Close the doors and take off." After stopping again, he did it for a third time.

Finally, Coach Felton walked away. I guess he called a cab. I didn't find it funny. Felton was the only Black coach on the staff. What message was that sending to us, his players?

I stayed in touch with Coach Shyatt and Coach Felton long after my undergraduate days at Clemson were finished. They were great guys. Around 2007, when Felton was a few years into his tenure as the head coach at the University of Georgia and I was working for Nike, we had a chance to catch up at the Peach Jam in North Augusta, South Carolina.

Peach Jam was an annual tournament, held in July, that featured the top AAU programs and ballers in the country. It has since been folded into Nike's summer Elite Youth Basketball League, more commonly referred to as the EYBL, as its culminating championship gauntlet.

During a break in one of the sessions, Coach Felton and I shot over to the K&W cafeteria, a buffet-style restaurant not far from the Riverview Park Activities Center, where the tournament was being played. As we were sitting there, I had a flashback to our time at Clemson. We were playing Georgia Tech and one of the refs made a terrible foul call against us. The ref was standing near our bench, and Felton, trying to encourage us, yelled, "Don't worry about it. That was a bad call, just keep on playing!" And the ref proceeded to hit him up with a technical.

Coach Felton was just trying to get our heads back in the game. But Rick exploded.

"If you open your mouth one more fucking time, if you open your motherfucking mouth again, your ass is fired!"

Felton tried to respond. "Rick, all I said was—"

But Rick cut him off, shrieking, "Shut the fuck up!"

As we began to dig into some heaping plates of our favorite Southern comfort food, I interrupted our small talk about how great Kemba Walker was playing for his New York Gauchos squad and asked him a serious question. It was one that had been bothering me for years.

"Why did you put up with Rick's shit for all of those years? It really bothered me, the way he treated you. And it seemed like it was reserved only for you because he never treated the white assistant coaches like that."

Coach Felton, in his normal mild-mannered and calm demeanor, simply said, "I had a goal in mind." And he left it at that.

But we both understood the essence of his statement, that in order for him to become a head coach of a major Division I basketball program, he had to sublimate his feelings and take whatever was being dished out, because ultimately athletic directors from other schools would be calling Rick for a reference.

I thought about the many other Black assistant coaches who perhaps weren't fortunate enough to work under men like John Thompson, Nolan Richardson, George Raveling, Tubby Smith, Clem Haskins, Shaka Smart, Tommy Amaker,

Johnny Dawkins and a select few others, who had to put up with god-knows-what in order to keep their jobs and hopefully one day get a shot at running their own programs.

The rest of my junior year after the injury was rough, but one bright spot was when we were playing against Wake Forest. Prior to tip-off, I was rehabbing my knee in the training room and Dave Odom and Tim Duncan walked in. They told me they were rooting for me, that they cared about me and that they hoped to see me back on the court that next season. That meant a lot to me. I maneuvered around campus on crutches that season, unable to walk. Clemson ranges across fourteen hundred acres and if you've got class on the other end of campus, it's a hike. When I asked the athletic department if I could have access to a golf cart to get to my classes, the compliance folks checked with the NCAA. My request was denied because they said it would be an impermissible benefit for an athlete.

But whenever the pain became too much, whenever I'd get down on myself because my body wasn't responding, I'd just look at the upcoming schedule. We were opening up my senior year against Kentucky at the RCA Dome in Indianapolis.

They'd just won the national championship with one of the most ridiculously talented rosters the NCAA had ever seen under their Hall of Fame head coach Rick Pitino. That Wildcats squad had nine players who'd eventually go on to cash NBA checks. So I was motivated to start my senior season off with a bang.

Little did I know that Rick Pitino and I would be linked up again two decades later. And the stakes, as it turned out, would be much greater than simply winning or losing a game.

4

September 26, 2017. After I was arrested and arraigned, I got back home and sat down with my father to watch the FBI press conference, which was the biggest story, not just in sports but in the entire sphere of news at the time.

Federal authorities charged me, adidas Global Director of Sports Marketing Jim Gatto and eight other people, four of them assistant coaches—Oklahoma State's Lamont Evans, Auburn's Chuck Person, Arizona's Emanuel "Book" Richardson and USC's Tony Bland—with fraud and corruption. They alleged that we took part in a scheme in which the coaches accepted bribes to funnel recruits to specific college programs, and then later to certain shoe companies, agents and marketing reps. Anyone on the inside, after reading the legal documents, knew that the case centered around high school recruit Brian Bowen and the $100,000 payment his family had been promised by adidas if he signed with the company's flagship program, the University of Louisville.

During the press conference at the US Attorney's Office, they had all of these fancy flowcharts in the background, revealing that it had utilized wiretaps, undercover agents, informants and other resources to blow the lid off a story about the greed and impurities of college sports, that the innocent colleges were being infiltrated and threatened by those who had the audacity to skirt around their wonderful concept of amateurism.

It was laughable. Schools, athletic departments, coaches, boosters and many others within the ecosystem of college sports, whether it's the shoe companies or prospective agents, have long had a brazen relationship with the truth as it relates to the NCAA's bullshit amateurism rules. Scandal, under-the-table cash and college athletics have long had an amorous relationship.

The laughable part about my situation was watching the look on the people's faces at that news conference as the words "We have your playbook" were uttered.

We have your playbook???

The investigation was supposed to shake college basketball to its core, they said. Wholesale changes were coming. Heads were promised to roll.

The Ringer's Mark Titus, when the news broke, wrote,

The higher-ups in the system have routinely exploited the fact that student-athletes don't get any piece of the billion-dollar college-sports-industry pie, and unless drastic changes are made, athletes receiving money through illegal back channels will remain inevitable.

And now, some five years later, where's the change? Oh, some heads definitely rolled, mostly African American middlemen like me and the assistant coaches. We lost our jobs, had to drain whatever savings we had for attorney fees, were sentenced to jail, had our reputations sullied and are left to figure where to go from here.

But what happened to the famous head coaches who not only knew about the payments, but who privately cursed me and other people out for not doing enough to ensure that they landed that one, singular, program-defining recruit, the ones who the FBI actually had on tape discussing payments, or bragging about the sweet deals they had offered to recruits and their families?

Their lives went on relatively unaffected.

"We have your playbook," the FBI's William Sweeney said at that press conference. "Our investigation is ongoing and we are conducting additional interviews as I speak."

And now, five years later, did the FBI come back to admit that their case was a bunch of shit, run by a bunch of rogue agents that basically entrapped Christian Dawkins, the aspiring agent, and his friends like me and the assistant coaches? Of course they didn't. But we'll get back to that later.

So what has really changed? As of now, not a damn thing. It's simply business as usual. And the worst-kept secret in all of sports, the dirty recruiting and the urinating on the NCAA rule book, continues unabated.

The show goes on.

After my junior year at Clemson was cut short due to injury, I was more determined than ever to get back on the court and be the same, if not a better, player as before.

But just because you want something doesn't mean you'll get it.

No matter how hard I attacked my rehab, no matter how determined I was, my leg was not responding. Physically, I was making progress and when I was cleared to return for workouts, it was a huge sigh of relief. But once I got back on that hardwood and started competing again, and believe me I worked my ass off to get to that point, the frustration became almost unbearable. I just couldn't do some of the things I was able to do instinctively prior to the injury.

Simple things like starting to sprint and stopping on a dime to change direction, or simply moving laterally, proved to be a chore. My mind was telling me to do things that my leg was not in agreement with. It felt great to be back, to get in game shape, to feel that leather in my hands and hear that beautiful sound of the net splashing after a perfect jumper. But I didn't have the same type of speed or explosiveness.

The coaching staff floated the idea of me taking a redshirt year, basically sitting out the full '96–'97 campaign and coming back the next year to play my final season. But emotionally and mentally I was tired. I contemplated the redshirt idea, but decided to finish up my degree and figure out my next steps.

Within the program, there was some understated excitement heading into my senior year. We started off ranked number twenty in the preseason polls and we knew we had some Final Four potential.

And we announced ourselves in our opening game against number-three-ranked Kentucky, the defending national champions, at the RCA Dome in Indianapolis. They had two exceptional guards in Ron Mercer and Derek Anderson and I thought that would be a good test for me, to see where

I physically matched up against two guys who were future pros. And it was going to be a good test for us as a team.

Well, we passed with flying colors. In front of over thirty thousand people, that adrenaline rush came back in full force. They held a six-point lead at halftime, but we had a furious run in overtime and won, 79–71. My teammate Harold Jamison played a great game, scoring twenty points, and everybody contributed. I played a decent game as the starting point guard, only took five shots, but it felt great to be out there for a strong thirty-four minutes, breaking Kentucky's vaunted press, grabbing some rebounds, handing out some assists and contributing to our team's success.

Mentally, I had to adjust to a new role because I wasn't the same player yet. It would take some time for me to get back to that, but I felt like it was just a matter of time before I regained all of the strength and mobility in my leg.

My confidence started coming back shortly after the Kentucky game when we went down to Puerto Rico to play in the San Juan Shootout and I was named to the all-tournament team.

After beating North Carolina State in mid-January, we were 17–1 and the number-two-ranked team in the country. The excitement on campus was bubbling. We'd previously beaten a very good Duke team with Jeff Capel, Roshown McLeod and Trajan Langdon, as well as a tough Maryland squad that had four future NBA players with Keith Booth, Laron Profit, Šarūnas Jasikevičius and Obinna Ekezie. We had it cooking.

On the surface, everything looked great. But there were some organizational dynamics at play and some fissures that would threaten and ultimately fracture our team chemistry.

When people wonder why good teams don't necessarily

reach their potential, there are a lot of underlying factors that can undermine a really good thing, many of which are hidden unless you are part of the day-to-day happenings within the family. And one of the things that happened to us still has me shaking my head all these years later.

A friend of mine was one of our team dancers. We were playing against Texas A&M over the Christmas break and she'd recently found out that she had a sister living in Houston that she'd never met. She told me that she was thinking of going to visit her over the break and bringing her to the game in College Station, and would I mind leaving them some tickets at will-call.

I said, "No problem."

But it turned out to be a huge problem.

I left my friend and her sister the tickets. We were on the court for warm-ups at Texas A&M's on-campus arena, the G. Rollie White Coliseum. It was a smaller Christmas break crowd, maybe three thousand people there, at most.

When my friend walked in with her sister, heading for their seats near the court, both teams stopped momentarily. Her sister was gorgeous; she literally had the whole arena buzzing. In the layup lines my teammates kept coming up to me saying, "Damn, Merl! Who is that!?"

The Aggies were asking themselves the same thing. This young woman was unbelievably beautiful; she lit up the whole damn place. We won the game pretty easily, but all anybody wanted to talk about for the remainder of the trip was my friend's long-lost sister.

We flew back to South Carolina and by the time students started returning to campus, this young woman had decided to move in with her sister at Clemson.

You would not believe the commotion that followed. One

of my teammates, a country boy who was fond of worn-out jeans and busted-up boots, all of a sudden was walking around campus in Gucci shoes, his whole wardrobe upgraded.

I shook my head, like, *What the hell is going on here?* I thought maybe the boosters were sliding him some cash or that he signed with an agent and got ahold of some money. I was wrong on both accounts. Turned out that him and ole girl had gotten together, and she was supporting him financially. With his size, build and the way he was playing, he had the looks of a future NBA player. We shared an apartment together, and before the Texas A&M game, dude was a homebody. Now, he was never in the room. I barely saw him outside of basketball activities.

But homegirl was just getting started. Football players and fraternity brothers were all in hot pursuit. It was crazy how fast she turned that town upside down. So you can imagine how fast my roommate's glee turned to sorrow when word started getting around that she was also shooting her shot with some of the NFL prospects on the football team. But she still had my man turned out and the circus and the drama ramped up when she claimed that she was pregnant.

She went to the coaching staff, telling them that they needed to give her cash to pay for an abortion. The coaching staff held a series of side meetings with my teammate, trying to get him to understand what he was dealing with. It turned out that he was not the only player caught up in the web.

I came home one day, and my teammates were in my living room screaming at each other. It got really tense as they squared up to brawl. I had to jump in the middle, telling them, "This is some bullshit, knock it off."

Prior to that, we were somewhat united in our disdain for Rick Barnes's verbal abuse. But after my friend's sister showed up, we splintered into various factions and became cliquish. Meanwhile, my friend was worried about her sister. "I'm getting some really strange phone calls for my sister at my place," she told me one day. "All of these NBA players have been calling here for her."

She named names, ones I will not repeat, but we're talking about some of the top and most popular young players in the league at the time.

"Why are all of these dudes calling my house?" she asked.

"Obviously they have something going on with your sister," I told her, which you didn't have to be Columbo or Hank, Walter White's DEA agent brother-in-law on *Breaking Bad*, to figure out.

My friend decided to take matters into her own hands and began to call some of these NBA players back. One told her, "I've been paying your sister every month to meet me here and there when we're on the road, but she hasn't been showing up lately."

In her naivete, my friend asked, "Paying her for what?"

Um, hello. They were paying her for sex. She was a high-end call girl, what NBA players call a "jump off," someone who meets them in different cities while they're on the road to service their sexual needs. We basically came to the conclusion that, just like the agents circling around the athletes in the hopes of signing them once they went pro, my friend's sister was playing the same game, seeking out some new future clients that she could add to her own roster.

It got so bad, the animosity and the friction within the Clemson basketball family, that the coaches told her to stay away from the team. As the team captain, I got updates on all this from the coaching staff, in addition to hearing about it from her sister. And homegirl agreed to keep her distance, but only if the coaching staff agreed to hit her off with a few thousand dollars.

So after going 17–1, we finish out the rest of the year going 5–7. Now what were you supposed to tell the media when they asked why things have suddenly fallen apart? *Um, yeah, we've got a high-end call girl that has basically destroyed our team chemistry.*

We had one away game where we played like shit. By the time we flew back to South Carolina and arrived on campus, it was around 1:00 a.m. Rick told us to go to the locker room and change into our practice gear. I had class the next morning at 8:00 a.m.

We did a drill called Eighty-Five and Two, a continuous layup drill where you have to make a total of eighty-five layups in two minutes. In order to do it successfully, you have to be flying down that court at full speed and not miss a layup. I mean, you really have to be moving fast. And if you don't get it done within the two minutes, you have to do it over and over again until you finally hit the mark.

After a round-trip flight and a game, we were already exhausted. We couldn't do it. Rick didn't care. By 3:00 a.m. we were beyond gassed. "Do it again!" Rick yelled.

Finally, around 4:00 a.m., our assistant coach Larry Shyatt intervened. Rick begrudgingly let us go, but as we left he shouted, "The first thing we're gonna do tomorrow at practice is Eighty-Five and Two, and we're gonna do it until you motherfuckers get it right!"

Then he added, as an afterthought, "You motherfuckers better not miss class!"

Even though my friend's sister was instructed to stay away, she showed up at our hotel in Kansas City for our first-round NCAA Tournament game against Miami of Ohio. When one of the coaches' wives saw her and asked her to leave, all hell broke loose. They got to yelling and screaming and had to be separated. Hotel security got called in, the coaches were pissed, their wives were pissed and the players that were in love with her were pissed. Meanwhile, we somehow managed to beat Miami of Ohio and Tulsa to advance to the Sweet Sixteen. The public had no idea about the drama unfolding off the court.

At the Alamodome in San Antonio, we faced a very tough Minnesota team coached by Clem Haskins. They'd only lost three games all year. They had four guys on that roster, including Bobby Jackson and Sam Jacobson, that would eventually play in the NBA.

Jackson and Jacobson lit us up, combining for fifty-five points, and we lost a double-overtime thriller, 90–84, missing out on our chance to get to the Elite Eight. I played one of my worst games, shooting just two for fourteen. It was a tough way to end my college career.

I was still in love with the game and wanted to try to keep playing, so I was excited to find out that I'd been invited to compete at the Portsmouth Invitational Tournament. The PIT is a postseason event strictly for college seniors with pro potential. A good showing at Portsmouth, in front of approximately two hundred representatives from every NBA team, helps a player to increase his chances of being drafted or in securing an invite to a training camp. Some of the alumni that catapulted out of the event include John Stockton, Scottie Pippen, Dennis Rodman, Tim Hardaway, Ben Wallace, Avery Johnson, Jeremy Lin and many others.

Something clicked for me in Portsmouth because I shot the shit out of the ball. Passing, defending, splashing jumpers, getting to the rim, I felt like my old self. My team won the championship and I walked out of there with an invite to the Denver Nuggets rookie–free agent camp. There I joined recent draft picks Tony Battie, Danny Fortson and Bobby Jackson, the exceptional guard from Minnesota who'd just lit us up for thirty-six points in the Sweet Sixteen. And I managed to play well enough to make the cut from thirty players to fifteen, which meant I'd head to Utah, on the Nuggets summer league roster.

At summer league, I remembered my father's words. *Make practices your games.* My job was strictly to facilitate and swing the ball to the open man. If I got an occasional basket here or there, cool. But I knew what they wanted from me and I just tried to be the best role player on the squad.

I didn't play a ton of minutes, but they must have seen potential in me because after summer league, they invited me to their full training camp. As other guys were getting cut, I kept hanging around. They encouraged me to start looking at an apartment near the practice facility. I was ecstatic, couldn't believe that I was on the cusp of being on an NBA opening day roster.

During the preseason I realized one of my dreams by getting to play against one of my childhood heroes, Joe Dumars. He was heading into his final year with the Pistons and I played against him in an exhibition game at, of all places, Freedom Hall, the University of Louisville's former off-campus arena. It's ironic, because that's the setting for one of my fondest hoops memories and accomplishments, and also the school where the shit would hit the fan many years later.

Ultimately a trade went down, the Nuggets brought in a couple of players and I got waived right before the roster was finalized.

That hurt. That was the first time in my life that I'd actually been cut by a team. But at the same time, I was thinking, "You came this close, keep working and one day soon you'll be in the NBA."

From there, Keith Smart, the head coach of the Fort Wayne Fury of the Continental Basketball Association, reached out and invited me to their training camp. I wound up making the team and was playing extremely well. I had just come out of the Nuggets training camp and I was in fantastic shape. I knew it was simply a matter of time before an NBA team reached out to call me up.

And the differences between the CBA and the NBA life were like night and day. Even though I was only with the Nuggets for the preseason, you realized that in the CBA, eating at Ruth's Chris, flying in customized planes and staying at the Ritz-Carlton were things of the past.

In the CBA, you were eating at the Golden Corral and the Ponderosa, flying to some rinky-dink town in raggedy puddle jumpers, sharing cheap four-bedroom apartments with your teammates that were actually a step down from how we, at least at Clemson, were living in college.

But hey, if this is what needed to be done to get to the NBA, I was all for it. So on the first day of training camp in Fort Wayne, about fifteen minutes in, one of the most hilarious things happened.

One of the guys expected to make the team was a guy named Thomas Hamilton. We called him Ham.

Hardcore basketball folks from Chicago know about Ham. He was a teammate of NBA player Rashard Griffith at Martin Luther King High School, which they'd led to the 1993 state championship. He was recruited to play at the University of Illinois but was ruled academically ineligible. He transferred to Pitt, never played a game for the Panthers, yet still managed to get signed by the Toronto Raptors in 1995.

He'd played a total of eleven games in the NBA up until that point with Boston, but had blown his chances with the Raptors, the Celtics and the Bulls by the time he got to Fort Wayne.

Ham stood seven-foot-two, weighed about 350 pounds. He was just a massive human being. He was in terrible shape, but you could see why the scouts were in love with his potential. He was huge, had great hands, could pass, shoot, rebound. The dude could play! But basketball and getting in shape were not priorities on his "Things To Do" list. The guy was a real character and you couldn't help, if you weren't a coach or an NBA general manager, taking a liking to him. He was really just a big kid.

So, we were in that first practice doing some running and some layup drills, and fifteen minutes in, Ham made a layup, didn't break stride, kept running out of the gym and yelled out, "I'm gone!!!"

He proceeded to hop in his car and drive back to Chicago. It was one of the funniest things I'd ever seen in all of my basketball experiences. We were cracking up. Coach Smart ran us through the rest of practice, then dispatched an assistant coach to drive to Chicago and find Ham's big ass.

He came back a week or two later and the first thing he said was, "Fuck that! I ain't doing all that damn running." But for like ten- or fifteen-minute stretches, the guy was remarkable. His son, Tommy Hamilton IV, wound up playing at DePaul and Texas Tech and is now a young pro over in Europe. Ham would have one more shot in the NBA, playing 22 games with the Houston Rockets during the 1999–2000 season. But by the age of 24, he'd exhausted any chance of ever playing in the NBA again.

But I had it cooking in Fort Wayne, knowing without a shadow of a doubt that the NBA would be calling any minute. And then, I hyperextended my knee, the same one I tore up at Clemson during my junior year.

In the CBA, there was no, "We'll put you on injured reserve and pay you while you rehab until you're fully healthy."

If you got hurt and couldn't play, they were going to replace your ass. And sure enough, they brought in a very talented young guard, Moochie Norris, to take my spot. He'd go on to have a nine-year run in the NBA as a dependable role player.

Me? I couldn't play, so they dropped me like a bad habit. I've got one leg that's fully healthy and another that is compromised. But I got a call from another CBA squad, the Sioux Falls Sky Force in South Dakota. There were some really talented guys on that team like Randy Woods and Anthony Avent, who would both go on to cash some NBA paychecks, but there were also some dudes on that squad who were certifiably insane!

One of my teammates out there was Victor Page, Allen Iverson's talented backcourt mate at Georgetown. He was another character who was lively and funny, but he loved to fight. Loved it! One game, we were playing against the Idaho Stampede and Vic attacked the rim strong, ready to bring down the house with a thunderous dunk. One of their players laid some serious wood on him. Vic hit the ground hard and all you heard was gasps for an instant. But somehow he bounced off the hardwood, was back on his feet, grabbed a dust mop that was behind the basket and started swinging at the dude's head that fouled him. It was one of the most bizarre things I've ever seen on a basketball court.

Vic's life eventually took a really sad and tragic turn. In 2003, while hanging out in his old neighborhood in Washington, DC, he got shot in the head, in his eye socket, and was lucky to survive. Ten years later, he was sentenced to ten years in prison for assault. Then, while out on parole a few years back, he was sentenced to twenty years for assaulting and attempting to rape a seventeen-year-old girl.

So, I was on the roster in Sioux Falls, getting some playing time, but I started noticing that my neck and shoulders were feeling really tight. I was trying to hide it because if the coaching staff found out that I was hurt, they were gonna send me home and bring someone else in to take my place. It got to the point where I couldn't even lift my arms above my shoulders. Finally, I went to see the team doctor, and he basically told me to, as we say in the Black community, to "rub some 'Tussin on it."

Seriously, they give me some Advil and some Robitussin.

And sure enough, the coaches said, "Hey, Merl, we really like you, but if you can't play we gotta send you home."

As soon as I got back to South Carolina, I went to see my doctor, who proceeded to tell me, "You've got pneumonia and a lung infection. Merl, you could have died behind this if left untreated." So for the next three months, I was on bed rest, doing what was prescribed so I could get healthy again.

Once I got that in the rearview mirror, my agent called and said he got a job for me in Europe. So I packed my bags, went over to Sweden for a year and had the time of my life. I mean, my housing and car were in my contract, and I was getting paid handsomely to play basketball in Sweden.

Stockholm is like New York, I was a celebrity on the nightclub scene, my body felt better and I was scoring close to 40 points a night. Had a great year in Sweden, then played the next year in Austria.

I had a ball over there and signed a contract to play the next season over in Spain. But I had to get my other knee scoped because it kept swelling up. I couldn't even run, my leg wasn't strong enough and I gave them every excuse in the book as to why I couldn't get to training camp on time, trying to stall. But then my dad got really sick and I knew that I had to stay close to home.

It became apparent that I was coming down the homestretch of my playing career. Once my knee healed up, I figured I had one more year to play before hanging up my kicks. At that time, I thought I'd go into coaching because I loved the game and wanted to stay involved with it. An offer for $8,000 a month came in from Venezuela and I seriously contemplated it. But with my dad's health situation, it didn't feel right going so far away.

The inaugural season of the NBA D-League, now known as the G-League, was about to tip off and they were going to have a team based in Greenville, South Carolina. Because I was a hometown guy who'd played at Clemson, they invited me to join the Greenville Groove.

I knew it would be my final year playing, my body was telling me to stop. After numerous surgeries on both of my legs, I wasn't the same player. I played sparingly, but it was pretty cool to be a part of the birth of what would become the G-League.

Our assistant coach, Stephanie Ready, who now works as an NBA sideline reporter, was the first ever female coach in a men's professional league. We wound up winning the league's first championship.

By then I was in excruciating pain every day. My numerous leg injuries and surgeries forced me to walk and run differently, favoring one side of my body, and years of doing that wreaked havoc on my hips, back, knees, shoulders and neck. I had nerve issues in my hands and needed cortisone shots in my neck at times. I'd wake up in the middle of the night and when I'd bend my back, it sounded like a bag of pretzels being crushed.

I felt a tinge of sadness, but also a slight sigh of relief because physically, I was in bad shape. I knew I was done. I started calling everyone who'd been a part of my journey, just to let them know that my playing days were over and to thank them for what they'd done for me along the way. Teammates, coaches, mentors, advisors, everyone who I felt had an impact and opened the doors for me that I eventually walked through.

One of those calls was to Lynn Merritt at Nike, who'd invited me to be a counselor at Jason Kidd's and Tim Hardaway's summer camps a few years back. A family friend, Lynn had been in my home when I was just a little kid and we'd reconnected years later at Clemson, when he was working for Nike and came to watch Grant Hill when I played against him and his Duke squad during my freshman season.

Lynn asked me, "So what are you planning to do now? Do you think you might want to work over here with us?"

I didn't know anything about the athletic shoe industry or the business behind what happens within the Nike basketball apparatus. All I knew was that some NBA players were signed to sponsorship deals.

So my uninformed response was, "No thanks, Lynn. I don't wanna sell no shoes."

"That ain't really what I do, Merl," Lynn told me. "Yes, ultimately we're in the business of selling shoes but there's a lot more that goes into it, I do a lot more than that. Why don't you meet me at our All-American Camp in Indianapolis and we'll talk."

I was intrigued and decided to attend during that summer of 2002. The Nike All-American Camp was a big deal. A few years prior, they brought Yao Ming over from China and that was the first time he played on American soil. They flew in two hundred of the most elite prep basketball prospects to the National Institute for Fitness and Sports on the campus of IUPU, Indiana University–Purdue University, for a week of drills, lectures, practices, mentoring and scrimmages. The top high school guys at the time were there like Rashad McCants, Chris Paul, Paul Millsap, Shannon Brown, Rudy Gay, Luol Deng, Booby Gibson, Adam Morrison and plenty of others.

But the best player there was an underclassman, a seventeen-year-old kid from Akron, Ohio. He was probably the most ballyhooed prep player since Moses Malone was playing at Virginia's Petersburg High School in the early 1970s, the one the sneaker companies were salivating over the most, the one they all saw as their twenty-first-century poster boy. The race to adorn his feet and body with shoes and apparel had already begun.

And he wasn't even competing. A few weeks earlier he'd broken his left wrist while playing at the Mac Irvin AAU Summer Basketball Classic in Chicago. But that didn't stop the increasingly loud buzz that followed him wherever he went.

His name was LeBron James. As a six-foot-three high school freshman in 2000, he led his St. Vincent–St. Mary squad to an undefeated season and a state title.

That summer, heading into his sophomore year, after he

played at the legendary Five-Star Camp, Howard Garfinkel, the camp's founder and a giant in the elite summer basketball space, said he'd never seen a better, more skilled player at that age, and he'd seen them all, from Michael Jordan to Isiah Thomas to Dominique Wilkins to Patrick Ewing to Grant Hill to Jamal Mashburn to Rasheed Wallace to Tim Duncan and practically everyone else in between.

Before suiting up for the basketball team as a sophomore that winter, LeBron, at six-foot-six and 205 pounds, was an All-State football player, with many regarding him as the greatest wide receiver prospect that the state of Ohio had ever produced.

A few months later, he was the first sophomore ever selected as Ohio's Mr. Basketball. It was a well-known and indisputable fact in professional hoops circles that, had he been eligible to enter the 2001 NBA draft after just two years of high school, he would have been the consensus top pick over the top three prospects that year: Kwame Brown, who eventually went number one, Pau Gasol and Tyson Chandler.

Many were predicting that LeBron would become a multimillionaire before graduating from high school via his first shoe deal, prior to affixing his name to his first NBA contract. Folks back then were estimating his first shoe contract to be in the $20–$25 million range.

The crazy thing is that adidas, led by the sneaker impresario Sonny Vaccaro, the man who helped Nike take over the college basketball space in the late '70s and early '80s, and who'd signed Michael Jordan and Kobe Bryant to their first sneaker deals with Nike and adidas respectively, was holding his ABCD Camp in Hackensack, New Jersey, at the exact same time. So Nike and adidas were flying LeBron and his mom back and forth between both camps that summer.

At the Nike camp, other than being intrigued at what was going on with the players, I met the logistics team to find out more about how the camp was put together. I met the folks on the product side, the grassroots side, the college side and the NBA side. The overall enthusiasm about finding that next crop of players that could lead a post–Michael Jordan resurgence was palpable.

Lynn Merritt was working on the pro side, but he also was heavily involved in the grassroots sector because the best players at the time were making the leap from high school straight into the NBA. The previous summer, he'd reached out to me and asked me to evaluate a few players for him, strictly from a skills perspective. He must have appreciated my notes because he offered me a consultant role for a year, with the stipulation that if I liked it and if they liked me, we'd move toward something more permanent. "If not," he told me, "no harm, no foul. How does that sound?"

It sounded good to me, and I officially signed on as a consultant with Nike in the summer of 2002, working in their NBA division. Guys were placed in various geographic regions and were responsible for handling and working with their sponsored pro players. I was assigned to handle the Midwest and moved to Chicago.

I was starting on my new path, and I was prepared to work my ass off. I was determined to leave my own mark on the game.

5

"It's gotta be the shoes!"

An iconic 1989 Nike commercial features an incredulous Spike Lee, asking Michael Jordan what makes him the best player in the universe. Holding up a pair of Air Jordan IIIs, Lee, who appears as his character Mars Blackmon from his first feature-length film, *She's Gotta Have It*, can only come up with one explanation.

The concept, however, was not new. In *The Wiz*, Dorothy's magical red slippers allow her to rid the world of the wicked witch Eveline and transport her and her beloved dog, Toto, back home to Harlem. Cinderella wasn't nothing but a poor stepkid until a glass slipper transformed her into a princess.

In the prologue to his book, *Kicks*, author Nicholas Smith talks about the symbolic power of footwear.

> It's embedded in our language. To understand each other we must "walk a mile in someone's shoes." A guess about one's character will prove true "if the shoe fits." Someone irreplaceable has "hard shoes to fill." ... An uncomfortable reversal means that "the shoe is on the other foot." Before the inevitable, we wait for "the other shoe to drop."

Basketball played a huge role in the rise of athletic sneakers. Shoes specifically made for hoops started appearing in 1894, three years after Dr. James Naismith invented the game in Springfield, Massachusetts, at the International Young Men's Christian Association Training School. Because of its affiliation with the national YMCA organization and Christianity, the game soon spread across America like wildfire, as did the need to have the best shoes, ones that could provide traction on the hardwood and maximize performance.

As sports became more popular in the early twentieth century, and not just as leisure activities for the wealthy, manufacturing techniques improved and the Converse Rubber Shoe Company, based in Malden, Massachusetts, was the first to effectively use a celebrity endorser to move its basketball kicks.

Chuck Taylor would probably be considered a marginal player by today's standards. But he was a former pro who had suited up for, among others, the Akron Firestone Non-Skids, the Original Celtics and the Buffalo Germans, popular barnstorming teams that would travel around the country to compete against other professional teams in the early 1900s prior to the founding of the NBA.

In 1922, he joined Converse as a sales representative and came upon a novel concept, one that sneaker czar Sonny Vaccaro would employ years later when Nike bum-rushed the college basketball establishment: he targeted coaches.

Taylor barnstormed the country, giving clinics and seminars with a unique showmanship. Since he was a former professional athlete, impressionable kids wanted to see him. Coaches too traveled from far and wide to hear his ideas about the game. After his clinics, he nudged those in attendance, as well as the owners of local sporting goods stores, to order Converse All-Stars.

Converse, seeing Taylor's impact on their bottom line, did something that had never been done before. They started affixing their shoes with an ankle patch containing Taylor's signature and rebranded them as the Chuck Taylor All-Stars.

But the Chucks did not have a monopoly on the market. They continually battled a formidable foe, Keds, their rival in nearby Waltham, Massachusetts. In essence, the battle between Converse and Keds was basketball's first so-called sneaker war. As early as the 1920s, Keds were being worn during competition by international tennis champions, college athletes and Olympians.

In addition to his Converse salesmanship and barnstorming tours, Taylor had other ways to make sure his kicks held the number one spot. He shelled out cold hard cash, sometimes giving the National Association of Basketball Coaches as much as $50,000, an exorbitant sum in those days, to help him remain in their good graces.

Within the larger landscape of athletic footwear, the race to outfit the best and most visible athletes was already fierce by the time Jesse Owens laced up his spikes for the 1936 Olympics in Berlin, Germany. Owens had set three world records and tied a fourth the year prior while running at Ohio State University. So when Adolf "Adi" Dassler, whose shoe company was outfitting the German national team, met Owens at the Olympic Village, he seized the moment and convinced him to try on his shoes.

So in one of the greatest athletic and cultural moments in Olympic history, where Owens obliterated Hitler's myth of Aryan superiority, he set his world records and stood on the stand to receive his four gold medals wearing Adi's shoes, which would translate into not only a marketing coup but a boon in sales as well. Every top runner in the world now wanted to compete in the shoes that Jesse Owens was wearing.

In 1948, Adi Dassler and his brother and business partner, Rudolf, would have a bitter falling-out. They divided their assets and went their separate ways. Rudolf started his own company, calling it Puma. Adi named his new venture adidas. Thus started the first major athletic shoe war on a global level.

On American soil, the Chuck Taylors ruled the basketball shoe market well into the 1960s. John Wooden's UCLA dynasty won those ten national championships from 1964 through 1975 wearing the Converse shoe. But more than 80 percent of Olympians at the 1968 games in Mexico City were rocking adidas, and those kicks would soon make the leap into basketball.

When Chuck Taylor passed away in 1969, his signature All-Star canvas shoes had sold a whopping four hundred million pairs. But the Converse days of dominance at that point had come to an end.

That same year, adidas signed one of the NBA's brightest young stars, the Milwaukee Bucks' Kareem Abdul-Jabbar, whose fame had already reached legendary proportions due to his schoolboy days in New York City at Power Memorial

Academy and his college dominance at UCLA. Kareem was paid a then-unheard-of $25,000 annually to wear and endorse the company's products.

Adidas had previously introduced a technologically superior leather basketball shoe, with better support, stronger grip and a wider base. Searching for a competitive advantage, Boston Celtics coach Red Auerbach tossed aside his team's Chuck Taylors and outfitted his squad in the adidas Pro Model midway through their astonishing run of eleven NBA championships in thirteen seasons in the late 1950s and through the 1960s.

Suddenly the canvas basketball shoe was a relic of the past, only to emerge much later as a fashion essential.

Adidas changed the name of the Pro Model, adding a shell toe and calling it the Superstar. By 1973, roughly 85 percent of NBA players were wearing adidas, with many college programs following suit.

In 1973 Puma debuted its iconic suede sneaker, the Clyde. With the New York Knicks being at the epicenter of the basketball universe at the time, their point guard Walt "Clyde" Frazier was the human embodiment of cool and thus became the very first NBA player with his own signature shoe.

For many people, it was the first suede sneaker they'd ever seen. And when the Knicks won the championship again in 1973, with Clyde rocking his Pumas on the court, the shoe became instantly iconic.

New York City playground legends, inspired by Clyde, began showing up to play at the Rucker Pro-Am in Harlem wearing Pumas. Execs took notice as their shoe became the most desired pair of kicks among NYC youth. That trend began in urban neighborhoods like Harlem, the South Bronx and Bed-Stuy in Brooklyn, and would later spread to the suburbs, where well-off white kids were begging their parents for Clyde's kicks.

The shoes had transcended on-court functionality to become a fixture in pop culture. On the streets, the Clyde had become a fashion statement.

Converse was still in the game though in the '70s and early '80s, with the NBA's marquee players like Julius Erving, Larry Bird, Isiah Thomas and Magic Johnson wearing the Dr. J Pro Leather and Secret Weapon models.

When Nike entered the fray in the 1970s, they were mostly a niche brand focused on track and field athletes, but they began to make inroads in basketball in 1978 with their introduction of the Nike Blazer, a forerunner for future iconic lines like Air Force 1s and Jordans.

Blazers were worn by the Spurs' George "the Iceman" Gervin and featured on one of the most iconic posters of all time, with Gervin, attired in a slick silver Nike warm-up suit, sitting on blocks of ice and palming two frozen basketballs.

Nike got some more skin in the game when Hall of Famer Moses Malone hit the court in 1982 wearing the very first model of the Air Force 1. Known as the Original Six, Malone, Michael Cooper, Bobby Jones, Jamaal Wilkes, Calvin Natt and Mychal Thompson, Klay Thompson's daddy, were among the first to disseminate the shoe's message. Charles Barkley would later join the family, because, well, he played with more force than folks were accustomed to seeing.

But everything changed when Michael Jordan signed with Nike ahead of his rookie year with the Chicago Bulls.

The Air Jordan brand, first launched in 1985, is the reason why Nike grew exponentially as a company, the reason why it's the top sneaker brand in the world today, the reason why it retains a stranglehold on the basketball shoe market.

But by the time I came on board as a consultant with Nike

in 2002, change was in the air. Michael Jordan, though his shoe sales would remain a force in the industry, was aging out. Reebok now had the most electric and exciting young player in the game, Allen Iverson.

Jordan was on his last legs with the Wizards, and as good as they were, Nike's younger marquee players like Jason Kidd and Tim Hardaway weren't moving product. The most mesmerizing up-and-comers were with other brands. Vince Carter had signed with Puma. The aforementioned Allen Iverson was with Reebok. Kobe and Tracy McGrady were with adidas. Stephon Marbury was with AND1.

When I joined Nike, I was part of the group tasked with bringing in the necessary assets to rebuild Nike basketball. Lynn Merritt assembled a group he dubbed "the SEALs," like the Navy SEALs, a covert force with specialized training that operated both in the shadows and in broad daylight, and on an array of terrain. So, in addition to me being tasked with the Midwest region, there was also Nico Harrison, who was stationed in Dallas, Keith Veney, who was in DC, and Marc Eversley, who was at the corporate campus in Beaverton, Oregon.

Today, after a long run as the vice president of Nike Basketball, Nico is now the general manager of the Dallas Mavericks. Keith is a high school coach and a personal trainer for NBA and WNBA players. Marc is the general manager of the Chicago Bulls.

The NBA guys started calling us the Nike Mafia because we were everywhere, on public and clandestine missions, in the grassroots, college and pro spaces. The pressure was to produce immediate results. And it was intense.

As I mentioned earlier, the Nike gig required that I move to Chicago and one of my responsibilities was to work with our NBA players in the Midwest. I coordinated with our footwear design and product folks to make sure every player on a team in my region had access to everything they needed for practices and games, as well as access to all our new sneakers.

But there was also a personal element to it. If a player's mom or wife or girlfriend or kid had a birthday coming up, I took care of any special arrangements. Ahead of commercial shoots, I'd walk players and their agents through all of the logistics. I was basically the conduit between the players, their families, their agents and the Nike brand. At the same time, I was also learning how to navigate the various organizational structures of each team, identifying and connecting with the go-to people, from the front office administrative assistants to the security guards to the assistant to the general manager. Because if Nancy with the Pistons holds the real juice in the office and you remember to send her grandson a package on his birthday, she's going to make sure that the hardest doors to walk through get opened for you.

So I was excited to get started and learn the business. I was always frugal and saved most of the money I'd made playing pro ball. It wasn't necessarily a small fortune, but I had enough to put a down payment on a nice town house in a swanky part of town. For a twenty-six-year-old Black man, I was feeling really good about where I was and where I was heading.

As part of my relocation package, Nike was moving all of my stuff from my place in South Carolina to Chicago. They planned to ship my car to me, along with my furniture and the entirety of my worldly possessions. While I was getting settled and waiting for my things to arrive, the company gave me a rental car for thirty days.

This was during LeBron's senior year of high school and as soon as I got to Chicago, my boss called. He told me to drive to Cleveland, pick him up from the airport and then we'd head to Akron to check in with LeBron, his mom and their crew.

On the day we were scheduled to make the trip, my Range Rover arrived. I decided to drive my own car to Cleveland but I didn't want the rental car sitting in the same spot on the street for a few days. I didn't know anybody in Chicago yet, so I called my old teammate from the CBA, Thomas Hamilton, aka Ham.

"Hey, Ham, I need a favor," I said. "I gotta drive to Cleveland this morning to pick up my boss, and my truck just got here. If I leave the keys for you, can you drop off my rental car to Hertz at Midway Airport?"

"No problem," he said. "I can do that for you."

I felt confident that everything was taken care of. On the way to Cleveland, my excitement grew. This was my first assignment, and all I needed to do was to be present, to absorb the workings of the business and to see how we attempt to sign a talent hailed as the next Michael Jordan.

I'll get into that Akron visit a little bit later, but when I got back home, the rental car was gone and everything seemed cool. A few weeks later, I flew out to Minnesota to watch the Timberwolves play and to meet with some of the players that I'd be working with.

Halfway through the trip, I got a call from the relocation department at Nike. "Hey," they said. "We're just checking in because you haven't turned in that rental car yet."

A wave of panic washed over me. I had assumed that Ham returned it two weeks prior. "Oh, okay, I'll get that taken care of," I said, and hung up.

I called Ham. No answer. I kept calling. No answer. Frantically, I called around to some folks in the Chicago hoops scene and everyone basically said the same thing: "Nope, we ain't seen him."

I closed out the rest of the trip, but the entire time my anxiety was mounting. *Where in the hell is this car?*

Another week passed, and the relocation department called again, asking more firmly about the car. Then my boss called. "Merl! Take the fucking car back! What the hell are you doing?"

By then I was sweating bullets and cursing Ham out even though I couldn't find him, thinking to myself, *This dude Ham is gonna get me fired before I even get started!*

I started calling everybody under the sun, ringing up every agent in Chicago, asking, "Do you know Thomas Hamilton? Do you represent him?"

I kept running into dead ends until finally I spoke to one agent who told me, "Hey, I don't represent Ham but I have his grandma's number."

Cool, so I called his grandma and in the sweetest little grandmotherly voice you've ever heard, she told me, "Oh, he's in China, baby."

HE'S FUCKING WHERE!!!???

In China???

Finally, I managed to get ahold of his agent and told him that I need to get his ass on the phone ASAP. So I got his number in China and finally got him on the phone. By then I was furious.

"Aye, Ham, where the fuck is that car?"

The dude said, "Oh, my man didn't take it back?"

"YOUR MAN!!!???" I screamed.

"Don't worry, Merl, I'll be home in a month and get everything squared away."

"A MONTH!!!??? Aw, hell no. You need to find that shit

now or I'm gonna have to call the police and tell them that you stole the damn car!"

"Aw, Merl, you ain't gonna do that shit."

"Ham, if it comes down to me losing this job because of this rental car, you're damn right I'm gonna do that shit. I'm about to get fired behind this. Find the damn car!" He gave me his friend's number, and I began to call him obsessively. Finally, a woman answered. I told her what was going on. "Look, I ain't tryna cause no problems but your man has a rental car that Thomas Hamilton let him hold. I need him to return it to Hertz at Midway right now or the police are going to be coming for him."

"Oh, okay," she said. "I don't know where he's at right now but when I talk to him I'll let him know."

For the next few days, radio silence. I didn't hear a thing. I was certain by that point that I was going to be fired. Hertz's insurance company was calling too and threatened to report me to the police for theft. Fifty days had passed. I was supposed to have it returned within thirty.

"If we don't get the car back within forty-eight hours, we're going to have to report it stolen and you're going to be responsible for whatever happens after that," they informed me.

Ham, his granny, his man, his man's girl, all stopped answering my calls.

Three weeks later, I was sitting in my office when a letter from Hertz arrived. I was trembling as I opened it. Pictures accompanied a note on letterhead, saying,

We regret to inform you that your rental privileges have been suspended because of the damages that were caused to the vehicle while it was in your possession.

I breathed a sigh of relief knowing that they'd finally re-turned the car, but the pictures were shocking.

They'd basically smoked the damn car out! The interior reeked of cigarette and marijuana smoke, the note stated, and there were burn marks all over the seats, all kinds of liquids spilled, staining all of the rugs. It was a damn mess. They trashed the shit out of the car, which was basically spanking new when I got it. But somehow Hertz took it back. And I'd dodged a bullet.

I never talked to Ham again after that, though I would eventually become cool with his son, who would blossom into a very good high school basketball player in Chicago.

Another mistake I made early on in my Nike tenure was in my dealings with Eddy Curry. Eddy was a young player with the Bulls at the time and one of my clients. He had been blessed with that special magic dust in terms of size, skills and talent, and I'm talking pure, unadulterated talent. The kid had the goods. But despite his all-star ability, he wasn't putting in the effort in workouts.

One day, his house was ransacked and robbed. He had an impressive collection of expensive throwback jerseys and they cleaned his ass out, along with some cash and jewelry. He called and told me what happened and I went over there to help him clean the place up. Afterward, we were outside on his basketball court, shooting around to blow off steam. He bet me that I couldn't make a certain amount of shots from various spots. We start off with just a handful of baskets. Ten dollars per shot. Then he upped it to $20, then $100. I warned him, "Hey, Eddy, I can shoot the shit outta this ball. You know I played. Let's take it easy before you wind up owing me a bunch of money."

Sure enough, he's started to get deeper in the hole, betting

$500 a shot. It got to the point where he owed me $10,000. I basically told him, "Look, man, we're gonna stop this right here. Just pay off my credit card and we're good."

I was still pretty young at the time, and it didn't seem like a big deal. NBA players gamble away far bigger sums than that on flights in between cities. Remember the crazy episode a few years back when the Wizards' Gilbert Arenas and Javaris Crittenton brought guns to the locker room in a dispute over some money owed over a card game?

Eddy and I were cool, laughing about how I had ten grand coming from him. But shortly thereafter, I got a call from my boss, Lynn. "Merl, what the fuck is wrong with you? You're asking your players for money?" I told Lynn what went down and he told me to knock it off and to never gamble with a client ever again.

Chicago is a tough city. Forget that Magnificent Mile stuff. A Black man can get killed for simply being in the wrong part of town at the wrong time if he's not careful.

I'm a South Carolina boy, so I didn't know a damn thing about the South Side, the West Side, the Gangster Disciples, the Vice Lords, none of that stuff. But I had to learn quick, because in addition to working with the NBA players in the region, another part of my job was running the Nike summer leagues, which would eventually become known as Pro City.

The leagues ran in eight cities. I was in charge of renting the venues, arranging for security, hiring referees and ordering every last T-shirt, sneaker, headband and sock. The Nike Pro City summer leagues don't generate any revenue; they're basically a community relations thing that provide the best competition for our guys during the off-season. A South Side kid's favorite player might be, let's say, Antoine Walker, Shawn

Marion, Shannon Brown or Will Bynum. Well, if that kid's family can't afford tickets to a Bulls game when those guys are in town to play them, they can come to Pro City during the summer and watch them play for free.

And the gear the players wear at Pro City might soon come down the consumer pipeline. In the same way that Clyde Frazier's Pumas started a trend with playground legends at Rucker Park, and by extension, kids throughout Harlem, these grassroots initiatives can really seed the market.

It took me a while to become fully acclimated to Chicago and to establish the kind of relationships you need to succeed in this business. The street guys saw who I was and what I was about. I gained credibility by playing pickup ball at a high level. I'd head down to Foster Park, which is in the middle of the hood, or over to Fosco Park on the West Side, which is in the middle of the projects, and get busy playing alongside guys who played in the NBA or overseas.

One of the ways I ingratiated myself with various communities was through workouts I'd hold for serious players that lived in the area. A buddy of mine, Tony McCoy, who worked in the city's department of recreation and parks and who would later oversee the Chicago Public Schools Athletics Department, would open the gym for me at 6:00 a.m., and we'd do some private workouts with college players, overseas pros and standout high school kids.

I'd load up my truck in the morning with Nike gear, shoes, socks, backpacks, shorts, T-shirts, whatever, and have a dumpster fire giveaway, blessing whoever showed up. Before long, the grassroots basketball community in the city accepted and welcomed me.

But that didn't mean the summer leagues ran smoothly. Out of all the Pro City operations, Chicago was the worst in terms of the financial piece. I couldn't understand how it was more expensive to run than the New York entity. The security bills alone were coming in at $100,000 and it took me a while to figure out what was going on.

One day, I got a call from a woman who was livid.

"My child's been working up there for Nike for three months and can't get no paycheck!" she said.

"I've already paid the director," I explained. "And everyone who works there should've already started receiving their checks. Let me find out why he hasn't been paid. Also, you need to know that your son doesn't work for Nike—he works for the summer Pro-Am. Give me a minute to see what's going on."

That same day I also received furious calls from the refs, complaining that they hadn't been paid yet either.

Ultimately we realized that one of the most powerful and vicious gangs in the city was extorting the director. Instead of paying the staff, the refs and some of the other bills, he was paying the gang to keep them off his ass.

I'd come to know one of the high-ranking guys in that gang and we got along well. I called him up, and he started laughing. He informed me that this was just the cost of doing business in the hood in Chicago. If major money was involved, the gang was gonna stake their claim to some of it.

I later found out that, once it became clear that I was trying to put an end to all that craziness, one of those dudes was asking around about me, asking where I lived. I guess he wanted to see me and extort me directly. I heard rumors that some people would be paying me a visit.

Somehow everything got ironed out and we managed to keep the gangster element at arm's length. I was finally starting to see what this one-year consulting agreement was all

123

about. Lynn Merritt, my boss who brought me into the Nike orbit, wanted to see if I'd get eaten alive. When he saw that I didn't, that I was handling my business in both the corporate world and the street, they made me an offer to be a full-time employee. But that audition involved some really wild shit.

Part of my job on the NBA side was to evaluate promising rookies coming into the league. That first draft class included LeBron, Carmelo Anthony, Chris Bosh, D. Wade and T. J. Ford. I had to evaluate each player and place them in certain categories based on their potential as a Nike-sponsored athlete.

The recruiting around LeBron was my first exposure to an athlete with stratospheric upside in the shoe market akin to Michael Jordan, someone who could move the needle globally. How committed were we? Lynn Merritt moved to Akron for LeBron's entire senior year in high school. Nike kept a dedicated hotel suite, stocked with shoes and products from floor to ceiling, and Bron and his folks were free to come by whenever they damn well pleased to take whatever they wanted.

My value came in my ability to assess guys who weren't yet the biggest names, but had some upswing. I fought for guys like Michael Redd, Carlos Boozer and Tayshaun Prince. In some of those debates, company execs laughed and dismissed me. But I knew basketball in ways that most of them didn't.

"I'm not saying these guys are gonna be market movers, but they're gonna make all-star teams down the road," I'd argue.

Despite the resistance, I believed in those guys and knew what I was looking at. My predictions about those three guys in particular gave me some credibility in terms of what I was able to project from a talent perspective. Sometimes I worked public relations angles. With Michael Redd, an early unsung talent from the Milwaukee Bucks, I connected him with the man who ran the *Milwaukee Journal Sentinel*'s sports section,

Garry D. Howard, my Omega Psi Phi fraternity brother. I knew he'd be the perfect person to help showcase Redd's humanity as he began emerging into an alite talent. He was reluctant to open up to the media, but Garry helped his profile blossom outside of just being a really good NBA player. Redd was one of the truly great people that I came across in my work with Nike.

Another early hiccup for me involved Sam Cassell. He'd won back-to-back titles during his first two seasons as a solid role player with the Houston Rockets. By his fifth year, then with the New Jersey Nets, Sam had established himself as a really good starting point guard.

Milwaukee, as I've said, was one of the teams in my Midwest market so I was there all the time servicing the Bucks roster. I had a good rapport with the organization, and by the time Sam got traded there, he was in the midst of the best four-year stretch of his career.

During his tenure in Milwaukee, we got along well. Sam didn't have a sneaker deal, but we'd send him shoes. We started talking about getting him a shoe contract during his last year with the Bucks because he was a really, really good player.

The conversations extended into the off-season, prior to him signing on with the Minnesota Timberwolves. I thought the timing was perfect because with Sam joining Kevin Garnett and Latrell Sprewell in Minnesota, they were poised to make a serious run in the Western Conference during the 2003–2004 season.

So I said, "Sam, let's get something done," and offered him a Nike deal worth $50,000.

It wasn't a big sum of money. Shoot, Chris Paul's rookie

deal with Nike came in at $650,000 annually. But Sam wasn't telegenic like that, nor did he have CP III's appeal as a commercial spokesman. No one was offering him any type of shoe deal, so to get that extra fifty grand was cool with him.

I sent the offer sheet to his agent and Sam said everything was kosher and we were good. Or so I thought.

A few months later, the Wolves were looking like they had a shot at the NBA Finals and Sam made the All-Star team. I was ecstatic for him. At the All-Star game in Los Angeles, Sam actually hooked me up with a room at the players' hotel. But as I was getting settled in, I received a call from an aggravated Lynn, who told me to get over to his room ASAP.

As soon as I walked through the door, he launched in. "Merl! Why the fuck is Sam's agent calling me saying that Sam's value has gone up now that he's an All-Star and now they want $150,000? He never signed that original contract that was drawn up!"

Normal protocol was that once everything had been agreed to, the player and his agent would finalize everything through Nike's legal department and my aspect of the job was done. I thought that's what had happened. So I'd moved on to other responsibilities I had with other players.

Lynn handed me a jar of Vaseline and said, "You might as well just bend over now and take it." He was laughing and giggling, but I didn't think it was funny.

"Don't worry, Merl. Consider it a lesson learned. I'll take care of it from here," he assured me. And to his credit, at least in that moment, he said it in an avuncular way, like we all go through something like this when learning the business. Sam eventually signed with Nike for more than the $50,000 we'd initially agreed upon.

Another big part of the job was reconnaissance, intel and

information gathering. I needed to get to know the scouts, the general managers, all of the decision makers from each franchise, the coaching staff, everybody.

I needed to know who was going to get traded and why, who was on their draft board, the players coming out of school that they were not fond of, the players they were bringing in for private workouts. I needed to be inside the building to gather all of these different perspectives in order to find out as much as I could about what was going on inside of the organization.

I learned early on that NBA teams would sometimes use us to talk to other teams so they could avoid any tampering charges. For example, I might get a call from my Nike colleague on the West Coast who'd say, "Hey, Team X is interested in unloading Player A, but they'd like to get Player B from Team Y in return. You work with the guys at Team Y—give them a buzz and see if they're interested."

I'd take that to the GMs and senior vice presidents of the teams that I had good relationships with. So we were utilized sometimes for cloak-and-dagger stuff while they explored their options on some potential moves.

At the same time, I needed to be plugged into the really good high school players. That was all part of Nike's intel machine. I had to know what kids in my markets had NBA potential, kids who might spend one or two years on a college campus before being a first-round draft pick.

Because those kids, you want to know if they're considering going to the highest profile colleges in Nike's NCAA portfolio. And if they're not, you need to figure out a way to change up that dynamic, by any means necessary.

If a high school kid in my region had pro potential, I started showering him with the flyest sneakers and gear at least once a month. Really good players would get boxes every three months or so. Solid players that you thought had a chance to develop down the line, they'd be blessed by the sneaker Santa every six months. Trust me, my FedEx budget was limitless, as was my allocation of product to spread around.

If there was a college kid in my region that had some first-round draft potential, I was calling up his coaches to tell them I was sending him a side package of the newest Air Jordans that had yet to hit the streets.

And there was a quid pro quo in that because when some of those college coaches were in hot pursuit of a five-star high school kid, they'd ask me to hit the kid off with boxes of the choicest Jordans, with a note saying, "Hey, man, coach XYZ at ABC University sends his love."

You have to be fully invested in getting those kids to consider Nike schools and you have to be a part of the process of making that happen.

That's how I eventually came to know a teenager from Chicago named Patrick Beverley.

Nowadays, he's known as one of the most tenacious defenders in the NBA, a guy who has carved out an enduring pro career due to his heart, tenacity, hustle and willingness to do the dirty work that might not necessarily appear on the stat sheet.

Back then, Pat Bev was the same hungry player hoping for a scholarship offer.

We met after I was tasked with running the Chicago side of a television documentary series called *Nike Battlegrounds: King of the Court*. Teams of the top high school players were assembled, and the series chronicled their practices and preparations leading up to the big game.

I loved Pat's tenaciousness. He was a pit bull, even back then. He played with a hunger that you just can't teach. Pat went to one of those schools on the West Side, Marshall, where they had to play the games in an empty gym with no fans early in the afternoon because they'd get to shooting if the students and the neighborhood folks were up in there.

His desire was off the charts and he had the athletic talent to warrant a scholarship to a good program, but things weren't working out for him the way that he wanted.

He'd be in the street, playing for teams that were sponsored by the drug dealers, what we called Dope Boy Games. And he'd get a few hundred bucks for his performance in each game. These were big-money games and dangerous, with tens of thousands of dollars being bet on the outcome.

I got to know Pat and his momma, Lisa, who was a fantastic individual. Oftentimes, he'd come over to my town house just to hang out and relax, eat some chicken wings and talk about life and basketball. I'd put him through workouts alongside some of the other really good players in the city at the time and our relationship was like a big and a little brother. He could confide in me without being judged, he respected where I'd been and what I'd done as a player and we got along well. My place was like a refuge for him, and he was always well-mannered and very respectful.

Even as a teenager, he was very intense and opinionated. He was going to listen to your advice, but he always had a mind of his own. He was a really good kid coming up in the middle of the hood, having to duck and dodge the negative elements that come with that, and I really liked him.

Around that same time, I'd been asked to do some work with Chris Bosh. I'd once gone down to Atlanta with Hall of Fame coach George Raveling, who was then Nike's global basketball sports marketing director, to watch one of Chris's games when he was a freshman at Georgia Tech. He signed with Converse, which was by then a Nike subsidiary, after being the fourth overall selection in the 2003 NBA draft.

He was now showing All-Star potential with the Toronto Raptors.

My colleague Marc Eversley, who had been working with Nike Canada, had recently accepted an assistant general manager position with the Raptors. Today, as I mentioned earlier, Marc is the general manager of the Chicago Bulls.

So with Marc leaving the company, I was asked to fill in the gaps until they could bring in his permanent replacement.

I already had a great relationship with Chris's agent, Hank Thomas, one of the most successful African American agents in the game at the time, who represented the likes of Michael Finley, Tim Hardaway and a few others. Hank was a really good brother, his offices were in Chicago and I'd been introduced to him when I first got to the city.

Chris was really great to work with. He was not a prima donna and once we'd built a rapport, he was extremely accessible. If he missed your call, he'd return it expeditiously. He had a responsible way of handling his business.

When the Raptors were coming into Chicago to play the Bulls, I promised Pat Beverley that I'd bring Chris to his high school game. Pat didn't believe me.

"Yeah, right, Merl," he said. "You're gonna bring Chris Bosh to my game? Sure, you are."

And sure enough, Chris came with me to Marshall High School to watch Pat play. He spoke to the team before the game, offering words of encouragement. And Pat was looking at me, nodding his head like, *Okay, bro. OKAY!*

We left at halftime and it's a good thing we did. Because as soon as the game was over, there was a shooting in the parking lot. I'm pretty certain that my bosses would not have been happy had Chris Bosh been in the middle of that cross fire, asking me what the hell I was thinking by bringing one of our prized young assets into the hood like that.

Now, back to Patrick Beverley. His mom, Lisa, called me one day in tears. After waiting and waiting for some college offers, one finally came through from the University of Toledo. Pat said he'd rather play in the Dope Boy Games than go play at Toledo.

"I don't know what I'm going to do with him, Merl," she told me. "If he stays here, these streets are going to get him."

I assured her that other offers would come, and she needed to believe in him the way that he believed in himself. The best-case scenario was that by his senior year he'd have his choice of schools. And that's exactly what happened. As a senior, he led the state in scoring, dropping thirty-seven points per game. But the college coaches really loved his bulldog mentality. He was afraid of nothing and backed down from no one.

Eventually, he got an offer from his dream school, the University of Michigan. Tommy Amaker, the great former guard at Duke, was the coach at Ann Arbor and both Pat and I really liked Tommy.

Now, you have to understand what Tommy meant to me when I was growing up. That Duke backcourt with him and Johnny Dawkins in the mid-1980s held a special place in my heart. I absolutely loved his game, studied it as a kid, and he was one of my stylistic role models. Plus, he was a stand-up guy, superrespected within the game both as a player and as a young coach.

But on his recruiting visit, Pat's host was a player that no one on the team liked. That friction bled into Pat's visit, where the Wolverine players barely paid any attention to him. He wasn't feeling that treatment; the guys who were already on the roster and who he'd potentially be playing with that next year, they didn't welcome him at all. So now Michigan was out the window.

People often wonder why kids pick one school over another. For Pat, even with Michigan being his dream school, when the players there treated him like a wet food stamp, that Chicago rumble in his blood would not allow it to slide. So he basically said, "Fuck ya'll."

Pat eventually chose to play at the University of Arkansas. Midway through his freshman year, his mom, a family friend and I went down to Fayetteville for a few days to visit with him and show him some love.

And after two years at Arkansas, he bounced to play overseas before eventually finding his way into the NBA and creating his own success—a true underdog story.

And there were other kids in Chicago that I got to know long before the spotlight found them. One of them was an unknown point guard.

A few months prior, he was a fringe college prospect that wasn't at one of the traditional city powerhouses. He had decent size for a high school point guard at six foot, but he wasn't really making any major noise.

Then, the boy had an eight-inch growth spurt. A colleague of mine called me up and said, "Hey, Merl, you need to come meet this kid and watch him work out. I can't believe what I'm seeing."

So I did. He was now six-foot-eight and still growing, but had lost none of his previous athleticism and point guard skills. My jaw dropped when I watched him play. Even some people deeply entrenched in the city's basketball scene had not seen or heard of him yet.

The first thing I said to myself when I saw him work out was, "Good Gawd."

His name was Anthony Davis.

6

On October 4, 2019, the Associated Press ran an article with the headline, "Merl Code gets 3 months in prison for role in NCAA bribery scheme." According to the article I was sentenced for supposedly steering young players toward handlers and managers. I was also described as an "amateur coach." First of all, I was never an amateur coach, I was an executive and a consultant for two multibillion-dollar international corporations. Second, if an outlet as prestigious as the Associated Press could get such a simple fact wrong, how else was my story being wildly distorted?

Regarding my professional prospects in the basketball industry, I was done. Forget toxic—I was considered radioactive. No company would touch me, given the stain of the federal charges, despite the fact that both of the cases were utter bullshit.

I'd worked hard to become respected in my field, had entertained numerous offers over the years to join NBA front offices and had performed my duties in the way that I was asked to, ultimately recognized as an asset to both Nike and adidas.

I wasn't some rogue employee that went off the grid for my own personal benefit. I simply did my job with the diligence to deliver the results. And I in no way was part of some conspiracy to steer players toward money managers that would handle their finances once they turned professional. My job was to help get the best players at Nike and adidas schools. Period.

But suddenly I was facing years in prison.

After the initial arraignment, and after watching the press conference on TV with my dad, I agreed to have one of my father's colleagues represent me. We sat down to strategize and I'll never forget what he told me: "The first person to talk gets the best deal."

I straight up told him that I was not going to be cooperating with the government. I was adamant about that because I honestly felt, with every ounce of blood in my body, that I'd done nothing wrong and had committed no federal crimes. Yes, everybody—the college coaches, the sneaker companies, the AAU folks, the players' families—was playing fast and loose to get around the NCAA's absurd charade of "shamateurism," but that did not cross over into the realm of federal crimes that warranted jail sentences.

And there was some precedent there. Many classic hip-hop fans might be familiar with the name Norby Walters from when Eric B. dropped his name—"Norby Walters is our agency, right?"—in his classic 1987 cut with Rakim, "Paid in Full."

But Norby Walters is someone that folks who have an interest in my case, who are fascinated by what goes on behind the scenes in the big-money world of college athletics, who have followed the FBI's foray into the world of major college basketball, should know.

In 1988, the FBI revealed that it had conducted a seventeen-month investigation into Walters and his business partner. Norby, a wildly successful booking agent in the music business who'd represented the likes of Janet Jackson, Patti La-Belle, Kool and the Gang and many others, had decided to expand his reach into the sports agent space.

And he did so with the subtlety of a bull in a china shop.

Walters allegedly offered college players, among other things, cash for them and their families, clothes, concert tickets, intros to celebrities in the entertainment business, cars, airline tickets, hotel accommodations, use of limousines, etc., as inducements to sign with him. Norby would then post-date the contracts, making it seem like they'd signed with him once their eligibility had expired.

Sports Illustrated's Bruce Selcraig wrote in September of 1988, "The indictment also alleges that nine colleges were defrauded by the agents and players, because the schools had awarded scholarship money to athletes who had been rendered ineligible to receive that money by signing the contracts. It is against NCAA regulations, not against federal law, for an athlete to sign with an agent while he has eligibility remaining. But the government is charging that players who accepted scholarships after signing statements attesting to their eligibility committed fraud."

Now, the Walters case was different from ours in that he allegedly had some serious ties to organized crime, along with allegations of theft, extortion and assault.

But the salient point I'm making is about the position that the government took in claiming that Norby had defrauded nine universities because the schools had awarded scholarships to players whose amateur status, defined by the NCAA, had been compromised.

So what eventually happened when the smoke cleared after Norby was charged and later convicted of conspiracy, racketeering and mail fraud charges?

The verdict was thrown out on appeal.

As brazen as he was, Walters may have taken a dump all over NCAA rules, but the appellate court basically said that no universities were defrauded.

So why would the FBI try to dust off that same, tired, worn-out theory and slap it on us some thirty years later?

Back in South Carolina, as my world was disintegrating around me, my dad's colleague, who I hadn't formally hired as my attorney, had already spoken to the FBI and told them that I was going to talk with them and tell them everything I knew.

The hell I was.

He did this prior to speaking with me and without my consent.

I don't know why he told them that without consulting with me, because that got me jammed up even more.

A federal agent flew down the next day to meet with me. And he seemed utterly shocked by my position that I was not going to meet with him, that I was not gonna work with them in order to cut a deal.

My dad, when we discussed the possibility of cooperating, said, "If you talk, you can't pick and choose what to talk about. You have to talk about everything."

I didn't know which way this thing was going to go and didn't trust that telling my side of the story at that time was going to be handled respectfully, without some hidden motive to ruin either my own or another individual's life. I didn't want anybody else to get jammed up. I'd built a lot of solid professional relationships over my years and who knew which rabbit hole the government would follow in terms of major college basketball recruiting?

But I do know one thing. Those federal agents, for some reason, had it out for Rick Pitino. I don't know the motivation behind it, whether it was a personal vendetta or a desire to grab the biggest headlines, but something definitely smelled fishy.

Less than a week after I refused to talk, they tried to further ramp up the pressure by hitting me with four more charges. They even folded me into another case that centered around bribing college coaches.

The first case was the Brian Bowen situation with Louisville, where adidas agreed to pay his father $100,000 for him to sign with the school. The most absurd thing to me was that the federal government was claiming that adidas and the company's executives had defrauded the university, making the kid ineligible to ever play a game of college basketball.

First and foremost, when Nike or adidas or whoever had sent that kid his first pair of sneakers when he was thirteen years old, if we're following the NCAA rules to the letter, the kid became ineligible. But we'll let that minor issue slide for a moment. Because if we're truly talking about defrauding a university and Bowen not being eligible to play college basketball, according to the NCAA rule book, that kid was ineligible going back to middle school. And the main culprit in that was his own father. I'll get to that in a minute.

So, you may be asking, how was I involved in the Brian Bowen situation?

I got a call from my guy Christian Dawkins. Christian, an aspiring agent at the time, had a relationship with the Bowen family. He told me he was helping out with the recruitment process and asked about the top adidas schools. I gave him my opinion from a basketball perspective of where he might fit in best, narrowing the choices down to our flagship programs: Louisville, Indiana and Kansas.

The Bowen kid was good, but he wasn't Carmelo Anthony or Anthony Davis, wasn't gonna deliver a national championship during his freshman year before riding off toward NBA riches as a top-five pick. But, I felt like with a couple of years of Rick Pitino's coaching, he'd develop into a solid NBA prospect. And again, my job was to make sure that elite prep players like him signed with an adidas school.

When we agreed that Louisville was probably the best school for him under the adidas umbrella, Christian asked me if I'd front him $100,000 to take care of Brian's family if he steered him there. He promised to return it to me. I just laughed and said, "I've got a hundred grand, but not to give you for no damn Brian Bowen."

He then asked if adidas might be willing to come up with the cash, wondering if I could talk to Jim Gatto, the company's director of global marketing.

I'd never met or talked to Brian Bowen or his daddy. He was the MVP of the prestigious Jordan Brand Classic after his senior season and the last top-ranked player in his class to commit. As I've said before, my job was to make sure that the very best players wound up at adidas schools. Had I not approached my bosses with this information, and had it come out later that I withheld that information, I would have been seen as a disloyal member of the adidas sports marketing team and could have been summarily released for negligence after my contract expired.

So I simply told Christian, as I mentioned before, "That's not a decision that I can make, that's an adidas decision and I will certainly ask Gatto and see what they want to do."

Which is what I did. I spoke to Gatto to let him know what was going on.

"I need to talk to Chris Rivers," Gatto said. "And the other folks internally and then talk to Rick Pitino."

He was basically telling me that he had to run it even higher up the flagpole. Later he called me back saying, "I spoke to Rick and he wants us to help him."

Rick Pitino has denied having any knowledge of or involvement in adidas facilitating a payment to the family to secure Bowen Jr.'s enrollment at Louisville.

The Bowen family had been going through some financial difficulties and their house had recently burned down. I relayed all the information Christian shared with me to Gatto. The family, who'd been offered money by a few other schools, settled on Louisville with the stipulation that adidas would pay his father in four $25,000 installments.

Gatto asked me to create an invoice, which confused me. He explained that to process these types of payments he had to take the money out of separate buckets of the budget. I was instructed to make out the invoice for the first $25,000 installment as a travel team expense.

"This is how we normally do this," he said.

I had previously invoiced a travel team expense for the Karolina Khaos, a lower-level squad run by two of my childhood friends. Adidas had committed a small amount of money and gear to get them through the spring and summer season and support the program as a platform for unseen talent in South Carolina.

So adidas wired $25,000 to the Karolina Khaos, who then sent a check to LOYD Management, which was Christian Dawkins's company, for the first of the four installments headed to Bowen's daddy.

As the FBI posed in front of their fancy charts and graphs for the television cameras, Louisville ran for cover. They declared Bowen ineligible. Even though it was Louisville who asked for our help in signing him, they took no responsibility. And Bowen, a promising talent, a teenager, was collateral damage.

Louisville's decision meant that Bowen could no longer work out at the team facilities; he couldn't practice or even eat meals with the team. His access to the training staff and all the other perks ceased immediately. I felt bad for him. He was simply hit with the shrapnel of a pretty common recruiting scenario, the details of which became part of the public record.

Bowen ultimately transferred to the University of South Carolina and practiced with the Gamecocks, but the NCAA too ruled him ineligible, and whatever dreams he may have harbored of March Madness heroics were up in smoke.

Now back to Brian Bowen Sr.

If you thought Zion Williamson's stepfather was doing the most, that dude didn't have a thing on Bowen's daddy. After being granted immunity, he testified in federal court that he was bartering his son's talent for cash as far back as middle school. When federal prosecutor Edward Diskant asked him why his son was not currently in college in early October of 2018, Bowen Sr. broke down in tears. He buried his face in a wad of tissues and began crying uncontrollably. In court-room 26B of the Manhattan federal courthouse, he eventu-ally composed himself to talk about his actions as it related to his family's navigation of the "amateur" hoops labyrinth.

He explained in his testimony that Creighton, Oklahoma State, Arizona and Texas, among others, had all offered pay-ment proposals to the family if his son signed to play with them. He also testified that he was paid copious amounts of cash for his son to play with various AAU teams and for him to attend La Lumiere, an elite boarding school in Indiana with a nationally ranked hoops squad. He said he was of-fered $25,000 by adidas program director T. J. Gassnola for his son to play with the Michigan Mustangs, between $5,000 and $8,000 for him to play for Nike-sponsored team Mean Streets, and $2,000 per month by former La Lumiere coach Shane Heirman.

After Bowen Jr. signed, the Bowen family relocated to Louisville and moved into a suite in the Galt House Hotel, a high-end spot with a monthly rent of $2,300. Bowen's father testified that he requested and received $1,300 from a Lou-isville assistant coach to help out with their rent in June of 2017. He testified that he never told his son about the adidas-Louisville arrangement. And he even used a secret phone, a "bat phone" as he called it, to broker the deal.

Brian Bowen's daddy freely admitted to all of this because he'd been granted immunity. He had pimped his own son for years, brokered the deal that led to the FBI case. He received protection so that they could convict me.

Brian Bowen's journey as a pro athlete is still playing out. He had a great showing in the G League with the Fort Wayne Mad Ants, where he averaged sixteen points and eight re-bounds per game and played in a total of twelve games for the Indiana Pacers during the 2019–20 and 2020–21 seasons. On April 23, 2021, the Pacers waived him. He sued adidas, me and a few others, claiming we derailed his NBA career. The judge dismissed the lawsuit.

I sincerely wish him nothing but the best in the years ahead. Unfortunately, like so many kids, he was a pawn in a much larger game, one his father and so many others gleefully engaged in and profited from. I know the way things unfolded for him, the loss of his college eligibility and the subsequent FBI mess, was not of his own doing. I hope to see him on an NBA roster in the near future, living out his childhood dreams.

7

On that initial assignment with Nike, as my rental car was getting trashed, I picked up my new boss, Lynn Merritt, at the Cleveland airport and we made our way to the rust belt city of Akron.

I'd recently retired from playing pro ball, so I wasn't super-plugged into the elite high school prospects in that 2003 senior class. But in the hoops world, you'd have to have been living under a rock to have not heard the astonishing praise swirling around seventeen-year-old LeBron James.

I'd read Grant Wahl's *Sports Illustrated* cover piece, "Ahead of His Class," the season prior and was aware of the immense hype. NBA general managers, whose teams might have a shot at the number one overall pick, were drooling over the kid, as were the executives at Nike, Reebok and adidas in what promised to be the biggest bidding war ever for a prospect who had yet to play his first professional game, let alone not a single college game.

Wahl wrote,

LeBron is thought to possess all the elements necessary to do for some apparel company what Jordan did for Nike... For now LeBron exists in a weird netherworld between high school student and multimillionaire, between dependent child and made man. He's both, of course.

So I knew that I was being thrust into a very exciting and enviable position, with this being my first assignment in my new job as I transitioned into being a player on the business side of basketball.

Lynn's flight landed at 10:00 a.m., so to make sure I wasn't late, I left Chicago at 2:00 a.m. for the approximate six-hour drive. This was in early November, so it was crisp out, the kind of chill that will put a giddyap in your step. As I settled in for the ride, I felt ready to embark on my first assignment with this new job.

I was definitely anxious to learn the business and knew that having a seat at the table during Nike's recruitment of LeBron was a great place for me to begin.

As I cruised through Gary, South Bend and Toledo, I blasted music, crooning at the top of my lungs to Carl Thomas, Jodeci, Patti LaBelle and Big Luther. I bumped some Nas, Outkast, Ludacris, EPMD, and Eric B. and Rakim.

I've always enjoyed being behind the wheel for long drives. They're therapeutic for me, where I do some of my best thinking. The ride was smooth and easy, and after scooping up Lynn, we shot over to the Marriott downtown. Lynn had his own suite, I had a room and then there was also the aforementioned Nike Room, which had boxes upon boxes of product stacked from the floor to the ceiling, all of which was free and accessible to LeBron and his people.

The sight of the sheer volume of stuff that they fit into that room was mind-blowing. Every type of athletic shoe, every make and model that you can imagine, Jordans, winter boots, shorts, T-shirts, sweatpants, hoodies, socks, headbands, wristbands, backpacks, winter coats, hats, I mean anything you can name, it was there. I'm talking close to $100,000 worth of the freshest Nike gear and apparel, enough stuff to make your jaw drop. You literally had to walk sideways through the narrow pathways to avoid knocking over the stacks of boxes. They had more inventory in that room than your average Foot Locker.

We had some time to get situated before meeting for lunch and then heading over to St. Vincent–St. Mary, the small private Catholic school on a hill at the edge of Akron that LeBron had now placed on the national map.

Lynn's itinerary was more detailed than mine. I was there simply to observe, ask questions and add my thoughts when queried. Lynn had some meetings and conversations that I was not privy to. He'd already been in close contact with LeBron, his mom, Gloria, and others in the James camp, so I was just there to see how the process worked.

There was no true road map for the race to sign LeBron. Sure, the footwear design and marketing folks were working on their mock-ups and storyboards, but from our perspective, it was about continuing to build that trust and deepening the connection and the relationship, by any means necessary.

We walked into the gym and LeBron and his teammates

were just starting to warm up. For the next two hours, I did everything in my power to tamp down my feverish exhilaration. I could not fully believe what I was seeing.

I'd played against the likes of Jerry Stackhouse, Tim Duncan and some other phenomenal talents in college. I'd been in an NBA training camp and played pro ball overseas. But never in my life had I witnessed this absurd level of talent in someone so young.

His skills, goodness gracious, his skills were off the charts. The ball handling, the passing, the footwork, the defensive intensity, the shot blocking, the elevation, the speed, the hands, the initial burst, the unbridled joy—coupled with a rare competitive fire and leadership ability—were unbelievable. When he was dribbling at full speed and soared to attack the rim in full flight, right before crashing the ball through the net, it was like watching a bird of prey soar.

But the bow that wrapped all of that up was his intelligence, his basketball IQ. The kid was a damn savant. I saw a guy whose dedication to the game and to being great were unquestionably embedded into his DNA. Even though his diminutive teammate Dru Joyce was the official point guard, LeBron was the main ball handler and facilitator. But he also played every other position on the floor and whether he was guarding a center, operating in the low post as a power forward, defending an agile wing on the perimeter or running a vicious fast break, he was going to be effective and leave his mark on the game.

I had to bite my bottom lip to keep from running around that shiny hardwood floor in delirium, as if propelled by the Holy Ghost at a Baptist revival.

I mean, I saw the damn light. And it wasn't no damn light bulb. It was the entire damn sunrise.

When practice was over, Lynn and I hopped into my car for the short ride over to LeBron and Gloria's apartment.

"So what do you think?" he asked. "Who would you compare him to?"

I'd heard the previous comparisons to Michael Jordan and Magic Johnson. Truth be told, he had elements of both. He had Magic's size, his vision, his leadership skills, his ability to see the floor and dominate without being a chuckwagon, i.e., a guy who just wanted to shoot and score and pile up numbers. He'd rather score eighteen points and play a flawless all-around game and win than scorch for fifty and lose. For him, winning was the bottom line. He also had MJ's fire, competitiveness and ruthless need to beat you into submission.

I summed up my observations by telling Lynn, "I saw a guy who, if he continues to dedicate himself and follows his current trajectory, he's going to be a force to be reckoned with from the very minute that he steps onto an NBA court. And from there, the sky is truly the limit."

We pulled into the parking lot of the Spring Hill Apartments, a public housing development that a *New York Times* writer once described as a "severe, Soviet-looking housing block." The place was rough and rugged, the type of environment where the weak get eaten alive. Lynn and I walked into the cramped two-bedroom apartment on the sixth floor and found a bunch of folks talking and laughing. LeBron and Gloria treated us warmly and then she lovingly turned to the others.

"Ya'll need to leave," she said, clearing out the room for us.

Gloria is a firecracker. She's tough and doesn't get enough credit for helping her son become what he eventually became. She don't take no shit from nobody and ain't gonna hold her tongue. She's gonna give it to you straight, with no chaser. I experienced her in full force that day.

In that same *New York Times* story, James told writer Charles McGrath about his home.

The apartment was about three hundred square feet, but the great thing was that from up there, you could see part of the city. This was where the stability started. I knew my mom was going to be there every single day. I had my own key that I wore around my neck. Having your own key to your own crib, that's the greatest thing in the world. And you learn responsibility, because you don't dare lose that key.

Bron's journey was like many other kids who emerge from America's forgotten pockets of urban despair. I saw his experiences replicated time and time again in my grassroots work for both adidas and Nike. And many of those stories did not have fairy-tale endings.

Back when he was in elementary school, nothing about LeBron Raymone James's destiny seemed predetermined. He missed one hundred days of school in the fourth grade. He and his mom, who gave birth to him when she was just sixteen years old, were essentially homeless, bouncing from friends' and relatives' couches with dizzying frequency.

Through sheer serendipity, a youth league football coach spotted him playing tag in the courtyard of a housing project. Soon, LeBron, who weighed less than 115 pounds, was suiting up for the East Dragons.

In his very first scrimmage, wearing a helmet and pads for the first time and playing running back, he took a handoff in the backfield and left every defender in his dust en route to an eighty-yard touchdown. Gloria screamed maniacally as she sprinted alongside him on the sideline. His coaches would store his equipment in the trunks of their cars and come to pick him up for practice, only to learn on some days that he and Gloria had moved again. "I was tired of picking him up at different addresses," his first coach Bruce Kelker once said, "or showing up at one junked-up place and finding out they had already moved to another."

Kelker decided to invite the young man and his mom to live with him and his family until she could get on better footing. LeBron eventually moved in with one of his teammates, whose loving parents provided him with the stability he needed to excel.

For the first time in his life, he was waking up at 6:30 a.m. every day, excited about school and completing his homework assignments on time. He had structure, chores and responsibilities and began to cultivate his own effective work habits. Gloria eventually secured her own apartment in Spring Hill when LeBron was in the sixth grade, just as Akron's youth sports community was beginning to recognize his prodigious talent.

Gloria and Bron had come up through some rough struggles and to meet him at the stage that I did when he was seventeen, seeing how smart and aware and playfully mischievous he was, how he genuinely seemed to care about other people, was heartwarming. They'd made it through the storms that swallow up so many talented kids, with generations of poverty, institutional racism, alcoholism, unemployment, substandard housing, drug abuse, police brutality and incarceration wreaking havoc on the desires of millions of families to achieve a simple slice of the American Dream. They were on the cusp of doing some monumental things, from both an athletic and a business perspective. The future was pregnant with possibility for them.

LeBron was not some naive kid content to play video games. He was at the table, genuinely interested and invested in the process, not just as a player. He understood, on a much deeper level than most kids his age, the commerce side of the equation.

We showed LeBron some of the concepts we'd been working on for him. We had some of the product design guys with us who shared prototypes that were LeBron-specific, factoring in stuff like his favorite car, his favorite animal and other bits and pieces of the people, places and things that had meaning to him, walking him through the various storyboards and planting the seeds for the big presentation that would come later at the Nike headquarters in Beaverton, Oregon. But the true goal of the visit was to simply deepen the connection and build on the relationship the company had already established with him.

Over the next few months, I made three or four of those trips to Akron with Lynn in the pursuit of LeBron. On one of those visits, I got a frantic early-evening call from Lynn.

"Meet me down in the lobby in fifteen minutes," he said. "We're going to dinner."

We walked into some high-end restaurant, the type of fancy spot that doesn't have the prices on the menu. LeBron, Gloria and some of their folks were seated at a round table. They were with Sonny Vaccaro and a bunch of adidas reps.

"Go grab a chair and pull up to the table," Lynn instructed as he sauntered toward them like George Jefferson, a little bop creeping more heavily into his step.

What the fuck? I thought to myself. *Are we just crashing a dinner that Sonny Vaccaro and the adidas guys are having for LeBron?*

The adidas guys were not pleased, but they chuckled at Lynn's brazenness. Gloria, however, loved it. She appreciated that type of confrontational approach. It was my first lesson that in the sneaker business, all is fair in love and war.

Damn, is this how we get down? I thought, as I uncomfortably pulled up a chair. "Hey, Merl, we got us a free dinner tonight, courtesy of adidas, so order everything you want!" Lynn said, and everybody laughed.

Sonny Vaccaro, whom LeBron refers to as "Uncle Sonny," is an exalted figure in the business, one of the most prominent and influential people in the entire history of the athletic shoe industry.

Along with Michael Jordan he was more or less responsible for Nike's ascension into a billion-dollar behemoth. He walked into Nike's headquarters in the mid-'70s, trying to pitch a sneaker-sandal design that was summarily laughed at and dismissed. But thanks to his founding of the Dapper Dan Roundball Classic in Pittsburgh and its success as the precursor to the McDonald's and Jordan Brand All-American games, Nike chairman Phil Knight, who was impressed with his hoops Rolodex and liked his bravado, his confidence and spunk, brought him on as a consultant.

Sonny's contacts with college coaches proved to be the match that ignited the fire. In 1977, when he started working with Nike, they were a small, Oregon-based company selling running shoes. Converse was the basketball bully at the time, but that changed when Sonny brought his Italian swagger, western Pennsylvania coal miner hunger and gambler's intuition into the game.

The friendships he'd cultivated over the years with the elite players, parents and college coaches at his Roundball Classic paid major dividends when, writing checks out of his bank accounts that were later reimbursed by Nike, he signed some of the top names in the game: Georgetown's John Thompson, Villanova's Rollie Massimino, Syracuse's Jim Boeheim, UNLV's Jerry Tarkanian and Iona's Jim Valvano, who would later gain fame and accolades in leading NC State to the '83 title.

Vaccaro's sales pitch was simple. Back then, coaches and schools had to purchase their own gear. He promised as much gear and sneakers as these teams needed at no cost.

It's taken for granted today, but back then that move was revolutionary. It flipped the entire script as it related to the relationship between shoe companies, coaches, athletic departments and recruits.

And with his Dapper Dan Roundball Classic being seen as a golden ticket at the time, Sonny used his influence with the best high school players to steer them toward Nike schools. By the early '80s, with Jordan on their roster, Nike had surpassed Converse as the marquee brand in basketball.

As the years wore on, the value of those contracts that Vaccaro first negotiated with the college coaches increased substantially. And those deals between Nike and the coaches, as well as the other sneaker companies, now include the entire universities. In December of 2020, after Under Armour backed out of its agreement with UCLA, the school inked a new $46.45 million deal with Nike to outfit their entire athletic department. Under the deal, the *Los Angeles Times* reported, the school received an estimated $7.7 million per year in cash and gear.

Vaccaro once told the *Pittsburgh Post-Gazette*,

It's an all-school deal at these kind of schools. Pitt has an all-school deal with Nike. They are their business partners. So why wouldn't Nike want Pitt to win or why wouldn't Nike want their schools to win? That's what it is. They did a business deal worth millions of dollars. They are your business partners. Nike and the shoe companies want to sell shoes. The athletic departments want to win bowl games and go to the NCAA tournament. To do that, there's one commodity that's relevant to both these elements: the athlete.

Lynn and Sonny had a relationship going back to Sonny's Nike days, before a bitter falling-out that led to his landing over at adidas. Since then he'd been chipping away at the Swoosh's dominance in the market, diving into high school markets and famously securing deals with prep-to-pro phenoms like Tracy McGrady and Kobe Bryant. And now, with Sonny and adidas sponsoring LeBron's high school squad, they were seen as the front-runners to sign him.

At the time, LeBron had connections with all the top three brands. During his 2003 McDonald's All-American game he wore a custom-made pair of red-and-white L23Js, Allen Iverson's signature Reeboks. Adidas had been down with him since his earliest high school days and even asked to help to design his team's uniforms. But he absolutely idolized Michael Jordan and saw how fruitful that partnership with Nike had been.

On his recruiting visit to Reebok's Canton, Massachusetts, headquarters, after presentations with execs and designers that featured fifty possible logos and designs for dozens of different shoes, the company's chairman and CEO Paul Fireman walked LeBron, his best friend, Maverick Carter, Gloria and his then-agent, Aaron Goodwin, into a private space and proceeded to produce a cashier's check for $10 million. Fireman said they could leave with it under two conditions: he'd sign with Reebok for $75 million and promise to call off his visits with Nike and adidas.

"LeBron understood that he had to give that check back to Paul Fireman," Goodwin told *The Undefeated*'s Aaron Dodson in 2018. "Gloria did not. Gloria wanted to keep that check and walk out. But even with that being offered, we had to see what Adidas had to say, and then finally what Nike had to say."

LeBron's next visit was out to a rented mansion in Malibu, California, where he met with "Uncle Sonny" and adidas amid a fresh ocean breeze and sounds of crashing waves. Vaccaro had promised Gloria that her son would sign an initial sneaker deal worth $100 million, a groundbreaking sum for a teenager who had yet to play his first professional game. Instead of promising that he'd be the next Michael Jordan, the adidas approach was that he would transcend sports like Muhammad Ali due to his already burgeoning concerns about social justice issues.

But despite receiving approval for a $100-million offer, the adidas CEO at the time, Herbert Hainer, at the last minute, and we're talking about hours before the presentation, got cold feet and lowered the offer to $70 million.

Vaccaro, on *The Ringer*'s NBA show podcast in 2016, said, after presenting the lower offer,

We went to a little corner of this mansion. Gloria, me, LeBron…and I apologized. I'll never forget what they did. They put their arms around me and they said, "Sonny, we understand. We know what you did. We're going to be fine."

Sonny was disgusted with what his bosses had done, saying it was "the biggest mistake ever made in corporate America."

He was so infuriated that hours later, he quit and was soon hired by Reebok.

After that, Nike was in the driver's seat. James and his camp walked into a massive wing in the Mia Hamm building on the picturesque Beaverton campus. As they walked down a long corridor with motion-activated videos playing, with each side boasting cases of iconic sneakers like the Jordans, Barkleys, Pippens and Pennys. Everywhere you went in the complex, there was an assortment of custom swag produced with LeBron as the focus. There were also boxes of Fruity Pebbles on hand, as it was learned that it was LeBron's favorite cereal and snack.

The Undefeated's Aaron Dodson wrote, "Walk right…and you entered essentially a king's treasure room. Its marvels included a mini model of James' 2003 pewter-colored H2 Hummer, and the pelt of a lion (think King Joffy Joffer's shawl in *Coming to America*). There were also sketches of sneakers crafted by the brand's top designers: Tinker Hatfield, Aaron Cooper and Eric Avar. It was here that Nike brass—most notably his future brand manager, Lynn Merritt—and James' team discussed product, and the potential of a partnership."

The Nike brass told Lynn, in no uncertain terms, that he was authorized to only go as high as $7 million a year for, at most, five years. But Reebok had upped their initial offer to well over $100 million. He knew Nike's offer wasn't going to cut it. Without consulting with his bosses, he drew up his own offer sheet. He had an intermediary present it to LeBron and Gloria, asking, "If we did seven years at $94 million, would that get it done?" And Team James said yes.

When the higher-ups learned what Lynn had done, they were furious. He was great at his job, but notoriously unpredictable. He was blunt and confrontational, with a street sensibility, and had no qualms about putting people in uncompromising situations. A few of his bosses were not very fond of him, despite his proven track record of working with the likes of Moses Malone, Ken Griffey Jr., Scottie Pippen and Charles Barkley.

So after the news of what he'd done hit headquarters, Lynn was immediately placed on review as discussions were being held about whether he'd be fired. He was barred from the corporate campus and all of his key cards had been deactivated. While he was hanging in limbo, he came to me and said, "Hey, Merl, I'm going to Reebok. Are you coming with me?"

This was the guy who'd played college football with my cousin; he had a relationship with my daddy going back to when I was eight years old. He'd hired me. He was my mentor. So without hesitation I told him, "Wherever you go, I'm going with you."

Eventually, word came back from the highest levels at Nike. Lynn came as close as he could come to getting fired, but some folks appreciated his brazenness and understood that missing out on LeBron was not an option. So he was retained, with one simple caveat: "This better work out."

And you gotta give the man credit because it all worked out beautifully for Nike and LeBron.

It's amazing how astutely LeBron and his inner circle of trusted friends planned their future on the business side of the ledger. Part of the Nike deal included an internship for his peer mentor Maverick Carter, with whom I sat in at many corporate orientation functions. Now Mav is LeBron's business partner in a number of wildly successful ventures. LeBron's other main man, Rich Paul, was already a forward-thinking businessman at the time. At nineteen he had already purchased his first home. He'd first met LeBron when he was running back and forth from Atlanta selling throwback jerseys out of his trunk in Cleveland, clearing close to $10,000 a week. Rich was a trusted member of LeBron's inner circle and when the time came for Lebron's NBA rookie contract to be extended, Rich took a job at Creative Artists Agency, CAA, working under Leon Rose, who is now the president of the New York Knicks. After learning the ropes, Paul started his own agency.

These guys did their due diligence, had a plan, put the work in and built something. Now Rich is the hottest NBA agent around. His Klutch Sports Group represents not only LeBron, but Draymond Green, Anthony Davis, Lonzo Ball, Ben Simmons and the breakout star of the 2021 playoffs, Trae Young, among others.

After the draft, our basketball group was buzzing with excitement. We'd gotten LeBron, Carmelo Anthony signed on with the Jordan Brand, and Dwyane Wade and Chris Bosh went with Converse, which Nike owned. Fred Whitfield, the man who was once in my Clemson dorm room year trying to lure my freshman roommate, asked me to spend some time with the Jordan Brand and be a part of Carmelo Anthony's internal management team. For his first two years in the league, I was the go-between, working with Melo, his adviser, Robert "Bay" Frazier, and his agent, Bill Duffy.

It was an exciting time.

But those halcyon days wouldn't last.

There was turbulence on the horizon in ways that I couldn't see coming. But in the mean and in-between time, I'd found my footing in this business and was poised to make my own mark on the industry.

8

The entire industry of elite high school, AAU and big-time college basketball, and football as well, is predicated on exploiting and profiting off of the talented unpaid labor force, the majority of whom are young Black men.

I'd experienced it as a player, but now that I was on the business side, I saw the innumerable ways in which people and entities—whether it be coaches, administrators, agents, people who ran their own AAU programs and hosted their own regional showcase events, financial planners, marketing reps, handlers, even the campus bookstore that was selling our jerseys or the local college bars that were packed to the seams whenever games were on TV—were making money, hand over fist. And lost in that equation were the players and their families.

My whole thing, once I got in a position to help kids like a Zion or a Pat Beverley during their formative stages, was that if they were certainly going to be exploited, then they needed to get some benefits during that process. If their parents were amenable, I felt it was my duty to help them understand the larger ramifications of what was going on, and how the industry really operated.

And what I saw alarmed me. Because of the nature of AAU ball, the top one hundred kids were fawned over from the moment they showed a hint of promise. The AAU coach who successfully lands a top kid has to keep recruiting him every year, every month, every week, every day because that kid can jump to another program whenever he wants.

So these "elite" kids are being showered with servile flattery and exaggerated attention on a consistent basis, sometimes before they've even reached puberty. That can engender a sense of entitlement that might ultimately come back and bite them in the ass when reality sets in a few years later.

If the next program that comes courting has something bigger or shinier, i.e., a bigger budget and product allocation, a more prestigious national and sometimes international schedule, lodging in four-star hotels on the road, access to a limitless supply of Air Jordans, whatever it may be, that's where the kid, his handler and his parents are going.

This kind of attention can have a massive negative psychological impact if a kid doesn't have the proper guidance. By the time he's sixteen, if he's only grown a few inches and his game hasn't improved or expanded, he's now a marginal prospect at best. Remember all that adulation from a few short years ago? It has disappeared faster than a hiccup. He gets dropped like a bad habit. Remember those dope out-fits and sweat suits that momma was getting, them new Air Maxes and Jordans and Weezys, them Steph Currys and KDs and Kyries? That has all ceased because everyone has already moved on to the next kid.

Young players need to insulate themselves from the deceitful glitz and glamour. They need to understand that if they're lucky enough to get a scholarship, they need to go to school and work toward a meaningful degree and emerge from school debt-free with a decent job in hand. People think the only people that win in these scenarios are the lucky ones that make it to the pros. We need to redefine what winning in this game really means.

So many parents are in such dire straits that they can't say no to the short money. But they're inadvertently setting their kids up for failure. Because that eight grand a month that a coaching staff has arranged for you, that five-bedroom house that a school's wealthy alum has provided for you, all of that shit is going to come to a screeching halt. Parents quit their jobs, live relatively rent free and think they've hit the jackpot.

But what happens when the kid tears his ACL? When the coach that brought him in gets fired? What happens when he underwhelms on the court? What happens if he does have a decent showing, puts his name in the draft when he's not yet ready and loses his remaining eligibility? He's not educated, has been listening to all this hype for years and now he's gotta go the long route, all while everyone still has their hands out expecting him to be the breadwinner.

It's a never-ending cycle. And very few will ever escape it long enough to cash an NBA paycheck.

There are only 350 or so NBA positions and only sixty young men get drafted every year, and the really good foreign players are gonna grab at least fifteen, if not more of those slots. Of those forty to forty-five American players, a bunch of them weren't highly ranked coming out of high school; they developed late. Maybe ten to twelve high school phenoms end up being drafted.

Even if you're lucky enough to be a lottery pick, that doesn't mean that you're going to be around for the type of career that's gonna effectuate generational wealth. Are you familiar with names like Doron Lamb? Joe Alexander? Rashad Vaughn? Justin Anderson? Chris McCullough? Malachi Richardson? Brice Johnson? Zhaire Smith? Jacob Evans? Adreian Payne? Tyler Ennis? P. J. Hairston? The list goes on and on of great high school players and really good college players that got taken in the first round, made some guaranteed money for a few years and then flamed out for one reason or another.

So for me, it was critical to have these conversations with the kids and parents that came into my orbit. Sadly, only a few were willing to listen and learn. Many were not. Many believed the hype.

Folks are so accustomed to how this system of exploitation works that it's become normalized to the point that they've accepted and become okay with it, in the same way that slavery and indentured servitude and tenant farming were once normalized and accepted.

What was it that John C. Calhoun said? Remember him, the guy whose slaves built the fortune and cultivated the land that Clemson University now sits on? Oh yeah, he said that peculiar institution that filled his family's coffers produced a "positive good." Your head coach makes $8 million a year, has one of his vacation homes in Hilton Head, has a separate mansion on a private island in Miami, but you're trying to figure out how to feed yourself, your girl and your infant child on the weekend? Where's the "positive good" in that? Something about that equation is supremely fucked up.

You have the billion-dollar TV deals, merchandising and marketing deals that are through the roof and yet the NCAA and individual conferences are somehow able to maintain a nonprofit status as a business entity. This whole amateurism conversation is bullshit. Amateur sports is washing cars, selling hot dogs and doing raffles to make enough money to fill the team van with gas. That's amateur sports.

Within the parameters of my job, I found what latent opportunities I could to help a few kids. I took that responsibility seriously. If I had a chance to mentor a young athlete, thinking about all of the great people I came across on my own journey, I was going to do my very best to help them.

I developed a tight bond with one young fella in particular named Murphy Holloway, aka Big Murph. I met him when he was about thirteen years old and in the eighth grade. Erik Glenn, one of my very best friends since childhood, was coaching Murph with the Carolina Ravens, a Nike-sponsored AAU program based in Columbia at the time. When I'd come home from Chicago, I'd spend some time with Erik around the program and would pop in when I could to watch the kids play.

Big Murph was the talk of the tight-knit local hoops community, a potential star. The more time I spent around him, the more I liked him. He was a great dude, low-key, cool, superrespectful, could light up a room when he smiled wide and was just a really nice person.

We developed a bond over the years and I stayed tight with him as he began blossoming into one of the top players in the country. His mom was a single parent, doing the very best that she could, and Murph's home life was stable. You can't help but pull for kids like that, especially the local ones that you get to know, because a lot of really talented guys, for many reasons, never make it out of the state of South Carolina.

By his junior year, Big Murph was a dynamic, powerful six-foot-seven, 225-pound forward who absolutely killed it at Dutch Fork High School, averaging twenty-five points and thirteen boards. As a senior, he put up twenty-eight points, fifteen rebounds and swatted four shots per game. He was named South Carolina's Mr. Basketball and the state Gatorade Player of the Year. I couldn't have been more proud of the kid.

The only problem was that Big Murph was not a good student at the time. He wasn't dumb. Far from it—the kid was actually very bright. But he had yet to form good study habits, folks hadn't prepared him for the academic requirements and there was a chance that he would not qualify to play D-I ball as a freshman. The main schools that coveted him the most were Ole Miss, Auburn, Clemson, South Carolina and Tennessee. But most of them backed away when it looked like he might have to spend two years at a junior college.

Ole Miss did not back away; they stuck with him. So when he qualified on his final SAT attempt, he chose to go to Oxford, Mississippi, to play for head coach Andy Kennedy. Murph had a really solid freshman year at Ole Miss, starting seventeen of their thirty-one games and averaging eight points and seven rebounds while only playing about twenty minutes, half the game.

Murph and I stayed in touch, spoke regularly and got together when we could. Our conversations were rarely basketball related. He had a daughter on the way during his freshman year in college, so we talked a lot about fatherhood, what it means to be a man and eventually a husband, and how to carve out a life once the athletic thing had run its course. Over the years he'd become like family to me.

Early during his sophomore year, I got a call from one of his assistant coaches. He knew one of my colleagues at Nike and was told that Murph and I were really close.

"Hey, man," the coach greeted me. "I heard that you and Murph are tight and I just needed to talk to you for a bit. The kid is being superdisrespectful. He's cursing the coaches out and it's getting a little out of hand."

As soon as we hung up, I got Murph on the phone.

"Hey, Murph," I said. "I just spoke to one of your coaches who tells me you're being really disrespectful. I don't know what's going on, but I do know that's not in your character."

Murph tried to tell me his side of the story, but I cut him off.

"We can work through that later, but the first thing you gonna do is go into the coaches' offices and apologize. They're trying to help you and they deserve a certain level of respect."

The next day, the assistant coach called back. "Damn, I was told that you were tight with the kid, but I didn't know it was to this extent. He came in, humbled himself, apologized, promised that it wouldn't happen again and we're good."

So I let it alone and at that time, did not get into why Murph had acted out. I didn't think it was anything major that I needed to get in the middle of. It happened, he apologized and it was over. Or so I thought.

After that Murph began to have a great sophomore season. He started twenty-nine games, had upped his field goal percentage and was averaging damn near a double-double. Erik and I had been talking about getting down to Oxford to go see him. In early January of 2010, we rented a car and drove down there to watch Murph play against Central Florida.

And that way, I could kill two birds with one stone because he had a teammate named Terrico White whose name was starting to percolate in NBA circles as a potential first-round pick. I wanted to evaluate him as a potential prospect for Nike.

So Erik and I booked a hotel for three days, and we were hyped to go show our young boy some of that home love. Murph too was excited and was looking forward to spending some time with us. I told him to put us on his ticket list and that we'd pick them up from will-call.

The day of the game, Murph called, sounding confused, and said, "They won't let me leave you tickets."

"What do you mean?"

"They said they don't know why you're coming down here?"

"Man, fuck them. They don't need to know why I'm coming down there and if that's the case, we'll just get our own damn tickets."

I don't know if the assistant coach who called me saw my name, or somebody else on the staff saw it and knew that I worked on the NBA side at Nike, but whatever it was, Murph's request for tickets was denied.

A few hours later, he called back and said, "They changed their mind. They're gonna let me leave you guys the tickets."

"Cool, we'll see you soon."

Murph didn't take many shots, but he played well, with three steals, eleven points and an impressive ten rebounds. They got the win, and we met him after the game and gave him some strong brotherly hugs.

Quickly his excitement turned to concern. "Coach wants to see you," he said.

Erik and I followed Murph to Andy Kennedy's office. He stood about six-foot-seven, a former high school All-

American and college basketball player, and he still possessed some of that residual baller swag.

The first thing he said to me was, "I don't really know you. Why are you here? Because I'm concerned that you came out here to talk to Murphy about turning pro."

"With all due respect, bruh, I don't really know you either. But since you wanna go there, we came down here to see our kid, someone we've known since he was in the eighth grade, someone who is like family to us, to show him some love and to be supportive."

Then I turn to Murph and say, "Man, have I ever had a conversation with you about the NBA and leaving school to turn pro?"

"Never."

"You goddamn right, never." Irritated, I turn back to Andy, whose tough-guy facade was beginning to recede. "I'm also here on official Nike business to scout Terrico."

At the mention of Terrico's name, Andy immediately started backpedaling, but I wasn't interested in engaging further. "Ya'll call me if Murph starts acting up again," I said, and left it at that.

Not too long after, Murph called me at my office in Chicago, clearly distressed. "Fuck these dudes, Merl," he said. "I gotta get up outta here. I'm transferring after this season."

I could hear the anger in his voice. Murph is not an angry-type dude—he's supremely even-keeled. And he's loyal. So I knew something had to be going on.

He told me that the assistant coach who had called me to discuss Murph's attitude, well, that dude was cheating on his wife with an Ole Miss student. The coach suspected that Murph had been sleeping with this young woman too, so he started giving him hell. Sometimes Andy Kennedy would summon Murph off the bench, and the assistant coach would intercede, "Nah, don't put him in, put such-and-such in." One game, Murph would play thirty minutes, and the next he'd play less than ten. The assistant was antagonizing him, confronting him about the girl, threatening Murph; the whole scenario was crazy.

So as we're talking this through, I asked Murph, "If you're 100 percent certain you wanna transfer, I'm behind you. Do you know where you wanna go?"

"I wanna be close to home," he says.

"Okay, we'll figure it out."

I did not tell him to go to Clemson. I did not tell him to go to South Carolina. We had yet to talk about the best options for him.

After Murph told Andy Kennedy about his intention to transfer, I received a call from my boss, Lynn, informing me that the compliance department in Nike's college basketball office just got a call from the NCAA accusing me of tampering. The NCAA was launching an investigation into whether I was steering Murph toward Clemson.

Murph had to sit down with NCAA investigators, and he grew worried that the Ole Miss coaches might be vengeful and mess with his eligibility.

"Murph, you have absolutely nothing to worry about," I told him. "Give them the God's honest truth. You know and I know that I wasn't trying to steer you to Clemson. I don't recruit for them nor any other school. I never told you where to go when you were coming out of high school because that was your decision. And the same is true right now. Sit down with them, answer all of their questions truthfully and I promise, you'll be good."

The NCAA ultimately concluded that there was nothing

to the accusation, and Ole Miss allowed Murph to transfer anywhere he wanted. Except Clemson. That still makes me giggle till this day.

Murph went to South Carolina and had to sit out a year. The whole time, Andy Kennedy was calling him, asking him to come back.

Murph finally admitted the truth. "I never really wanted to leave," he said. "But I was tired of the assistant coach's bullshit. So long as he's there, I ain't coming back."

Andy Kennedy fired the assistant coach, the married assistant coach who was sleeping with the student and who had been jerking Murph around his entire sophomore season. And Murph transferred back to Ole Miss, finished his last two years there and became one of the program's most beloved players.

It's funny looking back to see how the media framed Murph's story of transferring out of Ole Miss and then returning. According to the neatly packaged narrative, he wanted to be home to help his mom and the mother of his daughter. They made it sound like the script of a Disney special.

Murph is doing great today. He's a wonderful family man, made some good money playing pro ball overseas in Italy, France, Turkey, Israel, the Philippines, Korea, Bahrain and Germany, among others. The kid from Irmo, South Carolina, has traveled the globe, earning millions of dollars playing a game that he loves. Today, he's looking at the final stretch of his pro career with an entrepreneurial vision, having opened up a really chic physical fitness and personal training brick-and-mortar spot in downtown Columbia.

Another one of those kids that we tried to mentor was a young man named Marcus Goode.

Marcus was from the towns of Pomaria and Little Mountain, South Carolina. These are poverty-stricken, extremely rural areas. Pomaria has a population of less than two hundred people. Little Mountain may have three hundred residents, if that. These places are literally in the middle of nowhere.

My buddy Erik, as I'd mentioned earlier, was coaching the Carolina Ravens and that's how we got to know Big Murph back when he was in the eighth grade.

Marcus was a big kid playing for Erik and the Ravens who wasn't on anybody's radar. But the summer before his senior year in high school, he blew up overnight. In some meaningless early tournament game, he found himself matched up against the top-ranked power forward in the country at the time, Greg Monroe, a superskilled six-foot-ten lefty from Louisiana who later played at Georgetown. Monroe had a ten-year run in the NBA and he's still playing overseas, most recently in Moscow.

Something clicked for Marcus and he came alive. He was six-foot-ten, 315 pounds, and he was cooking Greg Monroe's ass. The boy had great soft hands, a delicate touch in the paint, he was splashing threes, tossing in skyhooks from ten feet out. He was like a dancing bear out there, light on his feet.

By halftime, Marcus had a double-double and the energy in the gym was palpable. Folks were on their cell phones talking about what they were witnessing. Everybody and their momma came up in there to see the top big man in the country, and now they were asking each other, "Who is this big dude that is giving Greg Monroe the business? This kid is legit. Who is he?"

Immediately after that game, coaches from top-twenty programs were calling the folks running the Ravens program, asking about him.

Erik pulled me aside and said, "Hey, Merl, we gotta help

this kid out. His home situation is really messed up and he ain't ready for all this attention. He has no idea how this process works. He's gonna need our support."

Kansas called. Georgetown called. Clemson, South Carolina and Penn State were all in love with him. And Erik was the closest thing he had to a father figure. Marcus's volatile family situation often affected his ability to show up for practices and games. Some weeks, he was just missing in action. We quickly ascertained that the kid was basically homeless. He'd be at his momma's for a few days and she'd grow tired of him eating all the food and then kick him out. He bounced around from different relatives' and friends' places, grabbing a couch whenever he could, but they'd soon tire of him and they'd tell him to get to stepping. He did not have a stable home environment.

So picking him up and dropping him off was always an adventure. Marcus would direct us by saying stuff like, "Turn off at the big tree and when we get ten rocks past that big black rock, near the bottom of the hill, you can drop me off." And then his big ass would hop out and disappear into the dense darkness of the woods like Bigfoot. To this day I've never met his momma, cousins, aunties, uncles, never heard a single mention of his father.

So prior to his senior year in high school, I had him come stay with me in Chicago for a few weeks. I took him over to Tim Grover's gym because I wanted to show him what putting in work to improve and become the best possible player looked like. My town house was literally a block away from Grover's gym. For those that don't know, Grover was Michael Jordan, Dwyane Wade and Kobe Bryant's personal trainer and his facility is both a shrine to and a lab that produces greatness. I had a good relationship with Tim and could use his facility whenever I wanted.

I wanted Marcus to see what being dedicated to the game looked like, how guys did their strength-and-conditioning workouts, how they ate, how they worked on their individual skills.

The kid didn't know how talented he was, how good he could eventually become, but talent alone gets you nowhere. I wanted him to see the effort that he was gonna have to put forth to succeed on the college level.

Dwyane Wade was there in Grover's gym, working out. So was Kobe and my client with the Milwaukee Bucks, Michael Redd. Marcus got to see, up close and personal, the amount of work that these guys put in to take care of their bodies and improve their games. I was trying to give him some inspiration. Outside the gym I was also trying to teach him how to eat better, introducing more vegetables and fish into his diet.

I'd given him specific instructions to stay away from the McDonald's down the street. One day I came home from the office to find Filet-O-Fish wrappers all over the floor. Marcus was stuffing another one in his mouth.

"Marcus! What the hell did I tell you about not eating McDonald's?"

"You said I could eat fish," he said incredulously, the corners of his mouth caked in tartar sauce.

At Grover's gym, I'd have him working out with personal trainers. He'd last all of eight minutes and collapse on the floor.

But now that Marcus had blown up, some guy said he was gonna pay his tuition at a prep school for his senior year in North Carolina. The catch was, the guy wanted his son to come along as a package deal. I guess he was hoping with all of the college coaches coming to see Marcus, his son would get a look too.

Well, the guy's son couldn't play worth a damn, and when he saw that the kid was gonna ride the bench all season, he withdrew him and stopped paying Marcus's tuition.

Erik and I needed to get Marcus into a new school, so our first task was to get ahold of his academic transcripts. Erik placed the request with Mid-Carolina High School and when he examined what was in the envelope, he called me. "Hey, Merl, um, they only gave me two years' worth of transcripts."

"Okay, run on up back there. They probably forgot to give you the other one."

He went back, asked for the missing year's grades and was told, "Ain't nothing missing. That's all we got."

We got Marcus on the phone. "Hey, Marcus, we're missing a whole transcript for an entire year."

"I know."

"What happened?"

"I ain't go."

"What do you mean you ain't go?"

"I ain't feel like it, so I ain't go."

"Gaaaaaat Dayumn, Marcus! You didn't feel like going to school, so you just didn't go? For an entire fucking year!?"

The school didn't call child services, nobody checked on the boy or asked about him. And even though he missed the whole year, they classified him as a junior when he showed up a year later. We thought he was heading into his senior year, and now we knew that was obviously not the case. And how did that prep school have him classified as a senior when he'd clearly only gone to Mid-Carolina for two years? The whole scenario stank. They were just pushing the kid along, for the sole purpose of winning basketball games.

So Kansas and Georgetown were interested and calling, but if they got a look at those transcripts, they couldn't have anything to do with the kid. Because when he was in school, he didn't do much academically and there was no way he was gonna pass anybody's SATs. So we had to avoid that for now and keep things on the hush.

An assistant coach at a midmajor D-I program and who I had a good relationship with reached out to us. They really wanted Marcus and due to the nature of the relationship I had with the guy, I was brutally honest with him and laid out the boy's situation. Told him everything, that we thought he was a senior but he'd only had two years of high school, that his grades were not up to par, that we had to get him from the prep school where he was enrolled because he was basically left stranded up there, and everything else in between, including him disappearing into the pitch-black woods like Sasquatch.

The assistant coach said, "We really like the big fella. Lemme make a few calls and try to put some things in motion."

He called back within a day or two and said, "I got a school for him up near Raleigh, North Carolina, and they've got a spot for him right now."

"Is he gonna have to stay up there for two years?"

"Naw, they're gonna make it happen. They're gonna make sure he's good."

Erik and I were relieved because this kid couldn't keep lurking around these small rural towns and backwoods. There was nothing for him there.

Erik drove him up to the school in North Carolina. Upon arrival, he called me.

"Hey, Merl," he said, "I think maybe we had the wrong address. 'Cause this ain't no school. It's just a raggedy-ass house. And these jokers give the kids city bus passes so they can go back and forth to the local recreation center to practice. There ain't no school, no campus, no gym. All of their games are on the road. I've never seen anything like this."

The place was a damn diploma mill with a good basketball team, plain and simple.

A few weeks later, the assistant coach called and said, "Merl, every time I turn around they're asking me for more money. I done already paid $2,500 and that was supposed to be it. Now they keep coming back asking for more."

"For what?"

"They're saying this class is gonna cost this, that class is gonna cost that, tacking on another $2,500, and there's some qualification or certification he needs that's gonna run another $2,500."

Those dudes were basically milking him for every penny.

Shortly thereafter, I got one of the most bizarre phone calls I've ever received. Erik was on the other end of the line, and with hints of shock and disbelief in his voice, he said, "Hey, Merl, you ain't gonna believe this. This MF'er done got stabbed."

"What? Who got stabbed?"

"Marcus big ass!"

"Whaaaaaat!!!"

"And you ain't gon' believe this part. Guess who stabbed him?"

"Who?"

"The coach!!!"

The damn coach got to brawling with one of the kids on the team. Marcus, who's really just a big soft teddy bear, tried to break up the fight. The coach thought he was coming for him so he stabbed him. It was the craziest thing I'd ever heard.

Erik ain't a big intimidating dude, but he's a tough five-foot-seven ball of muscle, a former college athlete who looks like NFL Hall of Fame running back Emmitt Smith. And he can and will knock the biggest man out in a street fight. He sped down the highway, on his cell phone barking at the coach. "Since ya in a fightin' mood, since ya like fightin' and stabbin' kids, I'm on my way up there to fight ya right now. I'll be there shortly."

When Erik got there, Marcus and the coach calmed him down, convincing him that it was all a huge misunderstanding. It was really some insane shit. But everything eventually settled down.

A few weeks later, we gave Marcus a call and he told us that he was going to Oklahoma to play at a junior college.

"Marcus, what are you talking about?"

Apparently, and I wish I was making this up but I'm not, the coach that stabbed him—THE COACH THAT STABBED HIM!—had been offered a JUCO job as an assistant, but only with the stipulation that he brought Marcus along with him. He had somehow convinced Marcus that he'd get him into Georgetown or Kansas prior to him becoming an NBA lottery pick. As you can guess, Erik was foaming at the mouth, ready to go back up there to really beat the dude's ass for real.

Erik and I had never once ever gassed Marcus up, telling him that he was going to be in the NBA. Because we know the reality, that 99.9% of these kids will never get close enough to sniff the league. We've helped out plenty of good local kids, helped them to get college scholarships at some pretty good schools, like Murph for example, but never once saw anybody as a damn meal ticket. That's not what it was about for us.

For us, it was about helping to get Marcus a scholarship,

helping him get out of his disastrous home environment, so he could possibly earn a degree and improve his station in life a few years down the road.

Eventually the JUCO scenario died down. But he was still being pursued by some high-level universities, who were talking to the guy that ran the Carolina Ravens AAU program that Marcus played for and that Erik coached with. But this guy was loving the attention of talking to all of these bigtime, famous coaches and he was feeding all this stuff to Marcus. Finally we sat the dude down and told him to back off.

"Hey, man," I said. "Stay out of this because once they find out about his background and his real academic situation, you're gonna get the kid jammed up."

Miraculously, the boy completed two years' worth of school in six months. While he still didn't qualify academically to play as a freshman, a donor was arranged to pay Marcus's first year of tuition, and the next year, when he was eligible, he'd be put on scholarship.

We were ecstatic. The plan was for Erik to pick up Marcus and I'd meet them at a McDonald's at about the halfway point to scoop him up and take him to the bus station.

But on the ride to McDonald's, Marcus had second thoughts. He and Erik began to argue.

"Boy, ya gotta go, ain't nothin' to talk about!" Erik emphasized. When they pulled into the parking lot, Erik was beyond furious. Marcus doubled down.

"I ain't going!" he shouted.

"I tell you what. Your big ass ain't getting back in my car to go home, so if you don't go with Merl I guess you're gonna have to walk them forty miles to get back home," Erik said.

"Get in my car and let's go to the bus station so we can get you off to college," I told him.

Finally, we coaxed him into my car and I managed to get him on the bus. We knew he was gonna be good once he got up there.

A few weeks in, everything was cool, and Marcus was acclimating well to college life. The coaching staff called, telling us we needed to pull the documentation together for his Pell Grant application. Erik met with his momma at the Waffle House where she worked, and she gave him her W2s. There was no way a single person could be expected to survive on what she grossed annually, let alone take care of anyone else. But I digress.

We turned everything in and Marcus was primed to get a few thousand dollars to help get him through the semester. Well, shortly thereafter, we get another call from the coaching staff.

"Hey, man, Marcus ain't got no money."

"What do you mean? Didn't he just get his Pell Grant money?"

Turns out that the check came in his momma's name. She gave him a little bit of money, and he proceeded to buy two PlayStations and a pair of shoes. Two PlayStations! She kept the rest. We sent him fifty bucks here, a hundred there, to make sure he had a little something in his pocket.

That year, Marcus made honor roll both semesters. Though he sometimes skipped practice, he was following a rigorous nutrition plan and workout routine and had dropped about fifty pounds. By the start of his second year, he was looking like a legit player.

In his very first Division I college game, he only played twelve minutes, but he was exceptional in that short spurt, scoring eight points and grabbing eleven rebounds. In their fourth game that year, they played Ole Miss. That game held special meaning for us because suiting up for the Rebels was another of our young boys, Murphy Holloway, Big Murph.

Marcus didn't play a lot, but he absolutely dazzled with fourteen points, making all seven of his shots and grabbing six strong boards in just fifteen minutes of action. Big Murph saw the court for about sixteen minutes, swiping four steals, grabbing three rebounds and scoring six points on 75 percent shooting. We were so excited for our hometown boys. Their futures were looking really bright.

Marcus followed that up with eleven points and eight rebounds in only seventeen minutes against Old Dominion. And that was the crescendo of his Division I basketball career. Because he went back to the bullshit of missing practices. As his playing time decreased, instead of working hard to get back into the coaching staff's good graces, he'd dug himself deeper into a hole.

Erik and I got a call from the coaching staff. "We've made a decision that he can't play or travel with the team because he's not showing commitment."

I tried to stall the coaches out, to give Erik and me a chance to get Marcus straightened out. "I can't tell you how to run your team," I told them. "And I understand completely where you are coming from. But I can tell you this—I know this kid and when you guys go on the road without him, there's a good chance he won't be there when you come back."

But they were tired of his bullshit.

So Erik and I got Marcus on the phone and dug in his ass for what felt like the thousandth time.

"Your ass hasn't been going to practice, and now here are the consequences. You have to be very careful, Marcus, because if you keep fucking up, they won't renew your scholarship next year."

"Well, fuck it," Marcus shot back. "I won't play basketball anymore. I'll just stay here and be a student. Or maybe I'll transfer to Georgetown and just go to school there."

The temperature had been rising, but at that point, we exploded. I had to take a minute to calm down and collect my thoughts. When Erik handed the phone back to me, I tried to be as measured as possible.

"Marcus," I said slowly, evenly, in as serious a tone as I could conjure, "all the shit that Erik and I have done for you the last two years has been an effort to help you improve your life. If you don't want it, we can't continue to fool ourselves into wanting it for you. So I tell you what. When the team goes on the road and leaves you, if you somehow manage to get a bus ticket and wind up back in Pomaria or Little Mountain, please do me a favor and lose my number. Because as much as I want it for you, I simply can't help you."

And Marcus got his big ass on that bus and went home. I haven't talked to him since.

But interestingly enough, his story didn't end in sorrow.

Erik had played point guard and graduated from Benedict College in Columbia, South Carolina, a small historically Black school with an enrollment of about two thousand students that competes in Division II athletics in the SIAC, the Southern Intercollegiate Athletic Conference. One of his former teammates was now the head coach and called him asking about Marcus, hoping to land him as a transfer student.

"Hey, Erik, can you help me get his high school transcripts."

"Ya better call his college and just get his transcript," Erik tells him.

"Nah, nah, I need his high school transcript."

"Bruh," Erik says, "ya not hearing me, listen to what I'm tellin' ya."

"Well, what high school did he graduate from?"

"Ya still not hearing me, bruh. When ya asked Marcus what high school he graduated from, what did he say?"

"He said, 'I don't know.'"

"Well, I don't either."

We still get a serious chuckle out of those times we spent with Marcus.

Marcus Goode wound up attending Benedict. During the 2010–11 season, he led all of NCAA Division II with 11.8 rebounds per game and was named the SIAC Player of the Year. He averaged 18.4 points, 11.3 rebounds and 2.7 blocks during the 2011–12 season and helped lead the Tigers to back-to-back SIAC Championships in 2012 and 2013.

Today, Marcus has a college degree and he's in the Benedict College Hall of Fame.

9

A while back, I mentioned Anthony Davis and how I saw him for the very first time when he was a growing teenager, before he sprouted to six-foot-ten and seemingly skyrocketed overnight into the consensus number one recruit in the country in the class of 2011.

My colleague Carlton DuBose, who previously ran Chicago's Mean Streets Nike AAU program along with former University of Michigan and NFL receiver Tai Streets, had been brought on board with Nike as a scout. Years later, he would become my second-in-command when I took over the Nike grassroots job as the director.

The Mean Streets program was once affiliated with adidas, but had jumped over to Nike. And to prove their appreciation and loyalty to the Swoosh, they sent four players from the program in the late 2000s to the University of Oregon, a Nike school: McDonald's and Jordan Brand All-American Mike Dunigan, Joevan Catron, Matthew Humphrey and Josh Crittle.

When was the last time you saw four kids from Chicago, from the same AAU program, go all the way across the country to play at Oregon? For people who wondered back then how that happened, that was a Nike machination. That's how the business works.

Carlton was close to a lot of the top kids coming out of Chicago and he was the one who told me to come and check Anthony out. He said, "I need you to see this kid and tell me what your eyes are looking at. I don't know if I've ever seen a kid like this."

And sure enough, I was blown away. I asked Carlton to bring Anthony over to Tim Grover's gym so I could work him out myself.

Jeezus Lawd Christ O'Mighty!!! I thought, *This damn kid is incredible! He's definitely going to be a lottery pick.*

Carlton gave me the backstory of how, just a few months prior, he was a decent six-foot guard who could shoot, handle and really pass the rock. But he was playing at Perspectives Charter in the Blue Division of the Chicago Public High School League, a strong academic school with no athletic pedigree that was virtually ignored by the local sports media. Now all of a sudden, he'd grown eight inches. This was during his junior year in high school. I was unequivocally blown away, literally humbled and intoxicated by how gifted he was. By the time the workout was over, I was convinced that in a few years, this kid was gonna be the number one pick in the NBA draft.

College coaches were always calling me, asking about kids in Chicago. I started going to watch the top kids in the city from the moment I got there, so if I knew of a kid like Pat Beverley that was being underrecruited, that wasn't on everybody's radar, I'd send them in that direction.

There are so many talented players in the city that there's bound to be some diamonds in the rough that fall through the recruiting cracks or who get missed entirely. I was respected within the coaching fraternity for my ability to assess, evaluate and project out talent in terms of what that player could become with a few more years of seasoning.

As soon as we wrapped up that workout, I called every college head and assistant coach that I was cool with and said, "Hey, man, there's this kid named Anthony Davis here in Chicago. He ain't at one of the top basketball schools but you need to start recruiting him right now!"

The standard response was, "Anthony Davis? Never heard of him."

"You will! Mark my words!"

Carlton had a strong relationship with Kenny Payne, the current assistant coach with the New York Knicks, who was working with John Calipari at Kentucky. Calipari had the inside track on AD and the direct access that no other college coach had.

Anthony didn't play much AAU ball so he didn't blow up over the summer like most kids do when their stock increases. I started to spend more time with him and got to know his mom, dad, his older sister and his twin sister. His dad and I became really cool. Big Anthony is a helluva father; nothing came before the love and desire he had to take care of his family. I came from that type of family environment and, from the get-go, we got along swell.

Big Ant loved football, so we had a standing date over at my place where AD and his pops would come to watch the Monday Night Football games. Big Ant would come through, smiling wide while carrying his own personal six-pack, and we'd order up some pizzas and sit in my basement watching the games. We'd just be chilling, talking, laughing, having a good time.

Anthony was a fantastic, bright young man, just a super-great kid. I really enjoyed being around him at that stage in his life and watching him develop. His high school team didn't have its own damn gym. They practiced at a church. During his junior year, his team won only eight of its twenty-three games. When I went to watch him play that season, there were maybe twenty people in the gym. But man oh man, did those twenty people witness one helluva show.

The kid jumped center, ran the point, grabbed every re-bound, splashed threes from the corners, blocked shots like it was ingrained in his DNA, dished out some lovely assists, established position in the post and with one lightning-quick move was throwing down a mean-ass dunk. The dude was virtually unknown for his first three years of high school. But by his senior year, the cat was out of the bag and his family started to get bombarded. I was thankful that I could be a resource to them during that time.

When Anthony's profile became national and his stock exploded, my boss at Nike, Lynn Merritt, gave me a shocking ultimatum. It was the first red flag that made me start looking at the dude differently. He told me to back off and distance myself from Big Ant, Anthony's momma and the rest of the family.

Now that AD was being seen as the future number one pick, before his freshman season at Kentucky, Lynn wanted to be the point man, in the same way that he was in pursuit of LeBron for his first sneaker deal. I had no problem with that, but his insistence that I cease and desist with my relationship with the family was problematic for me, to say the least. There was a genuine rapport that I had with them. I'd spent the last two years bonding and getting to know them, and our association with one another had transcended Anthony's potential as a product endorser. I not only questioned the directive, but it made me angry.

Lynn had been pushing me for a while to become the director of Nike's grassroots basketball operation. I'd rebuffed because I did not want the job. I was comfortable in Chicago, enjoyed my work with NBA clients, was making my mark in the region. In no way, shape or form did I desire to move to Beaverton, Oregon, which the grassroots job required. I pushed back, telling him in no uncertain terms that I did not want the job, that I was cool with where I was at.

Of all of my experiences working on the pro side in Chicago, absolutely nothing could compare to the very brief time I got to spend with Kobe Bryant. The Lakers were flying in late one night after a road game and they'd be in the city for a couple of days before playing the Bulls.

Nike and the Chicago public schools had partnered together on a really cool contest where elementary school students were given a chance at designing one of Kobe's signature shoes, with the winning sketch going into production for a limited run.

The day after arriving, after the team held an early-afternoon practice, Kobe was scheduled to go to one of the schools where they planned to announce the winner. My colleague Nico Harrison, who's now the general manager of the

Dallas Mavericks, was Kobe's brand manager at Nike. But due to a scheduling conflict, Nico couldn't make it, so he called and asked me if I could fill in.

I'd previously been around Kobe on a few occasions and his business manager at the time, Jerry Sawyer, was a friend of mine. Jerry had previously worked at Nike and was now working full-time for Kobe, handling his outside business interests. So we had enough familiarity to make Kobe feel comfortable.

Now, I've been around the game of basketball in one capacity or another for most of my life. As a player, I felt that I was as hard-driving as anyone. But what I saw from Kobe Bryant over the course of those couple of days was the most exhilarating and humbling thing I've ever seen in terms of an individual's work ethic.

The Lakers landed in Chicago well after midnight after just having played a game. As soon as they touched down, Kobe hit the gym. The next day, after practice, I got up with him to accompany him for his appearance at the elementary school. As soon as we wrapped that up, we went to the gym because he wanted to lift some weights. Afterward, we grabbed a late lunch and after a brief rest, we were back in Tim Grover's gym.

The workout he put himself through that evening was astonishing. He didn't touch a single basketball. He was going through the mechanics of every shot in his arsenal, visualizing innumerable permutations that he could go to based on how the defense responded. Pretending to dribble, he would touch all of his preferred spots on the floor, shooting imaginary jump shots, spin moves, pump fakes, head fakes, step backs, dream shakes, up-and-unders, all done with impeccable footwork and precise movement.

He did this for an hour and a half. It was like observing Ernie Barnes paint *Sugar Shack*, like staring at Robert De Niro rehearsing for *The Godfather Part II*, like watching Jay-Z step into a recording booth and drop his entire *Reasonable Doubt* album straight off the dome. Simply put, it was just pure, unadulterated genius.

From there, we went to Carmine's on the Gold Coast for dinner. After a fantastic meal, he wanted to lie down for a while. And at about midnight, we went back to the gym for him to get a few hundred shots up. To this day, I marvel at the recollection and feel blessed to have been in the presence of that level of dedication and excellence.

And that next night, as I watched from my courtside seat at the United Center, he dropped a vicious thirty-six points on the Bulls.

So anyway, back to me wanting to have no part of being brought on to run Nike's grassroots division. It began with Lynn calling me in Chicago, telling me, "Get your ass on a plane and come to Phoenix. We're having a grassroots meeting. This ain't up for debate and I ain't asking you—I'm telling you to get your ass on a plane and come to Phoenix!"

I got to the resort and I didn't know anyone. Everyone was looking at me, like, *Why are you here?*

"Your guess is as good as mine," was all I could offer up.

Rumors were already floating around that I'd soon be taking over. Lynn had been peppering me for a while now and I kept giving him the stiff arm. At that meeting, I just sat there, occasionally answering questions about my summer leagues and the Nike Pro City events, but I really didn't have too much to add to what was being discussed.

Part of the problem with the potential new job was that

George Raveling, the Hall of Fame former college basketball coach, was pulling all of the strings. I respect Coach Rav; he's a fascinating, brilliant and very accomplished man, a legendary figure. He'd spend his early childhood in Washington, DC, but was forced into an orphanage at thirteen after his father died and his mother was institutionalized. Rav went on to earn a basketball scholarship to Villanova, where he became one of the country's top rebounders. And in one of the most serendipitous moments ever, while walking the streets of his hometown of Washington, DC, the night prior to the March on Washington, he was spotted, due to his size and confident comportment, and asked if he'd like to provide security for the next day's event. When he showed up at the appointed time, he learned that he'd be situated directly behind the featured speakers for the day. So when Martin Luther King Jr. delivered his iconic "I Have a Dream" speech, with gospel music legend Mahalia Jackson standing nearby yelling, "Tell 'em about the dream, Martin! Tell 'em about the dream," Rav could literally reach out and touch him.

When he left the lectern, Rav asked Dr. King if he could have his handwritten speech. He obliged and handed it to him. To this day, it remains in his possession.

Rav would become the first Black coach in the history of the ACC, joining Lefty Driesell's staff as an assistant at the University of Maryland in 1969. From there he tracked through a remarkable career as a college head coach at Washington State, Iowa and Southern Cal while also serving as an assistant to Bobby Knight with the gold-medal-winning 1984 US Olympic basketball team, which featured collegians Michael Jordan, Patrick Ewing and Chris Mullin. Upon retiring from coaching after a horrific car crash that nearly took his life, Rav worked as a college hoops television broadcaster before coming on board with Nike, eventually ascending to the position of global sports marketing director for basketball.

The dude was beguiling and intellectually curious, his head always buried in a book. I had a ton of respect for him. But I wasn't going to be anybody's puppet. Whoever was running grassroots at the time was basically doing what he said. Whether or not they thought it was the right thing to do, they had to do it. I didn't want to be in that position. You can't ask me to be the director of something when I can't make the real decisions.

In Portland a few months later for a different meeting, Lynn told me, "You need to go talk to Coach Rav."

I walked into his office and he said, "Lynn tells me you're interested in the grassroots job."

I was momentarily frozen because I'd long told Lynn in no uncertain terms where I stood on that.

"With all due respect, Coach, I have no interest in that job whatsoever."

Rav sat behind his desk with a puzzled look on his face.

"Coach, I told Lynn several times that I'm not interested in the job. But I will tell you that if I was interested, what I'm not gonna do is be somebody's puppet. If you're gonna make the decisions, then you need to run it. But you can't ask me to take a job where I'm supposed to be in charge and there's another agenda where I have decisions being made over my head, decisions that I will ultimately have to be responsible for."

He sat there staring at me, completely unamused.

Later that night I got a call from Lynn in my hotel room. He was giggling his ass off. "I don't know what you said to Coach Rav, but he just finished roasting you for an hour!"

I told Lynn what I told Rav, verbatim, and did not hold my

tongue, telling him that if I didn't think it was right I simply was not going to do it.

"That's what I'm talking about, Merl. We need somebody like that!"

So they hired Kevin Eastman, who had previously been in charge of Nike Skills Academies.

And maaaaaaan, them dope dealers and street dudes in that AAU world that were running their own programs got on Kevin's ass so bad, he didn't last but six months before he quit. They brought in someone else to fill the gap, but that didn't work out either. So Lynn, still determined to jockey me into the position, came at me from a different angle.

"Merl, I need your help," he said over lunch one day. "I need you to take this grassroots job. Here's the thing, and I gotta say it to you, man, because I don't know how else to say it. If I tell you I need your help and you don't help me, the next time an opportunity or a promotion comes up, I can't say that your name will be thought of highly in terms of someone who is loyal."

So he basically threatened me, insinuating that I'd never get another promotion if I didn't accept the grassroots post. That was the way he positioned it. You need my help but you're threatening me at the same time? That didn't sit well with me. Not at all.

And that's how I ended up becoming Nike's director of grassroots basketball.

"Okay, Lynn, I'll do it. What do you need me to do?"

"First thing you gotta do is move your ass to Oregon."

In my head I screamed, *You motherfucker!*

My dad had been going through some health issues. He'd survived a heart attack and a battle with cancer. He'd had some of his surgeries in Chicago and lived with me for a few months while recovering. My man wasn't doing well; he was really going through it. He couldn't catch his breath, his chest was hurting all the time and it was a scary time for our whole family. When he went back home to Greenville, I'd make the ten-hour drive regularly to be with him, work remotely, then turn right back around in a day or two to head back to Chicago. I was doing that three or four times a month because my mother was still working. Sometimes I'd catch a flight into Charlotte or Atlanta and drive from there to Greenville. Lynn knew all of this.

But going to Oregon, there was no way I could see my dad on a consistent basis. It was just not geographically possible. In Chicago, I was good, I was hooping, I'd become part of the community, I'd forged a great network and I was doing well in my job. So well that when my friend Dell Demps left his job with the Spurs to become the GM of the New Orleans Pelicans, he told the Spurs, when they asked who should replace him, "You guys need to go and get Merl."

I had some conversations with the team president, R. C. Buford, and Danny Ferry, the vice president of basketball operations at the time. Ferry actually flew into Chicago to meet with me. And they did make me an offer. But it was for half of the salary that I was earning at Nike. When I balked at the number, I was told, "Sometimes you gotta take a step back to take two steps forward."

I wasn't feeling that, but took it to Lynn to get his thoughts and advice. He knew I had aspirations of one day working in an NBA front office. But his comment was, "Man, you ain't ready for that, Merl."

At the time, I was thinking, *Maybe Lynn is right, maybe I need some more experience before I jump into that space.*

In retrospect I realize that I probably was ready; Lynn just wanted to keep me for the grassroots gig. Dell Demps later asked me to come to New Orleans to be his assistant GM. Ultimately I didn't take the job. But in retrospect, I damn sure should have.

I took on the challenge of the grassroots job around the time that Lynn ordered me to stay away from Anthony Davis and his family. I was like, *Damn, I've been friends with these folks for a couple of years, we've gone to amusement parks, go-kart racing, they come over to my place to just chill and watch some football games, we've regularly gone out to eat and I've been a sounding board and a resource that's helped them out of a few jams.* Lynn didn't know the family at all, but now he wanted to manage the relationship for Nike. Once the kid's profile got that high, he wanted ownership.

But Lynn be damned, I'd still speak with Big Ant on the phone, albeit less frequently.

The first person I brought over was Carlton, who went from his scouting role to my second-in-command. With his experience running the Mean Streets program, he knew how this monster worked and would be a huge asset. He had the travel team background, knew how to operate around the street dudes and the corporate dudes, he knew the budgetary issues and the murky sides of the business and he helped me immensely through that learning curve.

I needed to grasp an extraordinary amount of information in a short period of time, like how do we identify kids? How do we make decisions on which teams to sponsor, at what levels of investment and in what markets? How do we determine the locations for our events? How do we staff and run them? How do we service our relationships with the colleges and universities as a direct feeder system? How do we select kids for the Brand Jordan All-American game? These questions are impossible to answer until you're in the thick of it.

As I was getting acclimated to my new responsibilities in Oregon, AD was absolutely killing it as a freshman at Kentucky. It was already apparent that he was a generational talent, a true cornerstone that an NBA franchise only dreams about. And I was ecstatic for the kid and his family, knowing what the future held for them.

As we were getting settled in Oregon, Carlton came to me and said, "Hey, man, we got a problem. Big Ant lost his job as the super at that apartment complex. He got laid off."

Anthony's mom was not working at the time and the family was on some real shaky financial footing with Big Ant now being unemployed.

"We gotta figure out a way to help the family," said Carlton. "It ain't gonna be for long because he's gonna be the number one pick in a few months, but we gotta help them out right now."

I took the information to Lynn and his simple response was, "You have to be an asset."

Now this was the same dude that previously told me to back off from the family so he could step in. But okay, whatever.

When I was on the pro side at Nike, I made numerous trips to Kentucky to see guys like Rajon Rondo, Eric Bledsoe, John Wall, DeMarcus Cousins and a few others. I had some solid relationships with folks in Lexington, so the first call I made was to a former assistant athletic director. He was no longer working in that capacity, but he was superconnected to some heavy hitters.

I told him the real deal, that the kid and his family needed some help, that Big Ant had lost his job and that we wanted to assist them financially. "It's just a short bridge so they can eat and keep their heads above water for the next couple of months because once he declares for the draft, the agents and marketing folks will take care of everything from there."

He thought on it and came back to me with a creative idea. He knew some guys that ran an apparel shop. "What if they created a T-shirt design? Would the family be okay if they got a healthy amount of the profits from the sales, so long as they don't come back and sue us? We wanna make a play on his unibrow."

"Cool," I told him. "Send me the schematics and designs and I'll run it by the family to make sure they're okay with how this is going down. And we can't take forever and a day—they need some relief immediately."

I took the proposal to Carlton. He liked the idea and presented it to Big Ant and the family, explaining to them how it would be promoted via the company's website and at various game-day events and on-campus sales, that the amount they'd receive would depend on the actual sales figures. The family was cool with it and so we went ahead. These conversations happened around Thanksgiving.

A few days later, those T-shirts were flying off the shelves. On December 9, my guy in Lexington called me and said, "They've had some movement, made some sales. They've got ten grand for the family right now. How do you wanna handle it?"

I was driving down to Bloomington that next day to check out the Kentucky vs Indiana game. Both teams were undefeated and the Wildcats were the number-one-ranked team in the country. It was John Calipari's third year and he was coming off consecutive Elite Eight and Final Four appearances. He'd restored the majestic glory that the rabid fan base had been dying for and the hype around the game, especially for an early-season contest and with AD looking like a mix between Bill Russell and Penny Hardaway, was off the charts.

So I asked the former assistant athletic director to meet me at the game in Bloomington. He handed me the envelope and I called AD's mom, who was at the game with AD's sisters. I met her, gave her the cash, and you could see the sense of relief washing over her face. We exchanged some quick pleasantries and before heading in separate directions to watch the game, she said, "We really appreciate ya'll helping us."

These are really good people. That kid and his family deserved an opportunity to live without constantly worrying about keeping a roof over their heads and food on the table, especially while AD was generating tens of millions of dollars for everyone except himself. His jerseys by then were ubiquitous in Lexington, the team went on to win the national championship, he'd been named the National Player of the Year, the Most Outstanding Player of the NCAA Tournament, won the Wooden and Naismith Awards and yet, it was the athletic director, Coach Cal and his staff and everyone else who got their hefty bonuses. All while the Davis family was facing temporary homelessness.

I have no qualms about what we did to help them. In my opinion, they deserved a helluva lot more. Now, with athletes being permitted to profit off their names, images and likenesses, I actually feel vindicated in helping that family in the way that we did. It was the right thing to do—to hell with what the NCAA would have said at the time.

It was a pretty cool moment for me recently, watching the new *Space Jam* movie with my sons and seeing Anthony Davis in the film, with his unibrow playing a pronounced role.

As I was getting settled into the grassroots role it became clear that Anthony Davis was going to be the consensus number one draft pick. In my previous role with our NBA clients, I got to know some of the prominent sports agents. Some had been calling, asking if I could help them get a meeting with him and his family. I told them I couldn't, and directed them to Carlton DuBose and Kenny Payne, his assistant coach at Kentucky.

As the AD sweepstakes were heating up, Lynn called a handful of us into his office.

"Somebody in here is trying to push an agent on Anthony Davis," he said, fixing his gaze on the first individual and asking, "Have you had discussions with agents around AD?"

"Nope."

"Okay, you can leave."

He did this with everyone else until it was just me and him in the room. He accused me directly of trying to steer kids to an NBA agent named Andy Miller, in exchange for a fee if they signed. I'd met Andy a couple of times, but I didn't know him like that. And I certainly wasn't trying to push his service on anybody. I told Lynn as much, returned to my cubicle and tried to calm down. But I was still livid. Lynn walked over and started poking me on the shoulder, now in a playful mood.

"Not the time, Lynn," I told him, rocking back and forth in anger. At this point, everything in my vision just went white. He kept poking me. "Now ain't the time. Knock it off, man, I'm serious!"

But he continued. And at that point, I lost it. I hopped out of my chair, grabbed him by the collar, lifted his ass off the floor and put him on the table.

"Lynn, I will fuck you up! You better stop playing with me!"

I'd had enough. Carlton was nearby, saying, "Oh shit, Merl!"

At that exact moment, I knew that my tenure at Nike was nearing its end. I didn't know how much longer I'd be there, but I did know that the clock was ticking.

Anthony Davis eventually retained Thad Foucher from Wasserman Media Group, the sports marketing and talent management company based out of Los Angeles that also represents the likes of Russell Westbrook. Right now, Wasserman trails only the venerable Creative Artists Agency for the top spot in the sports agency business, with $5.73 billion of contract value under management and its agents earning $334.1 million in commissions for the year at the close of 2020.

Go check those numbers again and you'll get a sense of why the elite "amateur" sports space is infested with agents, why they're trying to endear themselves to athletes while they're still in high school. Because a stable of transcendent, marketable athletes like AD and Russell Westbrook can bring in hundreds of millions in commissions alone. Annually.

So trust and believe, there were many folks in various roles, at Nike, at the University of Kentucky and within AD's inner circle, that were pushing for him to sign with a particular agent and agency, hoping to get a percentage of his rookie deal and the windfall that would soon follow on his subsequent contracts.

I was not one of them.

One of the biggest adjustments for me as I transitioned to grassroots was the breadth of folks I dealt with. On the NBA side, I was working with endorsers under the Nike umbrella, and their immediate circle of family, agents, financial advisers and the front office people for the teams that they play for in your region.

On the grassroots side?

The circle was humongous. For every high-profile kid, there's his AAU program and its coaching staff and hierarchy of parents, handlers, uncles, cousins, homeboys and hangers-on, not to mention university boosters, the ranking services, his high school coaching staff, the agents looking to represent him and all of the colleges in the Nike family that are recruiting him.

The influential circle and power structure is different for every kid. You have split households: some people are cozying up to Mom, while others are trying to get in tight with Dad or the stepdad. And you have to suss out who's really running the show, which can always change at a moment's notice. It's a delicate balance.

Sometimes, the college coaches could be among the worst folks to deal with. They're calling incessantly, badgering you to help them get a particular kid, or angrily accusing you of helping another school to their detriment. They ask who they should hire as assistants, or how they can get in the door with a certain kid and his family.

A coach from Ohio State might call, asking about a certain player, saying, "I'm trying to get close to the kid and I'm talking to his dad right now." Well, my staff's gotta be on point with their intel, letting me know that Dad's a drunk, him and Mom are separated, Mom has no clue what's going on and she's leaning on the new boyfriend, but the real person to talk to if you wanna get tight with the kid is the grandmother. My scouts better know all of that stuff.

During our All-American camps and skills academies, coaches would call repeatedly, asking for us to arrange for an uncommitted athlete to be roommates for the week with one that had signed with their program.

The coaches would be furious when I denied these requests. If I could help a coach out within certain parameters, I would. But not to the detriment of another school under our umbrella. And I never believed in pushing a kid to a particular school. They needed to make those decisions themselves so if things didn't work out, that was on him and his family. That's a part of growing up and becoming a man, making tough decisions and living with the consequences. Because if things went sour, they'd still have a line of suitors to choose from that snaked around the corner.

Recruiting is the lifeblood of any program. If the greatest coach in the world is coaching bums, he's fired within three years, if he's lucky enough to last that long. So the stakes are high to secure commitments from those so-called top-ten kids.

For example, when Billy Donovan was at the University of Florida, he'd taken that program from the Southeastern Conference basement to the absolute pinnacle of the college game, winning back-to-back national championships in 2006 and 2007. He won the school's first ever NCAA title with a sophomore-laden squad headlined by three future pros—Al Horford, Joakim Noah and Corey Brewer. When they won it again that next year, they became the first school to win consecutive titles since Duke in 1992. No program, as of this writing, has done it since.

Billy's pedigree and résumé cannot be questioned. As a player, coached by Rick Pitino, he was a First Team All–Big East point guard that led a Cinderella Providence College squad to the '87 Final Four. After a short stint as a player with the Knicks in the NBA and as a stockbroker on Wall Street, he apprenticed under Pitino at Kentucky as an assistant before landing his first head coaching gig at Marshall at the tender age of twenty-eight. After turning around the floundering

Thundering Herd program immediately upon his arrival, he went to Florida, where the program at the time was mediocre at best, and proceeded to build a powerhouse.

His top assistant on those national championship squads was my former assistant coach at Clemson, Larry Shyatt, one of the best people on this earth, just a great human being. I'd stayed connected with Coach Shyatt since my college playing days. I love that man and his entire family. When I was training ahead of going to the Denver Nuggets training camp, Larry invited me to spend a month with him at his house in Wyoming, where he was the head coach at the University of Wyoming at the time. He allowed me to work out in their facilities so I could get acclimated to the elevation. The man was always more than just a coach to me. To this day, I cherish our friendship and have a deep appreciation for him, his wife and his entire family.

So when I was working at Nike's NBA division, it was always great to see him when I'd go down to Gainesville to scout players like Brewer, Noah and Horford, all of whom had very long pro careers.

I didn't have a close personal relationship with Billy Donovan; we didn't know each other very well. But this is a fraternal business, so Larry Shyatt vouching for me made Billy comfortable. Florida was a Nike-sponsored school and I had access to the program, practices and the locker room. If I wanted to come down and get some prime seats to a big SEC football game, I was gonna get hooked up. Billy and I weren't friends like Larry and I were, we didn't talk every day or very often at all for that matter, but we did have a solid professional relationship.

So now that I was running Nike's grassroots operation, I had been down to Florida a few times to look at some of the top high school players in the state and if I could, I'd stop through Gainesville to say hello.

One day, I was in my office in Oregon and I got a call from Coach Shyatt.

"Hey, Merl," he said, "Billy's upset and wants to talk to you. Something about some kid's recruitment."

"No problem, tell him to hit me."

Shortly thereafter, Billy called, spitting fire through the phone.

"I'm sick and tired of this bullshit!" he yelled. Like in the cartoons, I could see the smoke coming out of his ears. "You motherfuckers keep helping Kentucky! This shit is ridiculous. I'm gonna call Phil Knight personally to talk about this shit because it's getting out of hand."

For those that don't know, Phil Knight is the billionaire cofounder and chairman emeritus at Nike, its former CEO and chairman, and was a track athlete at the University of Oregon back in the day. Phil is widely considered the most powerful man in the entire industry of sports.

I stayed quiet while Billy vented, because I knew there was some truth in what he was saying. With John Calipari getting an overabundance of the top recruits in the country at the time, Florida and every other program were fighting for scraps. One of the worst-kept secrets in the business was Nike's emphasis on helping Kentucky and Oregon, Phil Knight's alma mater, with everyone else falling in line after. For me, this perception created a never-ending cycle of conflict, messing up our relationships with some of the other top coaches.

Billy ended our conversation by saying, "So why are we even with Nike if you guys aren't gonna help us in the same way that you're helping them?"

I told Lynn about the call and how Billy was reevaluating Florida's relationship with Nike.

Not long after that, Lynn called me and said, "I talked to Phil Knight and he said, 'Fuck him! Tell him he can go somewhere else if he ain't happy.'"

"Lynn, I am not taking that message back to Billy Donovan."

I wasn't sure if Lynn was telling the truth about his supposed conversation with Phil Knight, or if he was just talking shit. Because Lynn was a notorious shit talker. But I do know that shortly thereafter, Billy left the University of Florida after nineteen seasons to become the head coach of the NBA's Oklahoma City Thunder. During his five years with the Thunder from 2015 to 2020, he never failed to lead them into the playoffs. Today, he's the head coach of the Chicago Bulls.

Were those two things, Billy's dissatisfaction with Nike and his jump to the NBA, related? Maybe, maybe not. But this was just one of many situations I had to address with the college coaches under our umbrella.

Tempers, conspiracy theories, tampering, poaching and cutthroat competition are par for the course when it comes to major college basketball recruiting. To quote the character Omar from the HBO series *The Wire*, "It's all in the game."

I'd often joke around and say that I was Dr. Phil for college basketball coaches. But there was some truth in that because I was often in the middle trying to settle serious disputes.

There was another situation that arose as it related to the recruitment of Stanley Johnson, a young man from California who was among the top-rated recruits in the class of 2014.

I'd hired a guy named Mike Mayo to be one of our West Coast scouts. He was a young dude from the Los Angeles area who'd played ball at Serra High School in Gardena and was close to guys like James Harden and Russell Westbrook. In my role, it was important to bring in young guys that were connected to the top prep players in our major markets. At this point, I was in my midthirties and didn't speak the same language as these high school kids. But Mike could. He related to them on their level and could kick it with them about their musical preferences, clothes and fashion. And he was a really good hire for us.

So Stanley Johnson fell under Mike's umbrella on the West Coast. Stanley was a force of nature in high school. Tough and rugged, he played an all-around game with passion, had some strength and some size at six-foot-six and 240 pounds. He could score, defend the post and the perimeter and rebound down low with the big boys. He was a one-and-done kid, meaning after his freshman year in college, if the stars aligned correctly, he was leaving for the NBA and would be among the top ten picks in the 2015 draft. He'd come to our camps as a kid, played for one of our marquee AAU programs, the Oakland Soldiers, which had flipped over from adidas to Nike, and was a really smart player. He was also a good person off the court. And every top program in the country was after him.

One day, I got a call from Sean Miller, then the head coach at Arizona. "You motherfuckers are helping Kentucky with Stanley Johnson!"

"Coach, I don't know what you're talking about," I told him. "I don't even talk to Stanley Johnson."

But he was pissed. "I know for a fact that you guys are trying to help Calipari get this kid."

Then I got a call from Lynn, who said that Calipari was

accusing me of trying to push Stanley to Arizona because my friend Book Richardson was an assistant coach there.

Then, Southern Cal started calling, saying I was helping Kentucky.

Then when Mike Mayo sent Stanley a pair of cardinal-and-gold shoes, somebody found out about the color scheme via one of Stanley's social media posts, and Kentucky and Arizona cited it as proof that we were helping USC, whose school colors are cardinal and gold, land the kid.

That's just a small example of the nonsense. The problem is, coaches are subject to NCAA rules about contacting kids, when they can visit them, talk to them, how often they can text and call them. But my guys at Nike weren't. So we could, if we wanted to, go sit in that kid's living room every damn day of the week, and twice on Sunday! Coaches were always asking for our help, or on the flip side angrily accusing us of helping somebody else. The whole damn thing was exhausting.

Every day, you're in the middle of these wars within your own college portfolio. After a while, it wears you out.

What's also important is that travel teams are allocated a certain amount for their travel budget every summer. They don't receive enough to sustain themselves and most programs have to figure out how to raise some extra cash. The folks running these programs aren't doing so out of the goodness of their hearts. They're running business entities and they ultimately want to make money.

For the few programs that are run and funded by wealthy individuals, there are other motivations. One may be as simple as a desire to get close to and live vicariously through the next LeBron. Others may be more sinister, like the rich pedophiles that funded New York's most prominent teams in the '80s, the Bronx Gauchos and the Riverside Church Hawks.

We had a program out of Alabama that current Phoenix Suns star Devin Booker used to play for. They'd had some high-profile kids that wound up playing at schools like LSU, Mississippi State, Alabama and Ole Miss. So let's say that team gets a cash allocation of $40,000. It sounds like a lot of money, but it's not when you're talking about twelve kids and four coaches that have to travel across the country.

That's sixteen people that need to be lodged at a decent hotel from a Wednesday through a Sunday. That's four or five nights on the road, folks gotta eat at least three meals a day, you gotta rent vans to get around town and so that $40,000 can get eaten up over two events. And we're asking them, at least the more high-profile organizations, to travel and play in at least four or five. So now, how do they make up the difference?

Most programs also have at least four separate elite travel teams for different age groups: seventeen-and-under down to fourteen-and-under. So costs elevate quickly.

Their best bet is to host their own events where they can sell tickets and programs, and keep all of the money generated by parking and get a cut of the concessions.

Some agents and agencies will donate to these programs, through other people, of course, so that there's no paper trail, especially if those teams are loaded with some of the top recruits. They'll say, "We'll give you $40,000, but we want access to the kids." And the folks running those programs are going to delightfully say okay.

That's a cheap investment for an agent or an agency to have access to kids like Devin Booker when they're young and impressionable at sixteen years old. They're trying to establish a strong early relationship with these elite players to sign them when they turn pro.

Now, if a university is heavily recruiting a kid like Devin Booker and they really, really want him, they're going to find a booster that's willing to put $50,000 into the program as a quid pro quo. And that check will be merrily accepted because the programs not only need the money, but they're also trying to make as much money as possible for themselves.

And don't you dare think for a minute that some of the bolder college coaches aren't assisting and advising in these transactions. They need access to the top kids because they need a competitive advantage on the recruiting trail because that's their lifeline to deep NCAA Tournament runs and ultimately, their own contract extensions. Simply put, if they don't secure the talent, they don't keep their jobs. This is a high-stakes business where people are playing chess, not checkers. When the chance arises, they cash in.

For example, there's a powerhouse college program with a Hall of Fame coach. One of the top agents in the game is an alum of the university, and he was donating $1 million a year to the school. Around the time when I was settling into the grassroots job, that school had a player projected to be a top-five pick. But the agent was pissed because he couldn't even get a meeting with the kid to pitch his services. It turns out that one of the school's assistant coaches, who'd been connected to the kid through relationships he had going back to his AAU days, soured him on this particular agent in favor of another.

So the agent called the head coach and said, "Why am I donating one million dollars a year if I can't even get a meeting with this kid?" He gave the coach an ultimatum. "Either your assistant takes a walk, or my annual contribution to the program does."

And so when the next job cycle opened up, the head coach, who didn't want to fire his assistant, worked feverishly to help him land a head coaching gig at a midmajor program in the Midwest. The bottom line was that he had to go. And folks looking in from the outside were none the wiser. That's how some scenarios really go down.

Once I'd gotten my feet wet in the grassroots space, I saw how the relationships really operated between the branded companies and their sponsored universities, how those schools leaned on you for the talent pool under your grassroots travel team system, and how those agents infiltrated spaces that were supposedly safe from their influence. It all works hand in hand. When you're just there as an observer, you don't understand all of that because you're just watching kids play.

And the sneaker companies are complicit because they're using all of the top-level kids as free marketing. So if I was given the directive to push KD's and LeBron's latest gear, I'm sending those products to those elite top-ten players. He wants it, his people want it, he's got a social media following and he's already an influencer, so he's gonna market and advertise our stuff. For free.

The fight for market dominance in the athletic footwear industry is never-ending, so we need to be visible at every level and we're going to utilize our colleges and universities, our AAU travel teams and the best high school teams in the country during the regular season. Our NBA channels reach more people globally, but I reach more people domestically through our grassroots and college basketball channels.

America loves its college hoops, and there's a huge trickle-down effect in the shoe business to the grassroots system, as it relates to licensing, apparel, coaching relationships and more. According to the NCAA, the college players aren't supposed to receive "impermissible benefits" from us; the shoe Santa is supposed to retire once they've left the grassroots system. But if you think the gift-giving stops, I have a really nice bridge in Brooklyn to sell you.

You find ways to keep the kids under your umbrella laced with the hottest stuff on the streets. And if a kid is at an adidas or Under Armour school and flashing top-ten draft potential, best believe he's also getting hit off with some Air Jordans as well. Since you can't send him stuff directly at his dorm, you're just sending his packages to an uncle, a handler, a former AAU coach that he's tight with or even the agent that's already locked him up years before he turns pro. That is your job. Because if you don't land the Devin Bookers or the Anthony Davises or the Kyrie Irvings, your boss is gonna be on your ass, saying that you didn't have a good enough relationship with him.

Another point of drama was determining who would participate in the Brand Jordan All-American game. Once the work was done, the event itself was phenomenal. The athletes would go to special screenings of Spike Lee movies hosted by the filmmaker himself. Michael Jordan, Spike, Mark Wahlberg, Kevin Durant, LL Cool J, Kanye, Carmelo, C. C. Sabathia, Chris Paul and other celebs are courtside. Fabolous, Drake, Rick Ross, J. Cole, Anthony Hamilton, Common, Akon and others were putting on halftime and postgame concerts in the arena.

But an unimaginable level of political maneuvering and fierce infighting goes into choosing the players for those coveted twenty-two slots. The college coaches want their soon-to-be incoming freshman in the game because it speaks highly to the level of talent they're attracting, and the AAU programs are pressuring you to pick their kids because they want the prestige, as do the parents and handlers and everybody in these kids' cipher that you've been dealing with for the last few years.

Other than Michael Jordan's sons, Jeffrey and Marcus, you have to be among the top twenty-five players in the country to be considered for the roster. Now, Jeffrey and Marcus were really good high school players in Chicago, and they both went on to play D-I in college. But when the all-star game bears your name, your kids get to play whether they deserve it or not.

For one reason or another, there were always people angling for kids that weren't ranked in that top twenty-five. And such was the case with a kid from Hackensack, New Jersey, named Reggie Cameron.

Reggie was a good kid who came out of Jimmy Salmon's New Jersey Playaz AAU program. He had some nice size for a shooting guard at six-foot-seven and his jumper was decent. He was slated to play in the regional game between the top New York and New Jersey kids because he was one of the higher-ranked players in the area. But according to the most reputable player rankings, along with our own scouts and internal evaluations, there were between seventy and ninety kids that were rated higher than him in that graduating class.

As we were finalizing the selection process for that 2013 game, we had players like Joel Embiid, Bobby Portis, Aaron Gordon, Andrew Wiggins, Jabari Parker, Julius Randle, Wayne Selden, Noah Vonleh and the Harrison twins, Andrew and Aaron, from Houston, as the big names in that recruiting class. So you can imagine my shock when I got a call from Jackie Thomas, Brand Jordan's global marketing director.

Initially, it seemed that she was just trying to get information, asking me what went into our player selection process. But the convo took a violent U-turn when she told me that we needed to put Reggie in the game.

"Um, yeah, Jackie. That ain't happening," I said. "There are at least seventy kids that are ranked higher and putting him in that game would destroy our credibility, my credibility. Now, we've already got him in the New York vs New Jersey game, the regional game. But I'm sorry, there's no way he's getting an invite to play in the All-American game. Ain't no way."

Jackie proceeded to call me back a couple of days later. She'd either ignored what I'd said or had completely forgotten about it, because she skipped all the opening pleasantries.

"Hey, Merl, we need to make sure that Reggie's in the All-American game. And I'm not asking you. I'm telling you."

"Jackie," I said. "We've already had this conversation. I'm not doing that. Do you have any idea what kind of backlash that would cause? The kind of mess that I'd have to clean up if a top-twenty kid got bumped in favor of Reggie Cameron? So you can say it until you're blue in the face, but I ain't doing it."

This tug-of-war went on for about three weeks. So here's the backstory. Reggie had committed to play at Georgetown. Big John Thompson, the legendary former Hoyas coach, was on Nike's powerful board of directors. His son, JT III, was now the head coach there, but after a surprising run to the Final Four in 2006–2007, they were regularly getting bounced out of the NIT and the early rounds of the NCAA Tournament.

So Big John wanted to help his son on the recruiting trail by telling the top kids and their people that he was bringing in Brand Jordan All-Americans, and that they should join them. Because the hot seat was getting hotter the more the program floundered. And *floundering* would be a flattering word for where they were at the time. The once mighty Georgetown was now a relic of the past, with the majority of the top recruits not having a damn clue as to who Patrick Ewing was. To them, the Hoyas' 1984 national championship might as well have taken place in the Stone Age.

So now Jackie was trying to tell me that the directive had come down directly from Big John. She was not asking or suggesting. She firmly told me to make it happen. Because if I didn't, someone else definitely would.

"It's our game, Merl. The Brand Jordan All-American game."

"Jackie, I understand that completely, but as long as the grassroots division determines who ultimately gets an invite, then we're gonna bring in the top kids. Period."

"Merl, if you don't do this, I just need you to know that Phil Knight is going to personally get involved and make sure that he gets put in the game."

"Well, then that's what it's going to take because as long as I'm in charge of grassroots and the selection process for the game, I'm not doing that."

So I gave a call to the most respected man at Brand Jordan, Howard White. The man known simply as H is a legendary figure. H hails from the Hampton Roads, Virginia, area, which produced the likes of Allen Iverson, and was a former college player himself at the University of Maryland. He was the quiet force behind Brand Jordan's meteoric rise.

In addition to being an ordained minister and a man of impeccable moral convictions, H is a motivational speaker nonpareil. Five minutes alone with him and he'll mesmerize you with quotes from the English philosopher Aldous Huxley; he'll have you convinced that you can set the whole damn world on fire in sixty seconds. He's a truly remarkable person.

Profanity is not part of his vocabulary, but that didn't stop me from saying, when he called me back, "H, you know this is some bullshit!"

H is just cool as a fan. He doesn't take any sides and doesn't tell me what to do. He calmly told me, "Yeah, Merl, they're adamant that they want him in the game."

"Yeah, H, and I'm adamant that he ain't playing!"

Now, I was used to some of the political bullshit because it was understood that if you had a kid on the borderline of that top twenty-five ranking, and they were going to Duke, North Carolina, Kentucky or Oregon, they were gonna get an invite over a kid that was ranked higher, but they had to at least be in that top thirty or so to make the cut. But telling me that Reggie Cameron needed to be in that game was preposterous.

I held my ground and eventually won that battle. Reggie, by all accounts a really good kid, never made an impact at Georgetown. He averaged 3.4 points and 1.3 rebounds per game over his four-year career. Today, he's on the coaching staff at St. Joseph's University in Philadelphia.

So the grassroots stuff was exhausting. I was becoming more physically and mentally drained, spending 250 days a year sleeping in hotel rooms away from my family.

Some of the experiences were great. A few of them were hilarious. Others were infuriating. And I met some of the most interesting folks on that path.

One of whom was Philip Esformes, the Miami Beach business mogul who was later convicted for playing a central role in the largest health care fraud in the history of the United States.

But back when I met Phil, before he was sentenced to twenty years in a federal prison on twenty felony counts for cycling elderly, destitute and drug-addicted patients through his sprawling network of health care facilities that stretched from Chicago to Miami and billing over a billion dollars to government programs for services that were often never rendered, he was just a filthy rich parent who'd stop at nothing to help his sons get Division I basketball scholarships.

10

I met Philip Esformes through a guy named Martin Fox, who was working with the Houston Hoops AAU program. The Hoops outfit is an unadulterated machine in the grassroots world that has cultivated and nurtured the likes of Kendrick Perkins, Booby Gibson, T. J. Ford, De'Aaron Fox, Stephen Jackson, Rashard Lewis, Kelly Oubre, Justise Winslow and many, many others.

Martin called me and said, "Hey, Merl, I got a guy in Florida that I want you to meet. When are you going to be down there?"

I told him I'd be down in Orlando in a few weeks. When I got there, I met Phil for dinner at one of the most expensive restaurants in town, and it was immediately apparent that the dude had plenty of money. He had the perpetual tan, he was in shape, he was wearing thousand-dollar shoes, his clothes were tailor-made and he had a driver wheeling him around in a $250,000 automobile.

He started talking about his kids, mentioning how a number of prominent NBA assistant coaches and relatives of some all-star players were working them out regularly. He alluded to the fact that he really wanted his kids to play on Nike's EYBL summer circuit and eventually hoped that they'd get scholarships to major D-I schools.

"Well, Phil, just because a kid plays in the EYBL doesn't guarantee that he's gonna get a scholarship," I explained. "Those offers are really based on how well a kid performs against some of the country's best competition."

He mentioned that he'd been having conversations with the guys that ran Florida's Each 1 Teach 1 AAU program, which was founded by former NBA player Amar'e Stoudemire, about having his kids play with them.

Each 1 Teach 1 is the real deal as it relates to elite summer basketball. Players like Ben Simmons, Brandon Knight, Austin Rivers, Jonathan Isaac, Kevin Knox, Joel Berry, Tony Bradley and D'Angelo Russell, to name a few, have suited up for them.

Without having seen his kids play, I didn't say anything. I let Phil do all the talking. But my antenna was raised when he mentioned Each 1 Teach 1. As we parted ways after dinner, he invited me to return to Miami with my fiancée a few weeks later so I could watch his sons work out.

On the second trip, Phil put us up at the historic Fontainebleau Hotel. We pulled up to the address of the workout and my then-fiancée Candance, who is now my wife, and I started shooting each other confused glances.

"I thought we were going to a gym to see these kids work out," I said as we idled in front of an expansive, opulent home with a long driveway lined with gleaming luxury automobiles.

As we were welcomed into the house Candance and I swapped glances again, this time ones of tempered shock.

The mansion had been gutted and turned into a sparkling basketball facility, complete with exact replicas of the Miami Heat's hardwood court from the American Airlines arena, along with the team's plush locker room.

Phil told me that he bought and gutted the house to build this miniature hoops shrine so his kids wouldn't have to go outside to play in the rain. At that point, I realized that Phil wasn't just rich; he had a staggeringly absurd amount of cash at his disposal.

We were playing it cool, but Candance's wide eyes said, *WTF!!! Can you believe this?* I just subtly shrugged my shoulders and pursed my lips, trying to mask my utter disbelief at what we were seeing.

As we watched his kids play for a few short minutes, Candance, who played ball in high school, looked at me seriously for a few seconds and whispered, "Merl, when are you gonna tell this man that his kids can't play?"

"I'm not," I told her. "That ain't my job. At some point, he'll figure that out."

After watching Phil's sons work out, Candance and I left and started walking toward our rental, a nice Buick Lacrosse. Phil came jogging out.

"Hey, take that one," he said, nodding toward one of the luxury cars in the driveway. "Keep it for a few days. You'll have some fun riding around town in that." He was pointing toward a glittering blue, brand-new Aston Martin that cost more than my damn house.

We got in the car and just sat there for a few minutes because I couldn't figure out how to start the damn thing. I ain't never been in, let alone driven an Aston Martin before. I was pushing every button I could see because there was no ignition key.

"What are you doing?" Candance asked.

"I don't know how to start it."

"Merl, don't you get out and ask that man how to start this car and embarrass me. You better figure it out," she chuckled as I scanned all of the controls, pushing whatever buttons I could see.

It took me a few minutes, but I figured it out. We wound up keeping the car for a few days and Phil was right: we sure did have some fun wheeling it around Miami Beach with the music blasting and every set of eyeballs in the vicinity glued to us as we idled at red lights and stop signs.

I called my guy Booby, who was running the Each 1 Teach 1 program, and said, "Hey, man, I know this dude has a boat-load of cash and I'm sure he's paying you and a few other folks a grip to work his kids out or whatever and I have no problem with that. But what I don't want to happen is for you to take this dude's money and make promises that you can't keep. If you're talking about his kids playing for one of your B or C teams, okay. But if you're talking about putting them on your top squad's EYBL roster, you need to stop that right now and just be honest with the dude."

Phil invited us over to one of his other houses for dinner and we were served a ten-course gourmet meal and every possible dessert that you could imagine.

"I didn't know what you guys liked, so I had the chefs prepare everything," Phil said.

One of the things that caught me off guard about his teenage sons wasn't the fact that they had their own BMW X6 and a Range Rover in the driveway. It was the fact that they kept calling their father by his first name, like, "Hey, Phil, guess what?" I am a child of the South and had I struck up the nerve when I was a teenager to call my father by his first name, I shudder to think of what the response would have been.

During dinner, I turned to Phil and told him, "I don't know what your conversations have been with Booby and I don't want to get in the middle of all that. But I will tell you that that program is stocked with some of the best and most talented players in the country. What you want to do is put your kids in a situation where they're gonna play and be successful. These Each 1 Teach 1 kids are superior athletes and superskilled and your kids aren't at that level. I'm just trying to be honest with you."

"I get it," he said, "but I've already got some schools that are looking at them."

"Okay, I'm just telling you," I said with a slightly raised eyebrow, highly dubious. "Don't put yourself in that situation. If they have a B or a C team where your kid can get on the floor and have some success, that's preferable. But don't stick them in the lion's den."

When some folks have a lot of money, they have a difficult time understanding the word *no*. It's simply not a part of their vocabulary.

So the first travel team event that summer was in Sacramento and when the Each 1 Teach 1 team walked into the gym, all swagged out in the latest, flyest Nike gear, I saw Phil's kid in uniform. The first thing I said to myself was, *Aw shit*. The next thing I see is Phil, who flew in on a private jet, walking into the gym. I nodded in his direction but didn't say a thing because I'd already given him my opinion and I was done with it.

The kid probably played twenty seconds, if that. In the second game, maybe he played thirty. Now Phil was pissed as he angrily walked toward me.

I cut him off before he launched in. "Phil, I told you!"

But Phil was resolute and unwavering. "He can play with those kids!"

"That's the coach's decision, Phil. I'm not the coach and I don't control that." But I really wanted to tell him that his son would play more, and probably have way more fun, at a less intense level.

"Well, you need to talk to Booby," he barked.

"I'm not talking to Booby. That's his team and he's gonna coach his team the way he sees fit. I tried to have this conversation with you prior to all of this, about you putting your kid in this situation. But you decided to do what you wanted to do. Again, I told you what I thought was best."

Phil had donated a lot of money to the program with the expectation that they'd feature his son. But some things you simply cannot buy. I tried to warn him. They gladly accepted his cash but definitely weren't ever going to play his kid for any real or meaningful minutes.

Next thing I know, Phil offered me $8,000 to personally come down to Miami and work his oldest son out. The offer was for eight grand per workout session.

"Phil, $8,000 to work your kid out is just ridiculous. I'm not taking your money. Anybody charging you that amount is simply taking advantage of you."

I refused to take a dime from Phil because had I done so, then we'd have had some business transactions going on. And he would definitely have been asking me to do some other things for him through my role as Nike's grassroots director. It would have put me in a compromising situation, and I wasn't gonna let that happen.

When Phil was arrested in 2016 at one of his Miami estates, he was charged with a massive $1.3 billion Medicaid and Medicare fraud scheme. At the time, it was the largest single criminal health care fraud case ever brought by the US Department of Justice. Federal prosecutors, in their presentencing memorandum, described his conduct as "pernicious, premeditated, and part of a life-long pattern of disrespect for the law... This was not one criminal act but hundreds of choices to break the law, even thousands, for more than a decade."

Upon the breaking news of his arrest, I immediately remembered one of his comments to me: "I've already got some schools that are looking at them."

It turned out that his son Morris's dream school was the University of Pennsylvania. It was later learned that Phil had convinced Penn's coach at the time, Jerome Allen, a former NBA player and two-time Ivy League Player of the Year for the Quakers in the mid-'90s, to come down to Miami to work his son out, flying him in on a private jet. At the conclusion of that workout, Phil handed him a plastic bag filled with $18,000 in cash. More visits and cash payments followed, with Jerome being put up in the swankiest hotels, having limousines at his disposal and receiving choice tickets to Miami Heat games.

Allen knew that Morris Esformes wasn't good enough to play D-I college ball, but I guess the money got good to him because he placed the kid on Penn's priority list of recruits. Ivy League schools don't offer scholarships, but by telling the admissions office that he was a preferred recruit for the basketball program, Morris was granted admission to the prestigious Wharton School of Business. Allen later testified that he'd received $300,000 from Esformes to help his son get into Penn, even though he had no chance of ever suiting up for the Quakers.

At trial, Allen said, "I just didn't think he was good enough. He was five-foot-eight, wasn't overly athletic. He could handle the ball fairly well and in my opinion at that time, he wasn't good enough to help our program win."

Allen, who was fined $200,000 but did not receive any prison time for his role in accepting Esformes's bribes, received a fifteen-year show-cause penalty from the NCAA, meaning he's not eligible to coach in college until 2035.

But he remains highly regarded in coaching circles, having spent the past six years as one of Brad Stevens's top assistants with the Boston Celtics. When Stevens resigned to step into the general manager role in Boston, Jerome was one of the candidates for the head coaching gig. He also interviewed for the Portland Trail Blazers job. In June of 2021, he left Boston and accepted an assistant coaching position with the Detroit Pistons.

I fully understand the depth of Philip Esformes's criminality as it related to his business, but I can say that as a man and a person, he was very good to me and my family. After I'd gotten to know Phil, Candance found a knot in her breast. She was in pain and her doctors in South Carolina said it would take a few months before they could schedule the necessary tests. In one of my conversations with Phil, we were talking about our families and I mentioned what was going on. Before we hung up, I told him that I'd be in Miami in a few days to check out some of the top kids down there.

"Okay," Phil said, "call me when you get down here."

When I touched down and called, he said, "Hey, can you get Candance down here now?"

"For what?"

"You said she's in pain and she needs to see a doctor to get some tests done," he said. "I'm concerned. I don't want this thing to be cancerous while the doctors up there are making her wait, saying that they can't get her in for tests until a few months. I'm gonna have my assistant call her."

Phil's assistant called her, they immediately arranged a flight to Miami that landed at 1:00 a.m. and he had his own personal doctor see her the very next morning at 9:00 a.m. She got X-rays, had the images of her breast put on a CD and shared all of the necessary information electronically with her doctors in South Carolina. In a few weeks, she was able to have a surgical procedure to remove the growth. To this day, we're super appreciative of what he did for us.

I know that there are many facets to people's personalities. As for Phil, I can say that, despite his crimes, we saw a piece of his humanity and compassion.

After Phil served close to five years in prison, Donald Trump commuted his twenty-year sentence to time served in December of 2020. But without a full pardon, his conviction still stands.

Another bizarre parent story involved a kid down south who was making some major noise on the prep basketball scene. I'd often visit his home city because it's a breeding ground for some of the top talent in the country, producing studs year after year. I went to one of his high school games and was impressed. He was definitely a future pro, with some suggesting that he could skip college altogether and go straight to the league. This was at the time when a crop of the best prep players were making that jump and by-passing the NCAA.

I tried to meet his momma, but she made it clear that she had no interest in talking to me. I'd been sending the kid some Nike packages for a minute, but his mom rebuffed and dismissed me at every turn when I tried to say hello. She finally agreed to meet me at an Applebee's for dinner. As we ate and chitchatted, I noticed that she was reserved, but with a quick tongue.

After some small talk, I cut to the chase.

"Did I do something over the last few months that made you uncomfortable or offended you?"

"Well," she says, "let's just say that I haven't heard good things about you."

"I don't know who you've been talking to, but I hope you give me the benefit of the doubt moving forward and judge me by my actions as opposed to what some folks have to say. Because in this business, everyone wants something and I can't please everybody."

The rest of the evening went well. She let her guard down and we had a good conversation. By the time we were heading to our cars, she was laughing. So after that, I put her son on that list of the most coveted recruits, those guys that get the best packages via FedEx every month.

Mom turned out to be supersweet and the more we talked, the more we got along. In addition to sending her son packages, I started sending her some of the best women's shoes and gear that the company had to offer, thousands of dollars' worth of product. Those packages were being sent to the kid's former youth coach, who was now serving as his personal trainer and Mom's de facto adviser. I'd check in with her every couple of weeks to keep the lines of communication open.

During one of those calls, I asked her, "Hey, how do you like that stuff you've been getting?"

"What stuff?"

"The stuff I've been sending you."

"Oh, the sneakers and the sweat suit you sent a few weeks back? Yeah."

"Sneakers and sweat suit? Is that all you've gotten?"

"Yeah."

"You've got to be kidding. I've been sending you boxes of stuff for about a month and a half now!"

It turns out that the youth coach/personal trainer/adviser had been stealing all the stuff I sent her and giving it to his wife.

Anyway, it got to the point where she invited me to the house and now we were cool. The kid and I got cool and as the season progressed, he just started annihilating the competition, putting up impressive numbers with an offensive arsenal that was tailor-made for the NBA.

At the close of the season, the kid was named the Naismith Prep Player of the Year and he was among the top ten recruits in his class. So of course, he gets invited to participate in the Jordan Brand All-American game.

On paper, only the players are flown in at no cost, with their hotels and meals all taken care of. And the swag bags they receive are ridiculous. But in some instances, the parents get the star treatment as well. Because when one of those top kids says, "I ain't coming unless my family gets flown in and gets a room at the hotel," guess what? You do what you have to do to make sure that kid shows up and plays in the game. So we took care of Mom and Stepdad's flight and hotel room.

One night in New York a few days prior to the game, when a few of my guys from Nike were stepping out on the town with our girlfriends, we invited Mom and Stepdad to come join us. It was a couples' thing. We were at this club in the Meatpacking District, jamming to the music, talking and laughing and having a good time. I ordered up some bottles for the table but the stepdad was drinking bourbon, so I asked our server to just get him another glass.

He began to shoot me some mad dog stares and then he got in Mom's ear and I could tell by her body language that he wasn't saying nothing pleasant. She started crying and a few seconds later she screamed out, "Merl, get him!"

As he approached I heard him shout, "You fucking her!"

I stood up and got in a position to defend myself. I didn't want to swing on the dude, but if he swung first, hey, he was gonna have to eat what was coming. He stopped short, looked at all of the guys that were with us, and yelled, "You fucking all of these dudes!"

We all just sat there, confused, looking at each other like, *What the hell is wrong with this dude?* The good time had come to a screeching halt. Finally, he fixed his unhinged look back on me and walked out of the club.

As you can imagine, Mom was a mess. We asked if she wanted to go back to the hotel and after composing herself, she said, "Fuck him. I'll deal with that later."

We somehow rallied enough to hit up a few more spots, grab a late-night meal and then get back to the hotel at around four in the morning. This fool had put the bolt lock on the door and haphazardly thrown all of her stuff out into the hallway. We went down to the front desk to ask if they had any vacant rooms, but there were none. We spent the next hour checking every nearby hotel in Manhattan, to no avail. Finally we gave up, and she came to the room that I shared with my girlfriend at the time and the three of us passed out.

A few hours later, dude checked out of the hotel and went back home. They got divorced shortly thereafter. As for the kid, he decided to bypass college, got drafted, and I helped him get his first sneaker deal. He went on to play fifteen-plus years in the league.

These are just a small sample of the many crazy stories that I could share regarding parents during the years I spent in the shoe business.

The EYBL was in its embryonic stage the year before I took the grassroots job at Nike. Prior to that, we had the All-American Camp that was competing with the adidas ABCD Camp. Both were pipelines for elite talent. We also had separate summer tournaments like the Hoop Jamboree and Peach Jam. But the model had gotten old after a really good ten-year run or so. We were trying to get ahead of the curve by instituting a new structure.

The idea of the EYBL was initially met with a lot of resistance by the folks running their own AAU programs because they'd been making a living off of running their own events. They'd cut a deal with their local hotels and reserve a block of rooms, getting a slice of every room that was booked by the visiting teams. They'd also come to an agreement with their local venue and get a cut of the gate and concessions and parking. They'd charge each college coach who attended $500 apiece for a flimsy packet while selling their scouting service subscriptions on top of that.

These folks, most of whom didn't have regular jobs, were making money hand over fist if they had a high-profile event. They could easily pocket six figures in a few months off of these events alone, some of which could be reinvested to attract the top talent and make the program stronger. The whole thing was a hustle.

They'd spread that cash around, telling the best kids, some of whom lived on the other side of the country, "Hey, come and play with me for the summer. Your folks won't have to worry about paying for travel, hotel rooms, food or rental cars when we hit the road. I'll fly you everywhere you need to go and you'll be well taken care of."

Long gone were the days in the '80s and '90s where the high school coach had all the juice as it related to recruiting. He was now as irrelevant to the process as the sixth-period earth sciences teacher. When I moved to Chicago, I'd heard the stories about the coach at one of the city's powerhouse schools who had a monopoly on the best talent at the time, and how he personally profited when college coaches were recruiting his players.

He actually had a menu printed up detailing the cost of each interaction. He charged $50 for a phone call, $500 for a home visit and $2,500 for a kid to sign a letter of intent. And that was just for him. The player and his family might have had a separate asking price.

But that power shifted when the shoe companies came in and took over the summer. Now the AAU guys flexed all the muscle. For example, there was a guy running one of the top AAU programs in America. I mean, they were kicking ass and for a minute seemingly had the best talent in the country. He sent one of his top players to a celebrated Big East program with the understanding that when the kid went to the league, he'd be the one handling his agent stuff and getting a cut of his rookie deal because he had a relationship with one of the top agents in the game.

Well, the head coach at the Big East program had his own

relationship with a top agent, where he was getting a cut of his top players' rookie deals. So when the player went pro, he signed with the coach's agent. And the AAU guy said, "Okay, you bastard, you'll never get another one of my kids ever again."

And sure enough, no one affiliated with that AAU program ever went to that school again. They basically alienated the university from one of its deepest and most robust talent pools. Once a major power that competed for national championships, that school is now a middling afterthought and hasn't been a player on the national scene since.

If you put it under a microscope, you can start to draw conclusions about how a certain program has a disproportionate amount of kids that sign with Franklin Street Partners over the years. Same with another program and CAA or the Wasserman Group to simply name a few. And it's not just agencies, but marketing reps and financial planners as well.

Certain coaches open their programs up to these people. It's not every coach, but there are definitely some that steer players to certain folks in exchange for a kickback and a percentage of their rookie deals. It's all one big money grab. If anyone thinks that there is such a thing as a clean big-time program, they need to wake up and smell the donkey shit. Somewhere along the line, even the so-called cleanest of programs has some dirt if you look close enough.

And when it comes to recruiting, everyone knows how the real game is played, and how the head coaches pass on those responsibilities to their Black assistant coaches. They know everything that's going on with a top player's recruitment; they're actually pulling the strings, but maintain enough distance to have some plausible deniability if shit hits the fan.

You mean to tell me that Rick Pitino was oblivious to

the fact that one of his Black assistants was paying strippers to have sex with prospective players during their recruiting visits? Or that he had no idea about the hundred grand payment from adidas to Brian Bowen Sr. to get his son to sign with Louisville? That Eddie Sutton wasn't aware that Emery Worldwide was picking up packages filled with cash from the Kentucky basketball offices in the '80s? That Tim Floyd had no clue that USC boosters were showering O. J. Mayo with jewelry, clothes and, oh yeah, two hundred grand? I mean, damn, Sean Miller was caught on tape talking about buying players, specifically mentioning the $100,000 payment to land Deandre Ayton. Will Wade down at LSU was recorded as well, speaking about the sweet deals he'd put together to acquire players. C'mon, folks, let's keep it real.

Will Wade and Sean Miller have also denied ever helping facilitate payments to secure recruits.

The other part of the hustle is when the AAU programs send their coaches on to become assistants at various universities. They charge a fee to the school that gets recycled back into the program and now they have a pipeline to its top talent. That's the lay of the land. And I'm okay with the hustle—it's how everyday business is conducted—but let's let the kid and his family also eat off the hustle without being vilified.

That's why this whole notion of defrauding a university is a crock of shit, because in reality, they are the actual ones who are defrauding the kids and themselves.

So if we're being honest, it ain't just Brian Bowen that should have been ineligible at the age of thirteen; it's every player at a high-profile program if we're following the NCAA rule book to the letter. Because they've been flying for free, eating for free, staying in hotels for free, their mommas and daddies as well, along with having been hit off with cash and tens of thousands of dollars' worth of free product for years.

Now, those opportunities for AAU teams to host those lucrative events would be few and far between because we were instituting this new structure, the EYBL, a uniform league played at various locations throughout the summer, eventually crowning a national champion. And it was met with a tsunami of opposition by the majority of our program directors because now we were taking food off of their table.

At the EYBL we went to a thirty-second shot clock about two or three years before the NCAA decided to institute it. My thought process was, *Look, even if we can't always prepare these athletes to play at the highest level, we can at least help them learn how to play faster.*

We also changed the format, moving away from marquee events where teams gained entry by featuring a top player or two, and focusing instead on the top all-round teams. No more riding the coattails of one supertalented kid. That wasn't gonna fly anymore. If your team was good enough and you qualified and got in? Cool. If not, sorry, bruh.

So we went to a league structure with a regular season and a playoff, ending with a national championship. Previously, you'd have ten or so events over the summer, all Nike-sponsored events, with each of those having a champion. So there was never really one team that could say it was the national champion that summer.

We were meticulous about how we broke up the conferences and divisions. We wanted to make it fair for every team so that no one conference was superstacked. We considered all angles in terms of how we built the infrastructure, how we picked the various geographic locations, how we staffed and ran them, while still allowing a short window for programs to host their own regional events so they could pocket some cash.

And all of these logistics were reevaluated every year because one summer, a team might be stacked and the next, not so much. The landscape was perpetually shifting, so we made sure to stay on top of it.

I created a map and went through each state, looking at the top fifty high school players, regardless of class, and asking my staff, "How many of these top-fifty kids are in our programs?" For the kids that were with adidas or Under Armour, the question we were asking ourselves was, *Why is that? What are the issues and how do we fix it? What is going on in each major market that we need to readjust?*

Maybe we needed a new organization in a certain state, or an existing organization needed an injection of new leadership. Maybe we needed to get more of the best high school coaches involved. And those were just the best forty programs in the EYBL. But a helluva lot more teams got smaller allocations of cash and gear under our umbrella because they had a player or two that we liked.

We also implemented a major change around team allegiance. Kids frequently jumped from program to program at the drop of a dime. They'd play with one team this weekend and at the next event, they'd be suiting up for an entirely different program from another state. And it was becoming a war among coaching staffs because everyone was trying to poach everyone else's top kid. We couldn't stop it, but we could levy some consequences and decided that if a kid started with one team and jumped to another, they'd have to sit out the next event before playing for their new team.

One of the first kids to do it was Grayson Allen, who went on to play at Duke and is now a member of the Milwaukee

Bucks after spending his first few years in the league with the Utah Jazz and the Memphis Grizzlies. He started out one summer with Atlanta's Southern Stampede. The next weekend, he showed up with Amar'e Stoudemire's crew from Florida, the aforementioned Each 1 Teach 1.

Grayson was a really nice kid. He told us beforehand that he was going to switch teams and we told him that he'd have to sit out the next event. That weekend that he sat out is when he committed to Duke, and he came back for the next event with Each 1 Teach 1, playing with them for the rest of the summer.

So we did an effective job discouraging all of that jumping around and the chaos that it brought about. Because you have to understand that it's not only the parents and coaches that are pissed when a kid jumps ship; some college coaches become enraged because they have an in with certain AAU programs, but now the kid is going to another team where another college coach has that in. We definitely didn't stop it, but we managed to deter it.

On the outside, everything looked great. We were killing it. But when you peeled back the surface, the job was not only mentally and physically draining; it was toxic. Candance could just look at me and tell the toll it was taking.

"Merl, if this is how this job is going to affect you, it isn't worth it," she said.

And there were three other incidents to come that convinced me that, sooner or later, it was gonna be time to move on.

11

The first scenario grew out of one of our annual analysis sessions. The glaring issue at that time was our presence, or lack thereof, in New York City.

The Gauchos program that we previously backed had a rich history dating back decades. They'd once been the gold standard of AAU basketball, suiting up the likes of Rod Strickland, Ed Pinckney, Pearl Washington, Kenny Anderson, Jamal Mashburn, God Shammgod, Felipe López, Lloyd Daniels, Mark Jackson, Stephon Marbury, Kemba Walker, John Salley and a slew of other New York City legends over the years.

But they were now in a state of disarray. They had severe mismanagement issues, their talent level was way down, they'd been busted having stripper parties in the gym, they faced major staff and player turnover, and we were not going to bring them back until they underwent a substantial overhaul.

So there was a huge void to fill. We had two really good programs in the Albany City Rocks and the Long Island Lightning. And Jimmy Salmon's program across the water in North Jersey, the Playaz, a former adidas outfit that we'd recently brought into the Nike fold, was a force. But he only had but so many spots on his roster. And you never wanted to be caught without having a flagship program in a fertile breeding ground like New York. So we started looking around for a new organization to bring in.

When you're assessing these potential partnerships, you want to make sure that you're bringing in an outfit that has a strong organizational infrastructure, that has a layered talent base starting at least with the fourteen-and-under division, that has reputable management and coaches and a proven track record for doing things the right way.

The last thing you want to do is bring a program on board simply because they've got a few talented kids, only later to find out that one of its directors or coaches has a history of pedophilia or violent felonies or drug trafficking convictions.

So we did our due diligence, looked at a lot of potential teams and programs that we could sponsor and only one checked all the boxes: Pro Scholars Athletics, better known as the PSA Cardinals.

I went to a couple of my trusted dudes in the coaching fraternity that knew the New York area inside and out: Tony Chiles, an assistant at St. John's at the time, and Book Richardson, who was on the staff at Arizona. Both gave the PSA Cardinals the thumbs-up.

So I went to New York to check them out. I watched their high school and middle school kids and they looked to have everything in place: good coaching and a solid outfit. They'd need a minute to ascend to that elite level, but they had everything we were looking for.

And with a major Nike sponsorship behind them, they'd be attracting some of the top kids in the market in short order. Because once those kids start posting on social media, showing off the latest Kobes, LeBrons, KDs, Kyries and the limited-edition EYBL league-exclusive shoes, they'd start attracting high-end talent.

During the negotiation, part of my pitch was that I would not be bringing in another team under our umbrella, that they'd be our flagship program in New York, that they wouldn't have to compete against another Nike team in the city for talent. So we agreed to terms and our New York issue had been solved.

Shortly after signing the deal, Lynn abruptly told me that he wanted me to sign another New York team. "They got a couple of kids who are really good and we need them under our grassroots umbrella," he said.

This particular group had one kid with major D-I potential and another who looked like he might be able to play at a midmajor. But the program had no feeder system in place, no proven track record like the PSA Cardinals had. Zip. Nada.

The truth was, Lynn wanted to do a favor for one of his influential friends in the entertainment industry, who was affiliated with the team. It went back to what I told Coach Raveling, that I refused to be anybody's puppet, that if I was going to be the director, then I needed to have the final say.

"See, Lynn, this is the same shit I had that conversation with Rav about. You're trying to bring this program in on the slick and I don't have a relationship or anything to do with them. When I made the PSA deal, I told them that we'd put all of our resources behind them as Nike's flagship New York City program," I explained. "And I'm not going against my word. So, no."

I told him, though, that we could compromise, give this other team some gear and a small stipend, but we were rocking with the PSA Cardinals as our New York City EYBL crew.

Lynn pushed back to the point that I told him if this kind of thing was going to continue I wanted to be sent back to Chicago on the NBA side or I was out.

It was all part of a constant stream of side hustles that were not for the company's benefit. I refused to budge and eventually, after a lot of back and forth, he left it alone. That other program is no longer in existence today. Meanwhile, the PSA Cardinals are one of the most respected teams in the land, sending players like Ty Jerome, Cole Anthony, Mo Bamba, Omari Spellman and, most recently, UConn's James Bouknight into the pros, along with a bunch of kids that played major college ball.

Despite winning that tug-of-war with Lynn, it continued to eat at me, especially knowing that it wouldn't be the last.

The second of those incidents involved Team Takeover in Washington, DC, one of our strongest programs that has produced the likes of Ty Lawson, Victor Oladipo and the Grant brothers, Jerami and Jerian. They weren't just producing pros; they also sent a ton of really talented kids to major colleges. Their deal was up and I was negotiating with their director, Keith Stevens, to bring them back under a new contract.

The Washington, DC, area has long been a hotbed for some of the country's best talent. So as far as we were concerned, Keith and his Team Takeover organization were extremely valuable. You never want to be without a top team in the DC market, which encompasses a lot of prime territory stretching from Maryland all the way through northern Virginia. It's a huge recruiting base for some of the top universities and Keith was the man to see now that the area's previous top program, an adidas outfit named DC Assault, had lost its luster.

There was no question whatsoever that it was critical to keep Team Takeover in the Nike family. But it was not going to be easy. Under Armour was in hot pursuit and offering Keith gobs of money. They already had a really good team in DC Premier and had they added Team Takeover, they would have owned that prime corridor.

Under Armour went all out with their offer. Keith and I had a great relationship and we were always honest with one another, even when the truth was uncomfortable. He sent me the offer details, and I was blown away when I read them.

The deal included a personal portion for Keith, including generous consulting fees, an enviable product allowance and a separate budget for personal travel, meals and lodging. On the team side, there were yearly stipends, a bountiful organizational product allowance, a bonus structure that would pay the team an extra $25,000 for every McDonald's All American that came out of the program, $10,000 for every tournament that they won and other incentives. When everything was factored in, without including the bonuses and incentives, Under Armour was offering Keith $300,000 a year.

And I knew that there was no way that we could ever get close to that number. On paper at least.

Boo Williams and his elite outfit down in Hampton, Virginia, which has churned out the likes of Allen Iverson, Alonzo Mourning, J. R. Reid, Jarrett Jack, J. J. Redick and Joe Smith, had the highest allocation of any program in our yearly budget at $100,000 a year. I knew I couldn't go any higher than that, but Carlton and I sat down and tried to come up with creative ways to at least get Keith to think about staying with us.

Team Takeover had been getting about $85,000 a year from us and I knew that getting that number even higher was going to be difficult. But we came up with some creative ways for Keith to pocket some serious cash. I was down in Baltimore having some conversations with Carmelo Anthony and his folks about establishing his own AAU outfit in that prime Bmore market, Team Melo, so when that wrapped up I jumped on the beltway and drove to the Marriott in Upper Marlboro to sit down with Keith and try to get the Team Takeover deal done.

"Keith, this is what we can do on the personal side of your deal," I told him. "We can give you $25,000 for your own live event in the summer. We'll continue to pay for the Christmas event that you already run, plus we'll throw in another $20,000 for you to host something around Thanksgiving. Whatever you make off the events is yours to keep."

Carlton had already negotiated the team side of the deal that Keith found acceptable. On paper, it was going to be in the $100,000 range, but with the Team Takeover events that we would fund at no expense to him, he had the potential to pocket a sweet chunk of change, well into six figures, for both him and the program.

And he was cool with that, so we shook hands and had a gentleman's agreement. The only thing we needed to do was draw up the contract.

Little did I know at the time that Lynn wanted Keith and Team Takeover to take the Under Armour deal. Because Kevin Durant's Nike contract was up for renegotiation. And KD and his people didn't mess with Keith's folks. I couldn't tell you why, but it's some old neighborhood, DC beef. There's some serious animosity there for whatever reason and KD wanted his own program, the DC Blue Devils, to bump Team Takeover out of that slot.

Lynn was trying to do everything he could to appease KD. And frankly, Kevin could not stand Lynn. Did not like the dude at all. He felt continually underappreciated due to Lynn and the company's focus on LeBron. But at that time, Kevin was proving that he was on LeBron's level, that he was one of the best players of all time, and the time had come for him to get top billing.

And Under Armour had just made KD a ridiculously lucrative offer to leave Nike and join them. They proposed close to $30 million a year for ten years, including stock options and other incentives, equity in the company and a community center in his hometown of Seat Pleasant, Maryland, that would bear his mother's name.

They also offered to make him the president of Under Armour's basketball division. In total, they were committing 10 percent of its annual marketing budget to him, despite the fact that only 1 percent of their close to $3 billion in revenues at the time came from hoops. Under Armour's shares were up over 96 percent from the previous year, with Nike's stock appreciating at a 21.5 percent clip. They were going all in.

Nike's offer would give KD a base and minimum royalty guarantee that would equal no less than $20 million a year. KD's, LeBron's, Kobe's and later Kyrie's products were the force behind the company's post–Michael Jordan resurgence in the basketball market. And if Nike were to somehow lose KD, who had ascended to that LeBron and Kobe category, it would have been a major source of corporate embarrassment. Heads were definitely gonna roll if that happened.

The previous year, Under Armour had only done $30 million in basketball shoe sales, while KD's signature Nike shoes generated $85 million alone in 2013.

So Lynn was trying to do everything possible to retain him, and if that meant kicking Keith Stevens and Team Takeover to the curb in the process to make KD happy, so be it.

At the time, I knew none of this. So when I called Lynn to let him know that Carlton and I had agreed with Keith on a new deal, I did not anticipate his response.

As I started walking through the details, he cut me off midsentence. "What? You don't have the authority to do that deal, Merl! You're gonna call him right now and tell him that you're sorry but you went ahead and made the deal without being authorized to do so. You need to tell him that the deal is being rescinded."

"Lynn, what are you talking about? I've been doing these deals for years and you know we can't lose our top program in the DC market. What the hell do you mean I don't have the authority?"

We angrily went back and forth, with him insisting that I call Keith and tell him the deal was dead. I refused.

"If that's how this is gonna go down, you need to call him yourself and tell him," I said.

Ultimately Lynn called one of my colleagues and directed him to call Keith and inform him that I didn't have the authority and that Nike wouldn't honor the deal. I was indignant. So what eventually happened? At the eleventh hour, Nike matched Under Armour's $300 million offer to Kevin Durant, along with the inclusion of other incentives like a $50 million retirement package. He opted to re-sign with the Swoosh. That deal runs through 2024.

As for Keith Stevens and Team Takeover, once KD signed and was firmly back in the fold, Nike went back to renegotiate his deal. But he held them to the fire and eventually signed for a lot more than the original deal that Carlton and I had put in place.

At Nike, when you hit your ten-year mark with the company, you're given a paid six-week sabbatical. As my tenth year was coming to a close, I went down to Chris Paul's camp in Winston-Salem, then to Atlanta to make my rounds. Once that wrapped, I went up to South Carolina to finish up some minor stuff before getting my sabbatical started. Back in Greenville, I got an agitated call from Lynn.

"Hey, Merl, where are you?" he asked, irritated.

"I'm down in South Carolina."

"What are you doing there?"

I explained to him that I'd been down at Chris Paul's camp, then in Atlanta for a few days and now I was back at home to get my sabbatical started.

"Your sabbatical doesn't start for another day. Get your ass on a plane and back to Portland. We need to sit down and do your annual performance review."

Every year that I'd been at Nike, my year-end review had always been done over the phone.

"Shit, Lynn, since we're on the phone let's just do my year-end review now," I told him, trying to hide my disgust.

"No! You need to get here so we can do it."

"Why do I need to come into the office to do this? We've always done these over the phone. Why now all of a sudden?"

"Because we haven't seen you in the office lately."

"That's because I've been on the road doing my damn job!"

"Well, your staff hasn't seen you."

"What the hell are you talking about, Lynn? My whole staff is on the road at this time of year!"

"Merl, your ass needs to be in Portland tomorrow. You better be here."

It was all part of the power struggle, with him taking every opportunity to remind me that he was the boss.

I'd already made arrangements for my older son to fly into Atlanta from Houston, where he lived with his mom, so I could spend the next six weeks with him and my parents in Greenville. I had to scramble to find someone to drive to Atlanta to scoop him up. I would be flying across the country for an hour meeting and then flying home the same day.

I tried to stay as calm as possible, but I was fuming. I flew six hours to sit across from Lynn at an Outback Steakhouse for an hour, just for him to tell me how I was doing in terms of my job performance.

The gist of my review? "You're doing a good job, Merl."

On that flight back from Portland, the resounding voice in my head kept getting louder and louder. *Get the hell up outta here.*

By the summer of 2014, I'd had enough. I knew those would be my final days at Nike. By the time we flew into Las Vegas for that year's LeBron James Skills Academy, I'd already cleaned out my office.

The LeBron camp is the culmination of all of Nike's skills academies. The Kyrie camp assembled all the best point guards, Amar'e Stoudemire's had the top big men, Kobe's gathered the most dynamic shooting guards, KD's was where the elite wings got it in and Bron's joint was the coup de grâce. It was where not only the best prep prospects regardless of position were summoned, but also where the crème de la crème of college players worked as counselors.

For the past few years, Candance, a small group of her girlfriends and some of my best friends from Greenville used the opportunity as a minivacation as well. My dudes would get their own hotel rooms. Candance and her crew would stay at my cousin's house nearby. My cousin was superconnected in the Vegas entertainment industry, and she always hooked us up with tickets to the hottest shows and concerts. Thanks to her we'd get on the VIP list and walk past the velvet ropes at the most exclusive clubs and rooftop lounges.

We all looked forward to that Vegas trip each year. The fellas would get some golf in, the ladies would get their hang on and at the end of the day when my business was conducted, we'd be out and about having a good time at a Nas concert or tearing up a sizzling dance floor.

So, as usual, I got a suite at the players' hotel, the Embassy Suites on Paradise Road, which is off of the strip. The camp ran from Wednesday through Sunday, but I was on the ground a week prior because it's my show. I had to ensure that everything ran smoothly.

I had a little extra pep in my step because it was always a great event, and a fun time in Vegas with family and friends. And I knew this was gonna be my swan song. I was tired. All of the drama over the last four years had worn me down. Mentally, I was running on fumes, just fatigued and exhausted. And I was ready for a change.

People saw the glitz and glamour, the courtside seats at NBA games and Final Fours, dinners with Hall of Famers at the most upscale restaurants, but they didn't see the flip side. Beyond everything, I just didn't enjoy the job anymore.

The day before camp officially started, as folks were arriving and checking into their hotels and getting settled, Lynn asked me to meet him for breakfast at his hotel.

As soon as I sat down, he cut right to the chase.

"I'm hearing all this stuff about how unhappy you are. And I noticed that you've cleaned out your cubicle and desk. People keep asking me if you're quitting, Merl. So if you're gonna quit, why don't you just go ahead and quit."

After all of his bullshit over the years and all of the animosity I'd built up, I just broke into a half grin. "Alright, cool," I replied. "I quit."

I got up and walked out, feeling like a thousand-pound weight had been lifted from my shoulders. I got back to the Embassy Suites, Candance helped me pack up my stuff, I checked out and then got another room on the strip so we could enjoy the rest of our vacation.

Within ten minutes of leaving that breakfast, my company cell phone was cut off, and my personal phone was ringing nonstop. Some of my former staff members were frantically calling, telling me that Lynn called hotel security and that they'd gone up to my suite to physically have me removed from the property.

Lynn was telling everyone, and these messages were being relayed to me in real time, that he'd just fired me.

So me and my crew just hung out in Vegas for a few days and made the most of it. The night I quit, the news was circulating as I had dinner with friends and colleagues that worked in a number of NBA front offices. They'd called, invited me out and showed me some real love. They didn't say one word about Nike or Lynn. We had a great meal, filled with laughter and encouragement about what lay ahead for me. It was a really nice release.

I never went back to Portland. My apartment was already mostly packed up. I hired a moving company, and Carlton and my former assistant helped me ship my car. I went straight to South Carolina to get some rest and decompress.

I wasn't looking to jump back into a new job right away. I knew that I needed to recharge.

I'd socked away a pretty decent rainy-day fund over my thirteen years at Nike. I owned some rental properties, had a nice 401K, a hardy personal savings account and some stock options. I wasn't pressed.

So for a little more than a year, I just chilled. And I loved it. I did some consulting work here and there, nothing major, but people kept calling to ask if I was interested in a number of projects and ventures. The majority of those I declined. One of the projects that I'd been asked to help out with involved an organizational push to get more head coaching opportunities for men of color in college basketball. So I worked on that for a little bit.

But for the most part, I was simply enjoying my family, living stress free, happy to walk around the supermarket in shorts and shower shoes for early-morning groceries. After so much time on the road, I savored the time at home.

One of the intriguing offers came from my friend Justin Zanik, an NBA agent who'd been working with Andy Miller. He informed me that he was planning to switch from agenting to an NBA front office job.

"I've been speaking to Andy about you. I think you'd make a fantastic agent. You wanna come over here and take my place? I'll give you my whole book of business."

I got a call from Andy Miller next. He said that he'd been talking to a lot of people who spoke very highly of me and that with Justin leaving, he wanted to talk to me about stepping into the position.

I gave some serious thought to it, but in the end I knew that I did not want to be a sports agent. I told Andy that I appreciated the offer and that I was gonna pass.

Andy called me shortly thereafter.

"Have you ever thought about working for another sneaker company? I'm working on Kristaps Porziŋġis's new deal with adidas. Their guy Jim Gatto and I were talking about you. He's coming to my office in New Jersey and I think the two of you should meet."

It sounded interesting, and I figured a meeting couldn't hurt. My batteries had been recharged and I felt like I was ready to do something. So I flew into Newark, and they had a limo waiting for me and put me up in a Manhattan hotel that night. This was late in the year, around September, some thirteen months after I'd bounced from Nike.

I'd previously only known Andy in passing, so it was good to finally have some substantive conversations with him. My talks with Jim Gatto went really well and I liked what he was proposing.

Because it was so late in the year, Gatto said that they'd like to bring me on as a consultant for three months, and when January came around we could put something more long-term together if it felt like a good fit. I was really pleased when he said I didn't have to manage anyone, I could work from home and they'd bring me in when my relationships and knowledge could be helpful. That sounded great to me.

So the first major thing was for me to attend at their annual late-fall–early-winter basketball meetings at the Nines Hotel in downtown Portland. I sat in on the various presentations and got a chance to meet the folks on the team. I'd known some of them by face because we'd been in the same sphere for years. It was good to get to know them beyond a passing wave.

And the offer was refreshing. I didn't have to manage an entire staff. I didn't have to be in the office for a sixty-hour work week. All I had to do was be available to work on certain projects when they called.

I was happy to be around the game again, without all the day-to-day bullshit. They'd ask me about certain markets, certain kids and things that I knew like the back of my hand. So after three months, Gatto came back with a six-figure offer, plus incentives for a three-year consulting deal.

"Merl, we really like you," he told me. "You've already proven to be a tremendous resource with a knowledge of this industry and a black book of relationships that could be really helpful to us. We're trying to grow and be ahead of the curve and feel like you're someone who can definitely help us get there."

I was excited and ready to get back in the game. So I signed a term sheet going into 2016 for a three-year consulting deal. I immediately went to work, studying and analyzing their summer events and how they could best expand their middle school apparatus, which had become a major adidas priority.

We were also in talks with the folks over at Cowboys Stadium to host the adidas Gauntlet, their version of Nike's EYBL, at the sparkling Dallas facility. In addition, I got to experience adidas Nations camp, where they bring in the best of their high school athletes, with college players serving as counselors.

I was slowly getting back in the mix and amped up for the new role. I felt fantastic.

But that feeling wouldn't last very long.

12

Early into my adidas tenure was when Giannis Antetokounmpo, now a two-time league MVP, world champion and the 2021 Finals MVP with the Milwaukee Bucks, had just completed his transition from a developing player with immense potential to being a certified global superstar.

He'd just been named Second Team All-NBA at the time, was a first-time All-Star and won the league's Most Improved Player award. His four-year, $100-million contract extension with the Bucks was about to kick in and everyone around the league was talking about his glowing future.

My friend Alex Saratsis was basically the guy who found Giannis when he was just a bony, angular young teenager playing in pickup basketball runs in Greece. His competition was subpar, but if you knew what you were looking at, you'd recognize his talent was rare. Several years before, while I was still at Nike, he'd sent me a grainy video of this painfully gawky six-foot-eight kid coming off ball screens and whipping passes with his left hand that went whizzing past his unsuspecting defenders' ears at light speed.

I tried to convince my Nike colleagues on the global side of the business, Susan Mulders, who was the company's international basketball marketing manager, and our international scout, Rich Sheubrooks, to invite him to play in the Nike Hoop Summit, which pits a team of the best young international kids against those from the eighteen-and-under Team USA development squad.

But they couldn't get past the weak competition in the clips that Alex had sent to me.

"I don't care who he's playing against," I told them. "What this kid is doing is gonna translate at every level."

Still, they weren't feeling me and the kid didn't receive an invite to compete in the game. Fast-forward a little bit, and now Giannis was playing semipro ball for the Filathlitikos club in Athens, where his raw athleticism and developing skills were drawing gasps from both NBA and international scouts. At the age of eighteen, he signed with CAI Zaragoza, one of the top European teams in Spain for four years, but his contract came with an NBA buyout clause.

Sure enough, the lanky teenager with sinewy arms that stretched as far as a pterodactyl's wings was selected with the fifteenth overall pick in the first round of the 2013 NBA draft.

So now Giannis was blossoming into the rarest of generational talents as a young, charismatic, handsome player that could single-handedly lift the spirits of not only a franchise and a city, but the entire country of Greece and his parents' homeland of Nigeria as well. Alex, who'd since become one of his agents, was frustrated about one aspect of his prized client's situation: his shoe deal.

The kid nicknamed the Greek Freak had ascended to an All-NBA level with the Nike swoosh embroidered on every stitch of his clothing, but his deal was only paying him $20,000 per year at the time. And that was about to change in a major way.

Adidas was paying larger and larger sums to compete with Nike for top-tier players. They were also trying to expand their point-guard-heavy lineup, which featured the likes of James Harden, Damian Lillard and Derrick Rose, to include more dynamic wing players. They'd paid just under $5 million a year for then-Knicks star Kristaps Porziņģis in the previous negotiation that Andy Miller told me he'd been working on. And if Porziņģis hit certain scoring benchmarks or became an All-Star starter, the deal could increase to $7 million.

Alex saw that as the floor for Giannis's next deal because despite playing in a small Midwest market like Milwaukee, his international appeal was massive.

"I've always said that I think he's one of those guys that has the potential to transcend his market," Alex told ESPN at the time. "I think he's one of the few players that could have a truly global appeal."

The stage was set for a bidding war. And with my relationship with Alex, I was poised to be right in the thick of it. Adidas's director of global sports, Jim Gatto, and Chris Rivers, the director of grassroots basketball, asked me to connect with Alex because they weren't having any luck making inroads. And it didn't take long to figure out why.

Unbeknownst to me, one of the company's marketing managers was working another angle.

One of Giannis's teammates at that time was Thon Maker, a seven-foot South Sudanese Australian who I'd known since he was in eighth grade, long before he became the tenth pick in the 2016 NBA draft. His guardian, Ed, had brought him and seven of his family members to the United States in pursuit of a better life.

I got a call one day from Ed, asking for $189,000, a bizarrely specific number.

"Well, damn, Ed," I said, trying to control my laughter, "I don't know how you arrived at that exact number, but you might as well round that shit up to a cool, even two hundred grand."

"You think so? Okay, then, I need $200,000."

He said the money would help him take care of the family until Thon's eventual pro money started rolling in, when he'd pay me back. The request made me giggle on the inside because I damn sure wasn't sending him no 200 grand.

Anyway, Thon was an adidas athlete by the time he joined the Bucks roster, so the marketing manager had enlisted him to coax Giannis away from Nike. In fact, the dude promised to buy Thon a new car for his efforts, whether Giannis came aboard or not. The problem was that by bypassing the usual channels, the dude was oblivious to the fact that he was causing some considerable issues.

"They're trying to go around me," Alex angrily told me. "That shit ain't cool, Merl!"

There was a specific window of time during which they were contractually allowed to consider competing offers, but it hadn't opened yet. Alex had also made it clear that they were going to hear everyone out, from Nike to adidas to Under Armour to the Chinese brand La-Ning and everyone else in between. So in my view, all this dude at adidas was doing was risking a tampering allegation and pissing off one of Giannis's most trusted advisers.

When I explained the situation to Gatto and Rivs, the company's basketball bosses, they agreed to tell the dude to stand down and abandon the Thon angle. And I assured them that I could secure a meeting for us to make an official pitch.

Alex agreed to the meeting but insisted that I be present because we had the relationship and he felt comfortable with me being at the table. He didn't have a real connection with the folks at adidas. So we drove together from Chicago to Milwaukee while the company's marketing team went to work spicing up its plans for the final presentation.

Shoe company pitches to athletes like Giannis, once they've proven themselves to be transcendent athletes with international commercial appeal, can morph into giant spectacles. Adidas was prepared to spend roughly a half-million dollars just to make its case, including renting an entire warehouse in downtown Milwaukee to create a unique experience for Giannis and his team. There were going to be custom shoes, slick marketing videos and a highly orchestrated presentation from the brand's top executives.

As for my own prep work, I scraped together any piece of relevant information that I thought could give us a leg up. One of the most important things I learned was that Giannis did not understand or appreciate the tendency for Americans to talk about family when they weren't talking about one's own literal nuclear family.

So trying to pitch him on joining the adidas family would be offensive to him. In an internal email, I fired off some bullet points that I felt were essential to making the best impression possible. I wrote,

- Stay away from "family" references. His immediate/ nuclear family is all he realizes as family!!!
- Is intrigued by expanding his market/presence in China, Greece, Nigeria (internationally).
- Nigeria is an important component to his mother.
- Wants his own clothing line/signature shoe.
- Loves the Kobe10. Should find footwear in our line that's similar and build off that platform.
- Wants involvement in the design process.
- Does not like flashy colors. Likes very basic color schemes.
- Not a lifestyle apparel guy at this point. More interested in upscale sweats and Ts. Could have some interest in lifestyle shoes (NMDs/Yeezys, etc.)
- No real hobbies!!! Ball really is life!!!
- Music… Chance the Rapper, Kendrick Lamar, Migos, etc.

Nike, adidas and Under Armour are like the Americans, Russians and Chinese running intelligence operations on potential assets. Any information that could give us an edge, we were all over it. Anyone we could leverage, we'd lean on. Anything we could do to undermine an adversary, we'd do in a heartbeat.

But just like in the intelligence community, not sharing certain information with internal rivals could sometimes lead to disaster. Such was the case in the Giannis situation.

The day of the big pitch in Milwaukee, I was just getting checked into my hotel room when Alex called me down to the lobby for a late lunch. We had just sat down at the bar when his phone buzzed. He stared at his screen with a disturbed look on his face.

Standing abruptly, staring at me, he yelled, "Y'all set me up!"

"What? What are you talking about, Alex?"

He showed me his phone. Giannis was streaming live on social media outside of the Bucks practice facility, where a giant van had pulled up with adidas gear stacked to the brim.

"Yo, man, adidas came with a truck!" Giannis smilingly declared. "Man, you got everything!"

Thon Maker was standing beside him, with a Cheshire cat's grin plastered on his face, snapping pics with the van's back doors swung wide open as Giannis scooped up numerous pairs of his absolute favorite shoe at the time, the Yeezys, Kanye West's signature line.

If somebody from Nike, who still had him under contract, was watching, they would have been pissed to the highest levels of pisstivity.

"Fuck this meeting!" Alex said, seething. "They're not getting anywhere near Giannis now. I told you I didn't trust them because they were going behind my back and now they've done the shit again! And it's streaming live on the damn internet!"

Instead of falling back like he'd been told, that marketing manager was trying to play hero ball, thinking his slick move would be like Jordan splashing a game-winning shot at the buzzer. But it backfired on him. Big-time.

Because now, a half dozen of adidas's top executives were sitting in a warehouse waiting to deliver a half-million-dollar presentation that wasn't going to happen. Meanwhile, I was listening to Alex take calls from Nike reps as he tried to convincingly explain that he didn't know anything about Giannis and a van full of adidas gear going viral on the internet.

The next several hours were a mad scramble to put the genie back in the bottle. I finally tracked Alex down later after he'd hastily stormed off from our aborted lunch. He was at a local high school gym with one of Giannis's younger brothers.

"Look, man," I said, easing my way in as I approached him, "I want to salvage my relationship with you. They obviously fucked this whole thing up. But at this point, we're all here. Why don't you just listen to the pitch? If it ain't right, oh well. At least it won't be a completely wasted trip."

To my utter surprise, he agreed, but he was as far from enthusiastic as one could get.

The adidas team breathed a sigh of relief. But we all knew that we had unwittingly been placed in a jacked-up position.

To their credit, the presentation was worth every bit of the $500,000. Even though I knew at that point that signing Giannis would be a minor miracle, I was happy to prove my own professional worth by making sure that he got to that presentation.

Giannis walked into the warehouse with his small entourage in tow. Alex was with him, along with his mother, two of his brothers and his girlfriend. Oh, and Thon Maker was there too. He was going to make damn sure he got that car he'd been promised.

It was pitch-black upon entering the warehouse, to the point that you couldn't see your hand if it was raised in front of you. Deeper into the room, spotlights lit up enormous photographs of the company's legendary athletes in action: Muhammad Ali, Kareem Abdul-Jabbar, Pelé and Lionel Messi, among a slew of others.

Set out in front of each photograph was a glass case containing some of the actual shoes that those icons had previously worn in competition. Giannis's eyes were popping out of his head. "They got Ali? THEY GOT ALI!!!" he exclaimed in awe as he peered into the glass case at Ali's calf-length boxing shoes with adidas's three-stripe logo on the side.

A member of the marketing team then guided the group over to an industrial elevator that took us up to the second floor, where the rest of the team was anxiously awaiting. For the next hour, he was the proverbial kid in a candy store. There were prototypes of shoes no one else in the world had seen yet, which he excitedly passed back and forth between his brothers. Storyboard drawings showed the starting point of a Giannis signature shoe and apparel line. And he was loving it. They all were.

Then, out of the blue, I hear, "Hey, Merl, we're about to talk numbers, so would you mind stepping outside?"

I almost looked at the adidas executive like he had seven heads, but managed to maintain my composure. I then looked across the table at Alex, who only agreed to bring Giannis based on our relationship. From his perspective, adidas had proven themselves to be untrustworthy, but he came because we had a history and I pleaded with him. And now they were asking me to leave? Alex laughed sarcastically and threw his hands up. And I knew, if no one else in the room did, what that gesture meant as I slowly walked out, shaking my head.

Giannis went on to re-sign with Nike for $9 million per year, with increasing monetary increments as the contract matured, along with promises of his first signature shoe, which eventually dropped in 2019.

In the summer of 2021, he hoisted the Bill Russell NBA Finals MVP Award after beating Chris Paul's Phoenix Suns. He scored fifty points, snagged fourteen rebounds and blocked five shots in a decisive game six, wearing his Zoom Freak 2 signature Nike shoe. The Zoom Freak 3 model hit retail stores later that summer.

And I'm still laughing at the thought that somewhere in his native Greece or his parents' homeland of Nigeria, there are entire towns of children running through the streets wearing those too-large size-16 shoes, along with whatever other extra-large gear was left over from that adidas van that popped up at the Bucks practice facility back in 2016.

Oh, and as for Thon Maker, I don't know if he ever did get that car.

As I was getting acclimated to the way adidas did business, I got a call from my friend and colleague Raphael Chillious, an assistant coach with Kevin Ollie at the University of Connecticut. Raphael and I had worked together at Nike for a spell before he returned to coaching. He'd made his name in the hoops world previously as the head coach at South Kent, a western Connecticut boarding school that he'd turned into a national powerhouse.

In his five seasons at South Kent, he'd coached the likes of Isaiah Thomas, the five-foot-eight dynamo who went on to star in college at the University of Washington before becoming an All-Star with the Boston Celtics, and Dorell Wright, who played in the NBA for eleven seasons. Chill also coached Dion Walters and Andray Blatche, both future pros.

Chill called to tell me that he was recruiting a six-foot-nine high schooler from Mali, Mamoudou Diarra, who was playing not too far from me at a place called 22 Feet Academy in Anderson, South Carolina. I went to watch him play and liked what I saw. He was long and talented, a good athlete with a very slim build. With some strength training and the proper skill development, he looked like he had the potential to be a solid role player on the college level.

I took another drive out to Anderson to watch him play

again and this time, he was at the end of the bench in street clothes. I called Chill, "Hey, man, the kid didn't play. What's going on?"

"They think he broke his hand."

He didn't have a cast on, and when I asked what the doctors were saying, Chill said he hadn't been to see a doctor because he didn't have insurance.

"Damn, the school didn't send him to see a doctor that they'd pay for?"

Turns out that they hadn't. Instead of making sure that his health was a top priority, they were just sitting the kid out, hoping his hand would eventually feel better. It was wrong. He needed to be seen by a doctor and have some X-rays taken. Because had they put him back out there not knowing the extent of his injury, he could really harm himself.

So I called a good friend of mine who was a doctor and explained the situation. He told me that he wasn't supposed to see the kid if he didn't have insurance and I assured him that I'd take care of the cost of the visit. It turned out that his hand was not broken; it was just a really bad bruise that had the potential to morph into something bigger if it wasn't cared for properly.

Luckily, Mamoudou didn't suffer any long-term damage, and he wound up accepting a scholarship to the University of Cincinnati. But that one minor episode with him at 22 Feet Academy spoke to a larger trend at these fly-by-night "prep schools" that field teams with solid prospects, many of them from overseas.

"Every single day there was something we had to deal with that was outside of our realm of responsibility as coaches," the school's former coach, Richard Gatewood, told the *Louisville Courier Journal* in 2018. "[The players] were living in a converted barn out back of Mike's [school founder and owner Mike Rawson's] house that he had just thrown some plywood and carpet into. None of them were in the correct classes. They were being given plain turkey sandwiches for breakfast. It was just a mess."

Rawson eventually pleaded guilty to conspiracy to commit visa fraud, with one of his international players from Turkey having to spend time in jail due to the school's fraudulent handling of his student visa. Rawson and his wife were also accused of telling the school's players and coaches to lie to law enforcement officials if they were questioned about the academy's living conditions, operations and academic irregularities.

I bring this up to simply say that for every international success story like Giannis Antetokounmpo, there are thousands of untold stories of athletes lured to America to play at places like 22 Feet Academy, which aren't much more than diploma mills with good basketball teams, where players are being taken advantage of while their owners charge exorbitant fees to their families and international handlers, where the kids are being housed in substandard conditions and they're lucky if they're being fed one healthy meal per day.

This is the landscape where some truly sad tales of exploitation are regularly taking place.

Shortly after I started consulting with adidas, I got a call from Andy Miller, the agent who'd previously connected me with adidas. Andy was enthusiastic about a young man who was now working for him by the name of Christian Dawkins, and he asked me if I wouldn't mind being a resource and a mentor to him.

Young aspiring agents like Christian play an essential role in a lot of agencies, similar to the young Black assistant coaches on D-I college staffs whose main job responsibilities are re-cruiting. He can connect with young players in ways that a guy like Andy Miller can't. He can open the necessary doors and build the rapport that gives the agency a better chance of landing big clients. And Christian had a leg up because he wasn't starting from scratch. He was already in possession of an enviable network.

Christian was incredibly bright and remarkably connected. His father, Lou, once a star college player who helped lead the University of Tulsa to the Sweet Sixteen in 1994, was a legendary coach at Saginaw High School in Michigan.

Christian was high school teammates with NBA champion Draymond Green at Saginaw. He'd literally grown up in the school gymnasium, forging relationships with great players along the way.

Always in possession of an entrepreneurial spirit, he started his own AAU team and scouting service as a young teenager. He secured a sneaker deal with Under Armour to outfit his team, and his mother was astonished at the stream of checks made out to her son's company, LOYD Management, that landed in the family mailbox from individuals, high school and even college coaches who paid to subscribe to his scout-ing service.

Christian's younger brother Dorian was a true hoops phe-nom, a preternaturally gifted point guard who'd received a scholarship offer from UCLA as a mere eighth grader. He was presumably the next great player to rise out of Saginaw, but in a summer tournament game held on the campus of Mich-igan State prior to his freshman year in high school, Dorian collapsed and died. It was later revealed that he had a heart defect that had gone undetected.

Christian rebranded his AAU squad, calling it Dorian's

Pride. Some of the players that suited up for the program included Josh Jackson, currently with the Detroit Pistons, the Washington Wizards' Kyle Kuzma and a then-burgeoning young player, Brian Bowen. The relationships that Christian built along the way, dating all the way back to elementary school, were estimable.

He proved himself as a young associate straight out of the gate, working for the firm International Management Advisors, which at one point represented Vince Carter and provided financial management services to LeBron James. There he signed Elfrid Payton, the current Phoenix Suns guard who was the number ten pick out of Louisiana at Lafayette in 2014.

When Christian left IMA to join Andy Miller's agency, ASM Sports, he found himself at the center of a contentious federal lawsuit, with IMA accusing him of steering prospects to ASM while still being employed with them. Christian had also been accused of using Elfrid Payton's credit card to rack up more than $42,000 in Uber rides, which he later explained as being a simple misunderstanding.

The situation soon took on its own name, Ubergate, and when the news surfaced, Andy Miller had to publicly part ways with Christian. But notice that I said publicly. Because despite Christian's name being scrubbed from the ASM website, he was still recruiting and signing players for Andy.

I'd heard about the Uber scandal and some of the things being said about Christian's departure from IMA, but I've heard of crazier things happening in the agency world. The young man was talented, signing and sitting with his first-round picks and their families at the draft when most dudes his age were playing beer pong in the basement of a frat house.

Per Andy's request, I started talking to Christian semiregularly and went about introducing him to my NBA network of general managers, directors of scouting and directors of player personnel.

Christian was superintelligent and aggressive, with a quick, sharp wit. On occasion, I had to remind him of certain protocols because he was not shy about calling people at any time. I received a few messages from my NBA folks that I'd introduced him to, saying things to the effect of, "Hey, man, the young fella needs to slow down. He's calling me at seven on a damn Sunday morning."

Christian's impressive network extended beyond talented players. He was friendly with a lot of folks in the college coaching ranks as well. An assistant coach at Creighton named Preston Murphy used to babysit him when he was a kid back in Saginaw, so Christian was able to leverage that relationship into signing Justin Patton, a seven-footer who'd just completed an outstanding freshman season for the Bluejays and would be selected with the sixteenth overall pick in the 2017 NBA draft.

In that same draft class, Christian had also signed Edmond Sumner, a really good point guard out of Xavier, and Jaron Blossomgame, a solid six-foot-six forward out of Clemson, who were both selected in the second round. The year prior, he'd signed Brice Johnson, who was taken in the first round. So the young fella was making moves and people were noticing.

As I was getting started in my consulting role with adidas, Christian and I were talking sporadically, maybe once or twice a week. I quickly learned that it was not going to be a one-sided relationship. He was very helpful to me as well.

I was impressed with how many kids he knew, how deep his relationships were. I'd been removed from the scene for over a year before I started working with adidas, so the flow of information I received at that time wasn't the same as it had been when I was at Nike.

So to have someone as plugged in as Christian was invaluable. His insights helped me go back to my bosses and say, "Hey, this is a player we might want to consider bringing in once they get to the league."

Within a few months, Christian and I were speaking pretty regularly and he started talking about his desire to leave Andy Miller and start his own agency. Around Christmas, he called and said, "Hey, I'm coming down your way to see my kid that plays for La Lumiere at the Chick-fil-A event in Columbia." He was referring to Brian Bowen.

This was around the time that I was dealing with Zion Williamson and his family. Zion's team from Spartanburg Day was playing in the event. And Brian Bowen was playing on a monster squad with three teammates at La Lumiere: six-foot-five shooting guard Jordan Poole, who went on to play at the University of Michigan and was a first-round pick by the Golden State Warriors in 2019; six-foot-eleven big man Jaren Jackson, who'd gone to Michigan State for his one-and-done season and was a lottery pick as the fourth-overall selection in the 2018 draft by the Memphis Grizzlies; and the diminutive floor general Tyger Campbell, who made a big name for himself while dazzling during UCLA's improbable run from the First Four to the Final Four in the 2021 NCAA Tournament.

So I met up with Christian in Columbia and saw the Bowen kid play for the very first time. He was a decent athlete at six-foot-seven who could really shoot the ball. But he didn't seem to take any pride in being dominant on the defensive end. Which was cool, because you'll find that a lot of the top kids aren't wired that way defensively in high school. You could see that, with time and development, he had a chance to be really good down the line.

Christian would refer to Big Brian, the Bowen kid's daddy, as "Alonzo from *Training Day*," a former police officer that perhaps made his own rules. He told me he'd been coming out of his own pocket and doing some things to help the family for a while now. Supposedly the dad was constantly hitting him up for cash.

So when we started talking about what schools under the adidas umbrella might be a good fit for Bowen, Christian asked about the company facilitating a $100,000 payment to the family to secure his enrollment at Louisville. In this business, that is not an absurd ask. Believe it or not, it's pretty commonplace.

So as I stated earlier, I took it to my bosses, who ran it up the corporate ladder and the answer came back yes.

A few months later, in May of 2017, I was invited to a coaches retreat that adidas was having at the Andaz Peninsula Papagayo resort in Costa Rica. Most of the big-name guys were there with their wives, except for Rick Pitino. Among others in attendance, which included adidas executives Michael Ladinig and Chris McGuire, were Arizona State's Bobby Hurley, Miami's Jim Larrañaga and Kansas's Bill Self.

We were pampered with spa treatments, delicious meals at outdoor restaurants with monkeys jumping and swinging from nearby trees. A DJ rocked great music at a barbecue held on a private beach accessible by Jet Ski. We played volleyball and cornhole, and had access to kayaks, paddleboards and snorkeling gear. We went mountain climbing, zip lining, played golf and got massages. Every night, there was an open bar from 9:00 p.m. to midnight.

But there was also business to be conducted, with Kansas's

Bill Self being among the most vocal. His sentiment at one meeting was basically that Nike was kicking our ass and we needed more resources and more help on the recruiting trail. Adidas needed to help them get more of the high-profile kids.

Some of the biggest names in the coaching game were captured on tape, either expressing direct knowledge of recruits receiving payment offers, or of actually requesting the monetary assistance, or of facilitating the payments themselves. But none of those coaches were allowed to testify in court to claim that we defrauded the universities.

The wild thing is that when we went to trial, despite the clear evidence on the FBI's wiretaps and even though all of those coaches were subpoenaed, the government would not allow them to testify. I'll touch on some specifics in a little bit.

But the overall arc of those wiretaps showed that the coaches were in cahoots and it demonstrated that paying players is a long-held, widespread practice that they were well aware of, sometimes even bragging about the "strong-ass" offers that they themselves were making out of their own pockets.

So if these head coaches and athletics departments were considered to be representatives of the university, to simply say that guys like me and the Black assistant coaches who all got jammed up were acting in a rogue fashion is a crock of shit.

Let's take the University of Kansas, for instance. Despite the fact that their coaching staff was on tape having conversations with me about their recruitment of Zion Williamson, the jury was not allowed to hear those conversations.

In October of 2018, CBS Sports' Matt Norlander wrote,

After the prosecution rested its case, defense lawyers for James Gatto, Merl Code and Christian Dawkins prepared arguments and fought for inclusion of evidence

that would be seen and heard by the jury. As they lob-
bied for this with Judge Lewis A. Kaplan, the jury was
not present in the courtroom. Kaplan first had to rule if
the evidence the defense was fighting for was relevant
to the fundamental arguments and facts of the case. The
prosecution, naturally, was fighting the inclusion of said
evidence.

Ultimately, the judge didn't allow the most damning wiretapped calls into evidence, the ones that showed that the
coaches were not innocent bystanders, but active participants.
So the jury was forced to make its verdict without knowing
the existence of those calls and that evidence. It was a huge
blow to our defense because it proved that the coaches were
knowledgeable and active in facilitating payments to prospects and their families.

Following his in-home visit with Zion, Kansas assistant
Kurt Townsend called me to discuss how the visit went. The
following are excerpts of the conversation, which were recorded on September 13, 2017.

Kurt Townsend: "Hey, but between me and you, you
know, he [Lee, Zion's stepfather] asked about some stuff.
You know? And I said well, I mean, we'll talk about that
if you decide."

Me: "I know what he's asking. He's asking about opportunities from an occupational perspective. He's asking
for money in the pocket. And he's asking for housing
for him and the family. He's asking for—"

Kurt Townsend: "Yeah, cause they gonna move there. You already know."

Me: "Yeah, I know. I already know."

Kurt Townsend: "Yeah, but the one that I didn't know was the kid that's at Clemson [Zion's brother] coming to Kansas... So I'll just try to work to figure out a way. Because if that's what it takes to get him for ten months, we're going to have to do it some way... I don't want that to be this deal-breaker, because if that's what we got to do to get him—"

Me: "No, I understand. I understand... Did he give you, did he give you, did he throw out a number?"

Kurt Townsend: "Not at all. Just said, they want to go live there for the time he's there. And they needed money for, you know, the kid [Zion's brother] to go to school there for a year, which is about $35,000 out of state, you know?"

When relaying that Zion's stepfather wants the other brother to accompany them on the official recruiting visit out to Lawrence, Kansas, to see if he likes the school, Kurt told me,

And I said, "Well, he could come but we're not allowed to pay for it." But I said, "You know we could, shit, I don't know if they could throw some money into your budget from your AAU team to pay for him to go." He said, "Well, you know, that would be big, Coach."

But him saying that he wanted to bring him, makes me think they're thinking serious about it, if he wants to look at the school. But I'm just throwing everything out at you…and you know, it's my job, so I'll talk with Jimmy and see what we can do.

Members of the coaching staff were constantly kept abreast from the higher-ups at adidas in terms of what was happening in the Jayhawks' pursuit of Zion. It's all in the transcripts of the intercepted text messages. But again, the jury never saw or heard any of it. Self has subsequently denied any wrongdoing in the matter.

But the higher-ups at Kansas saw it and heard it. And they swiftly rewarded Bill Self with a lifetime contract, which included a very interesting clause that stated the coach who'd delivered them a national championship in 2008 would not be fired "due to any current infractions matter."

When the contract was announced during the 2021 Final Four in early April, CBS Sports's Dennis Dodd wrote about how KU was charged with five serious violations related to the 2017 scandal. Kansas and Self both disagreed with a significant portion of the allegations. But the NCAA claimed that Self and an assistant, Kurtis Townsend, "'embraced, welcomed and encouraged' Adidas to influence recruits to sign with Kansas."

Shortly after I got back from Costa Rica, Christian told me he was going to strike out on his own, and asked me to come meet with some of his potential investors in New York.

I told him there was really no need for me to meet with them. "This is your company," I reminded him.

"What if I get them to pay you a consulting fee for coming to the meeting—let's say five grand?"

That sounded fine by me. I'd long been taught that your network is your net worth. If they were willing to pay me consulting fees because of my knowledge and my network, which was what adidas was doing, I was all in.

So I paid my own way to New York, paid for my own hotel room and at the meeting, his "investors" informed me that they wanted to be able to meet with college coaches. I mean, anyone who knows this business knows that inroads to the top kids in most instances ain't through their college coaches. These elite kids are only gonna be on campus for a little more than a single semester, so the real power brokers are the folks who've been in their lives years prior.

The meeting, I later learned, was secretly recorded. One of Christian's investors handed me an envelope with $5,000 in it that later surfaced after my arrest. They showed it at trial as proof that I was taking a bribe. A bribe for what? They were paying me a consulting fee, as far as I was concerned, for my expertise, knowledge and connections in the industry. I claimed that $5,000 consulting fee on my taxes. Now who in their right damn mind goes ahead and claims a damn bribe on their taxes?

After that initial meeting in New York, I hit Christian up because I noticed that there were a bunch of cash-filled envelopes on the table. And I told him straight up, "If these folks are thinking about paying coaches, I'm out. Don't be giving my dudes no envelopes."

He told me that the company was open to paying me a consulting fee of $3,000 per month, along with a $5,000 bonus for each coach that I introduced them to. And I couldn't understand the apparent strategy that they were looking to enact. I clearly voiced these concerns to Christian. I told them if they wanted to meet my coaches and pay me for that privilege, I was cool with that. I actually told Christian, "We might as well just go on ahead and take these fools' money." And I'd made it abundantly clear that if they were going to try to pay my guys, I was unequivocally not cool with that and didn't want to be involved with any of it.

His basic response to me was essentially, "Merl, these guys are idiots. I told them that paying coaches as a business model makes no sense. I'm the one with the relationships with the kids and their families. I've told them over and over again that the strategy is dumb. But they're not listening to me. So what I'm going to do is just basically take these guys' money and go about business as I normally would."

"Christian, I don't have a problem collecting a consulting fee and facilitating meetings with my network of coaches. But you're not gonna be offering my guys cash. I ain't cool with that."

"I hear you, bro. These fools are stubborn and insistent. They're going to put cash on the table, and I'm just going to take it and use it to run the business. We're just gonna take these fools' money."

At this point, if you haven't watched the HBO documentary *The Scheme*, where Christian lays his story bare, I highly recommend you do so.

So how did we wind up in handcuffs, arrested by tactical teams sporting assault rifles at the crack of dawn? How exactly did our worlds get completely turned upside down?

It all starts with a huckster by the name of Marty Blazer.

Marty was a con man financial adviser out of Pittsburgh who worked with professional athletes and harbored dreams of becoming a big-time Hollywood movie producer. He de-frauded a few of his clients out of $2.35 million so he could make two terrible and forgettable films in 2013. The first was called *A Resurrection*, which grossed a little more than $10,000, and one called *Mafia*, which starred Ving Rhames and went straight to DVD. If twenty people bought that piece of shit outside of Marty Blazer's family, I'd be thoroughly surprised.

He basically stole from his clients, invested their money in his failed movie projects, and when the producers kept call-ing, needing more money, he stole more. Facing fraud charges after his clients realized that their hard-earned cash had disap-peared, Marty started working for the federal government as an informant as early as 2014. In order to avoid prison time, he promised he could help them uncover the supposed mas-sive corruption going on in college basketball. He claimed he could snag some of the biggest coaches in the game for paying players and their families to attend their schools.

So when Christian left Andy Miller to start his own agency at twenty-three years old, Marty Blazer introduced him to a guy by the name of Jeff DeAngelo, a supposed wealthy real estate tycoon who wanted to invest in the business. But Jeff DeAngelo was not really Jeff DeAngelo; he was an under-cover FBI agent whose main operative asset in this world was Marty Blazer.

A meeting was arranged on an ostentatious two-story yacht that was docked in Manhattan's affluent Battery Park area not far from Wall Street, the epicenter of global commerce. It had to be a pretty impressive setting for Christian. He later admit-ted as much on the witness stand, saying, "When I stepped on [the yacht]…I thought 'Wow! This dude must have some real money.'" His youthful naivete had gotten the best of him within that moment as folks stood around sipping on their top-shelf liquor. "Ain't no yachts in Saginaw," he said.

At the meeting, in addition to Marty Blazer and the undercover FBI agent, was financial adviser Munish Sood, who Christian was partnering with. Christian was handed an envelope with $25,000 in cash, which he deposited into his business account. Jeff DeAngelo, or whatever his real name is because the federal government never presented him as a witness at our trials, was hell-bent on paying college coaches, which Christian consistently scoffed at, privately mocking the dude for his stupidity.

Christian was adamant that paying the coaches served no purpose. But DeAngelo was also insistent, saying that he was the investor and that was how he wanted the business to be conducted. Christian kept arguing that paying the players and their families was the way to go, often laughing at DeAngelo's dumb hubris as it related to the business model that he wanted to pursue.

And he even told him as much, on a recorded wiretapped call, saying directly and sarcastically to him, "If you just wanna be Santa Claus and just give people money, well [expletive] let's just take the money to the strip club and just pay for hookers."

"I'm funding you," D'Angelo told him. "This is what you're going to do."

Now, I'm no legal scholar, but anyone who's seen an episode of *Law and Order* will tell you that that sounds a helluva lot like entrapment. Christian is telling him it's dumb, it makes no sense, it's not what he's going to do. DeAngelo says he's the moneyman, so that is in fact what he's going to do.

So Christian, desperate to get his company off the ground,

told the dude what he wanted to hear, even though he had no intention of doing it.

At this point, as Christian was sharing all of this information with me, I was growing more concerned about Jeff DeAngelo, along with his supposed business partner, a woman named Jill. I voiced those concerns, telling Christian that he needed to conduct official background checks because my little Google searches were not producing any information. Christian proceeded to call a buddy of his who worked for the FBI, who did the background check. Of course, it came back clean, so Christian felt he didn't have anything to worry about.

So, looking back, yes we were baffled that this dude wanted to undertake a terrible business strategy, one that was 100 percent certain to fail. But Christian's goal, as is the goal of most agencies in this business, was to provide financial assistance to the players and their families, maintain relationships with them while they were in school and ultimately have those players sign with his company so he could manage their professional careers. Whether you like it or not, that's how the game is played. He didn't make up that blueprint. He was simply following it.

Now, was Christian breaking NCAA rules? Hell to the yes he was, in the same way that agents were in my dorm room trying to sign my roommate. Damn near everyone breaks those bullshit rules. But he damn sure wasn't bribing any coaches.

And as we all know, it all culminated with the arrest of Christian, myself and nine other coaches and adidas employees, the majority of whom were Black middlemen.

When Christian was arrested, the FBI told him that he could be an informant and avoid prison time if he wore a wire and helped them build a case against Rick Pitino, Sean

Miller, who was then the head coach at Arizona, and Andy Miller. Boy oh boy, would those names grab some headlines and advance the careers of whoever was involved in investigating and prosecuting them.

But it ain't what happened because Christian refused to do it. I was asked to cooperate, and I refused too. So we had our day in court.

Marty Blazer, the con man who helped the FBI entrap Christian, received probation, was ordered to forfeit $2.4 million and to pay $1.56 million in restitution to the former clients that he robbed in order to fund his shitty movies. He didn't have to spend a day in prison.

Meanwhile, the people that he got jammed up, that the FBI basically entrapped, depleted our resources to fight for our innocence.

Dan Wetzel, the *Yahoo! Sports* columnist, dove into how the sneaker companies were operating in the high school and AAU space in order to secure the next Michael Jordan, i.e., a player who could potentially move billions of dollars into their bottom line while selling millions of shoes and other products to youth consumers around the globe in the book that he co-wrote with Don Yaeger, *Sole Influence*. Wetzel covered Christian's court cases extensively. He also appeared as a talking head in the HBO documentary *The Scheme*.

In his March 31, 2020, column entitled "All we got out of the FBI's college basketball investigation is an entertaining movie," Wetzel wrote:

"At their initial press conference detailing the investigation, way back in 2017, the FBI and the Southern District of New York promised to blow up college basketball and pursue any coach who was breaking NCAA rules.

"'We have your playbook,' was the most memorable line. They at least sounded serious.

"Instead, they got a few assistant coaches, a few anonymous middle men and in an effort to win those cases, hid most of the most damning evidence that would actually (possibly) cause college sports to clean up its act."

That's correct. After all that time and money and resources, after their big show of a press conference with their fancy graphs and flowcharts, where they promised to upend the world of college basketball as we know it, what really changed?

Not a damn thing.

13

As I headed to the first trial to face felony wire fraud and conspiracy to commit wire fraud charges, I was very confident about my innocence. My dad could see the stress I was under and was very upbeat, focusing on the evidence we'd present and the witnesses who would be called to testify, and how ultimately none of my actions met the standard of conviction on those charges.

But my confidence was tempered as I walked into the court building through a phalanx of film crews and photographers. The whole thing felt surreal.

My positive thoughts and affirmations got assaulted pretty quickly, with the combination of the media attention and the vibe I felt when I first got settled into the defendant's chair. It was like *The Twilight Zone*. There was no way that this could actually be happening to me. My nerves were shot, and my face was drawn with anxiety.

But I kept reminding myself that I hadn't broken any laws. Yes, I along with many others played fast and loose with the NCAA's antiquated rules. But never in a million years, and even to this day, will I ever see any criminality in that.

I had faith that once we put the big-time head coaches and athletic directors that we'd subpoenaed on the stand, once we presented evidence from the government's wiretaps, intercepted emails and text messages, we'd prove beyond a reasonable doubt that the representatives of the universities asked for our assistance and were willing participants in the widespread practice of paying players to attend their schools. I was confident the truth would exonerate me.

The gist of the prosecution was that, as it related to me, my actions made Brian Bowen ineligible, thus defrauding the University of Louisville. As a consultant with adidas, I did not act on my own, nor could I have done so. I simply ran the proposition by my bosses, who did the same after consulting with Rick Pitino, and the answer that came back from up high was, "Rick wants our help. Get it done."

So, as we got settled in, my mind raced with conflicting thoughts. I knew I had the evidence and the actual letter of the law on my side, but my confidence dissolved when the judge began to grill Jim Gatto's attorney. He started explaining the realities of the NCAA and how the organization has exploited underprivileged African American athletes for decades, with billions of dollars pouring in off their unpaid labor. Judge Lewis Kaplan responded with the following statement: "You're not gonna talk about poor Black kids in my courtroom." I knew from there on out I wasn't going to get a fair shake.

My worst fears came to fruition when I saw that each piece of evidence that would exonerate me, the ones that corroborated my side of the story, was not allowed to be shown to the jury. The FBI had wiretaps of me telling my friends in the coaching fraternity, "If these dudes try to give you money, do not accept it." But those conversations were not allowed to be presented to the jury.

Here's the thing. In order for wire fraud to exist, there had to be an intent on my behalf to defraud or take something away from the other party. And that something has to benefit me personally, something of monetary value. So in this case, the government said we defrauded the University of Louisville. But the blocked text messages, conversations and emails showed that the Louisville coaching staff was not only in on the transaction, but they encouraged it. And none of it benefited me personally. I gained nothing of monetary value.

But when the government, the FBI and the US attorney spends roughly $43 million on the investigation and fails to ensnare the famous coaches that they promised, you better believe that to save face, somebody is going to get banged in the head.

An exchange of text messages that was recorded between Rick Pitino and his assistant coach Jordan Fair on May 5, 2017, shows them discussing a top-level recruit, where Pitino asserts that he's going to pass on bringing the player in to be a part of the Louisville program.

The correspondence is as follows:

Pitino: Thought about it most of the night–didn't like his body language–Kenny said brother told scar he had 50,000 on the table.

Fair: Oh wow. I did most of the recruitment and they never mentioned that. I agree on his body language.

Pitino: We will be better off without…. We don't need any possible issues. Too good of a group.

Fair: And who THE HELL would be dumb enough to pay $50,000 for that kid for one year!?!?!?!?!?!? Lol.

Clearly Pitino had knowledge of this specific recruit, and the notion that schools offer payments. The player's brother obviously thought it was a common enough practice to casually raise the issue around Pitino and the Louisville coaches. Because it is.

Later, when Pitino did land Bowen, he received a congratulatory text from someone named Ralph Lnu: "Great get in Bowen."

Pititno hit him back with, "Yep, never spent a penny—most athletic talent I've had since 96 UK."

He never spent a penny on Bowen; adidas did. But how many others had his program shelled out for?

The other interesting tidbit here is that several members of Louisville's coaching team instructed a staffer to alter the official paperwork of Bowen's unofficial visit to keep Christian Dawkins's presence on that visit unknown. The document initially said that Bowen was only accompanied by his parents.

The program's director of operations, Michael Bowden, said during a court deposition that he was told to keep Dawkins's name off the form. Bowden said he later changed the form to show that Christian was present on the visit after the FBI investigation became public knowledge in September of 2017 and that he was directed to do so by the university's compliance office.

The fraud was on them.

As far as compromising Brian Bowen's eligibility, his own father admitted on the stand that he'd been bartering his son's athletic talent for cash, from AAU teams and his high school team, since the boy was thirteen years old.

And if the university was harmed, why are they still business partners with adidas? But what about that lead FBI agent, "Jeff DeAngelo"? As *Sports Illustrated* reported in May of 2018, he had been removed from his undercover duties near the end of the operation because he was accused of misappropriating investigative funds, allegedly "spending the money on gambling, food and beverages during the probe. Reverse engineering the dates, this alleged misconduct occurred during the July 2017 trip to Las Vegas."

We filed a motion requesting specific information on the scope of DeAngelo's corruption, but the government declined our request.

We all want to have faith in our judicial system, in the standards and morals of our FBI, but history has proven, especially for people of color or marginalized folks in America, that we're not always playing on a level field. We need to look no further than the recent scandal involving USA Gymnastics and how the FBI handled the claims of the abused athletes at the hands of team doctor and convicted sexual predator Larry Nassar.

The gymnasts asserted that the FBI agents who handled their investigation deserved to be indicted.

"What's even more upsetting to me is that we know that these FBI agents have committed an obvious crime," said Team USA member McKayla Maroney. "They falsified my statement, and that is illegal in itself. Yet no recourse has been taken against them. The Department of Justice refused to prosecute these individuals. Why?… These individuals clearly violated policies and were negligent in executing their duties, and in doing so, more girls were abused by Larry Nassar for over a year."

FBI Director Chris Wray said that he felt heartsick and furious once he understood the depth of the agency's failures. And yet, he placed blame on individuals rather taking accountability as an agency.

In March 2021, our lawyers received correspondence from the United States Attorney's Southern District of New York office that they had access to information that was never shared with us. They had withheld evidence for three years. We got a terse mea culpa.

What also hurt me emotionally was the choice I and my legal team had of whether or not to subpoena my friends in the coaching fraternity. I'd already heard from many of them, who all basically said, "Merl, if I testify on your behalf, they've already told me that I'll be fired."

These were friends, people I'd respected and known for decades, people who were providing for their families, one of whom was the sole breadwinner who was taking care of his sick mother. In the end I couldn't do that because I felt like I'd just be throwing another Black man under the bus.

And if I wanted to, if I REALLY wanted to, I could create a real shitstorm in this space by mentioning the names of the coaches, athletic directors and big-time recruits at a number of high-profile universities in the ACC, the Big 12, the Pac 12, the Big Ten, the SEC and other major D-I conferences over the years whose texts, emails and phone conversations were intercepted by the FBI, who the government so deftly kept away from the jury because it exonerated us.

But doing that would serve no purpose.

I will simply say that a massive amount of evidence was never presented to the jury.

Adidas refused to honor the terms of my consulting contract. They've asserted that I didn't have an actual contract despite the fact that I have the 1099s to prove that they were paying me according to the contract and term sheet that we'd signed and agreed to.

They simply cut me loose, as if I was the one who was responsible for all of this, when in reality the decisions to facilitate these payments come from the very highest up on the corporate ladder.

So here I stand. A federal appeals court has upheld our convictions in the wire fraud and conspiracy to commit wire fraud case, and we're currently appealing the convictions in the second case of bribery conspiracy, which said that we were paying coaches to steer NBA-bound athletes to a favored group of handlers.

I've said what I have to say and I'll go to prison if I have to, and even my grave, knowing that I'm innocent of those felonious crimes. I damn sure ain't the first Black man facing the specter of incarceration for something I did not do, nor will I be the last. At the end of the day, I take solace in knowing that the situation I got ensnared in will continue to reverberate. The truth will eventually come out and absolve me. I'll be vindicated.

And the time is running out for the NCAA to continue to rake in billions on the backs of its unpaid labor force without having to offer something back in return. And we're not just talking about individual players getting paid for their names, images and likenesses, which some states are already working on legislation to limit.

I'm talking about the players and their families, the future Zion Williamsons and Anthony Davises actually receiving a fair and living wage and a true percentage that speaks to their value and what they generate for the NCAA and their universities.

During these days, as I sit back and reflect on everything I've been through to arrive at this specific juncture in my life, I take solace in the words from one of my favorite poems, "Invictus," by William Ernest Henley.

Out of the night that covers me,
    Black as the pit from pole to pole,
I thank whatever gods may be
    For my unconquerable soul.

In the fell clutch of circumstance
    I have not winced nor cried aloud.
Under the bludgeonings of chance
    My head is bloody, but unbowed.

Beyond this place of wrath and tears
    Looms but the Horror of the shade,
And yet the menace of the years
    Finds and shall find me unafraid.

It matters not how strait the gate,
    How charged with punishments the scroll,
I am the master of my fate,
    I am the captain of my soul.

So, as I said before, if you want to have an honest conversation about what happens in the areas of grassroots and major college basketball, and what needs to happen moving forward, how about I pull up a seat at that table.

Because what I've shared here is only the tip of the iceberg. I have so many more stories I could tell. Perhaps one day, I'll tell more.

And I keep asking myself the same question. Ultimately, what did I really do to wind up here in this situation?

I did my damn job, plain and simple.

★ ★ ★ ★ ★

ACKNOWLEDGMENTS

First and foremost, praises and thanks to God the Almighty for his showers of blessings and mercy over my life. This project could not have reached successful completion without his grace, which is sufficient.

I would like to express my deep and sincere love and gratitude to my wife (Candance), my boys (Lleyton and August), my mother (Denise), my father (Merl), my sister (Whitney), my aunt (Andrea), my mother-in-law (Blondell), my sister-in-law (Kelavor), my grandmother (Jean) and my cousins (Ron, Nancy, Rhonda, Kim, Audra, Darren, Dennis, Kim, Warren, Adrienne, Rachel and Ali). Your prayers, support and understanding helped me through the storm. I appreciate each of you more than I can express on paper!